The 2015 Book of Baby Names

Hannah Crawford

ISBN:1507501188

ISBN-13: 978-1507501184

Penguinies@outlook.com

DEDICATED

This book is dedicated to my son, friends and family.

Introduction

The 2015 Book of Baby Names has over 1700 first names to help you to decide on the right name for your baby. There is a wide variety to choose from with both modern and classic names listed alphabetically. With pronunciations, origins and meanings all included to give you a better understanding of each name.

The 2015 Book of Baby Names can help you to pick a suitable baby name that suits your baby and family surname. Each name is divided into easily readable sections. Agreeing on a special baby name can be one of the most difficult yet rewarding decisions that any parent can make during their lifetime. This book can help make choosing a baby name easy and lots of fun.

A-Z

Baby Boy

Names

For

2015

A

Aaden

Pronunciation: Ay-din.
The name originates from Irish Gaelic, origin of the
name Aidan. The name means, "fire", "fiery."

Aamir

Pronunciation: Aa-mir
Aamir is a modernised counterpart of the Arabic and
Hebrew name Amir, which means "treetop."

Aaron

Pronunciation: Aa-ron
The name Aaron is of Greek origin. The name is also
linked to Ancient Egypt. Aaron is a biblical name and
appears in the Old Testament borne by the brother of
Moses. The name Aaron means "Strong mountain."

Abdul

Pronunciation: AB-dul
The name Abdul is of Arabic origin and means
"servant of God", "servant". The name Abdul also
signifies a religious service and devotion.

Abdullah

Pronunciation: Ab-dul-ah

Abdullah is of Arabic origin and means "God's servant".

Abraham

Pronunciation: Ay-bra-ham, Ahb-rahm

The name Abraham comes from the Hebrew *av haomon goyim*. The name Abraham means, "Father of a multitude", "many nations". Abraham is a biblical name; borne in the Old Testament and originally named Abram, was bestowed the name of Abraham by God. He is said to be the father of Jewish nations, the great Jewish patriarchs. Abraham received God's promise that his people would possess the land of Canaan.

Abran

Pronunciation: a-BRAHN

Abran originates from Spain and means, "father of a mighty nation", "father of a multitude", "high father". Abran is a variant the Hebrew name Abraham.

Ace

Pronunciation: Ayce

Ace is of English origin and also an English surname meaning "Noble". The name Ace means, "Number one". Additionally an ace is a playing card with the highest face value in many card games, making the ace the most powerful card to hold.

Achilles
Pronunciation: ah-KILL-eez
Achilles is of Greek origin. Achilles was the son of the sea nymph Thetis and Peleus, King of the Myrmidons. Achilles was a hero of the Trojan War, the central character and a supreme warrior in Homer's Iliad. Famous for his courage and manly beauty, Achilles was invulnerable on all of his body except for his heel. Achilles was dipped in the River Styx by his mother Thetis, she held him by heel which became his one weak point, "Achilles' Heel".

Adair
Pronunciation: ah-DARE
The name Adair is of German origin. The meaning of the name Adair is, "wealthy spear". Adair is also a Scottish surname from the Gaelic word 'doire', which means "oak grove.

Adam

Pronunciation: AD-am

Adam is of Hebrew origin and means "earth". In Hebrew, it is a generic word for "man". Adam is a biblical name; borne in the Old Testament by the father of the human race, he was the first man created from the red earth of Eden by God. Adam and Eve were the first humans and lived in the Garden of Eden until they committed sin.

Adan

Pronunciation: ah-DAHN

The name is of Spanish origin and is a variant of the Hebrew name Adam. The name Adan has the meaning of "earth", "fire". In Spanish, the meaning of the name Adan is "from the red earth".

Adolfo

Pronunciation: ah-DOLE-foh

The name Adolfo is a Latin name. The Latin meaning of Adolfo is "noble wolf", "majestic wolf".
Additionally Adolfo is a Spanish and Italian variant of the German name, Adolf.

Adrian

Pronunciation: Ay-dree-an

Adrian is of Latin origin, the name is derived from the Latin name "Hadrianus". The meaning of the name Adrian is "from Hadria", a town in northern Italy which gave its name to the Adriatic Sea. Adrian is also the name of several early Christian saints and Martyrs.

Agustin

Pronunciation: ah-goos-teen

Agustin has Latin origins. The Latin meaning of Agustin is "deserving of respect". Agustin is a popular Spanish name. The Spanish meanings of Agustin are "majestic", "great".

Aidan

Pronunciation: AY-den

Aidan is of Irish Gaelic origins. The meaning of Aidan is "fire". Aidan is the name of several early Irish saints, one of whom established the greatest centres of learning of its time, The monastery of Lindisfarne which is also known as The Holy Island of Lindisfarne.

Ainsley

Pronunciation: AYNS-lee

The name Ainsley is of Old English origin. The meaning of the name is "clearing", "only hermitage wood". Originally a place name Annesley or Ansley.

Alan

Pronunciation: AL-an

The name Alan is of Celtic origin. In Celtic, the meaning of the name Alan is, "noble", "harmony", "stone". The name could also be derived from the Gaelic name 'Ailin', which means "little rock". Alan was originally a saint's name and was reborn in Britain during the Normal Conquest.

Alasdair

Pronunciation: AL-as-dare

Alasdair is of Greek origin. In Greek, the meaning of the name Alasdair is "defender", "protector of mankind". Other variations of the name include: Alastair, Alistair, Allaster.

Albert

Pronunciation: AL-burt

Albert is a Norman French name of German Origin. The meaning of the name is "noble", "bright". The name was brought to England by the Normans and replaced the Old English name Ethelbert.

Albin

Pronunciation: AL-bin

The name Albin is taken from the Latin name Albinus derived from '*albus*'. The meaning of Albin is "white", "pale-skinned" Albin is also a variant of the name 'Alban'.

Alexander
Pronunciation: al-ek-ZAN-der
The name Alexander is of Greek origin, taken from the Latin form of the Greek name '*alexandros*'. The meaning of Alexander is "man's defender", "warrior". Alexander appears in the Bible as the one who helps Jesus bear the cross on the journey to Calvary.

Alexis
Pronunciation: a-LEX-iss
Alexis is of Greek origin and means "defender". The name is often used a shortened variation of the name Alexander. Although Alexis is traditionally a male name, it is now also used for girls in the modern world. Saint Alexis was a popular saint of Edessa, admired as a 'man of God.'

Alfonso
Pronunciation: al-FON-so
Alfonso is of Spanish and Italian origin. The name Alfonso is a variant of the German word, 'Alphonse'

which means "ready for battle. The Spanish meaning of the name Alfonso is "eager for war".

Alfred

Pronunciation: AL-fred

The name Alfred is of Anglo-Saxon origin and means, "name of a king".

Ali

Pronunciation: ah-LEE

Ali is of Arabic origin. Borne by a cousin the prophet of Muhammad, was also known as the first male convert to Islam. The name Ali is also borne by the hero in 'Ali Baba and the Forty Thieves'. The meaning of the name Ali is "excellent", "noble".

Alton

Pronunciation: ALL-tun

Alton is of English origin. The meaning of the name is "old town".

Alvin

Pronunciation: AL-vin

Alvin is of English origin. The meaning of the name is "friend", "magical being".

Amos

Pronunciation: AYM-ess

The name Amos is of Hebrew origin. The meaning of the name is, "to carry", "carried". A biblical name; borne by one of the twelve minor prophets of the Old Testament, who wrote the Book of Amos. It is the oldest of the prophetic books.

Andrew

Pronunciation: AN-droo

The name Andrew is of Greek origin, from the root andr-, 'man' giving the meaning "manly", "strong" or "Warrior". English form of the Greek name Andreas. A biblical name; borne by one of the first of Jesus's disciples, the first chosen of the 12 apostles. Saint Andrew is the patron saint of Scotland, Greece and Russia. His feast day is 30th November.

Angel

Pronunciation: AIN-jel

The name Angel is of Greek origin. The meaning of the name Angel is "messenger of God". A biblical name; borne as the name for the spirit creatures sent to men by God as his messengers. Angel is used for both female and male names. Derived for the Greek "angelos".

Angus

Pronunciation: ANG-guss

Angus is of Celtic origin. The meaning of Angus is "one choice", "one strength". Angus is the anglicized for of the Irish and Scottish Gaelic name Aonghus. In Celtic mythology, Angus Og is a god of love and beauty. Angus is both a first name and surname.

Anthony

Pronunciation: AN-tha-nee

Anthony is of Latin origin, adopted from the Roman family name Antonius. The 'h' was introduced in the 17th century. Ruler of the Roman Empire and lover of Cleopatra, Marcus Antonius (82-30BC) was an early bearer of the name. Saint Anthony was an Egyptian hermit monk renowned for his resistance to the devil and founded the first Christian monastic order.

Apollo

Pronunciation: er-POH-loh

The name Apollo is of Greek origin. The name comes from *Apollyon*, Greek translation of the Hebrew word "Abaddon". The meaning of the name is "destroyer". A biblical name; borne as one of the early Christian disciples. The name Apollo has come to symbolise the classical and intellectual aspects of thought.

Archer

Pronunciation: AR-cher

Archer is of Latin origin, derived from the Latin *arcus* meaning "bow". Archer is an adopted English surname from medieval times, originally an occupational name for skilled archer.

Archibald

Pronunciation: Ar-chi-bald

Archibald is of Old French and Old German origin. The name Archibald means "genuine", "bold", "brave". The name is particularly popular in Scotland.

Arden

Pronunciation: ARD-en

The name Arden is of Latin origin. The name means "great forest". It is the name of the magical forest in Shakespeare's "As You Like It". Arden is also the surname of Shakespeare's mother.

Ariel

Pronunciation: AR-ee-el

Ariel is of Hebrew origin. The meaning of Ariel is "lion of God". A biblical place name; used in Isaiah 29 to refer to Jerusalem. Ariel is also the scriptural name for a place in Sumeria. The name is used in literature to identify various spirits. Shakespeare gave this name to a spirit who can disappear at will in "The Tempest". Ariel is given to both male and females as a name.

Aries

Pronunciation: A-ries

The name Aries is of Latin origin. The meaning of the name is "ram". Aries is the name of the astrological sign for those born from March 21 to April 19.

Arnold

Pronunciation: AR-nold

Arnold is of Old French and Old German origin. The meaning of the name Arnold is "eagle power". A Puritan adoption, an early saint of this name was a musician at the court of Charlemagne. The name died out during the Middle Ages, and was revived in the 19th Century.

Arthur

Pronunciation: AR-ther

The name Arthur is of Celtic origin. The name could possibly have been derived from the Celtic word "artos", which means "bear". The 6th-century King Arthur and his Round Table of Knights have become renowned figures. The name was first found in the Latin form Artorius, which is of obscure origin.

Ashely

Pronunciation: ASH-lee

Ashley is an adopted surname and place name, of Old English origin. The meaning of the name Ashley is "ash meadow". Initially used as a boy's name, Ashley is now used more commonly for girl's names. Ashley is an English saint's name from the 17h century. The name was first recorded as a given name in the 16th Century. Earl of Shaftesbury, Anthony Ashley Cooper made the name more popular in the early 19thcentury. The humanitarian was renowned for the legislation designed to improve conditions among the working classes.

Asher

Pronunciation: ASH-er

The name Asher is of Hebrew origin. The meaning of the name Ashe is "happy". A biblical name; borne as the eighth son of Jacob, was promised a life blessed with an abundance. The Puritans brought the name Asher to England.

Ashton

Pronunciation: ASH-ten

Ashton is an adopted surname of Old English origin. The meaning of the name is "ash tree town". Although the name has been used as a boy's name since the 1600's, the name is commonly given to girls.

Aston

Pronunciation: AS-ton

The name Aston is of Old English origin, and the meaning of the name is "east town", "ash tree settlement". Aston is also a place name.

Atlas

Pronunciation: AT-las

The name Atlas is of Greek origin. The meaning of Atlas is "to carry". The name bears connotations of great strength. Atlas was a mythical Titan who bore the weight of the world on his shoulders.

Auberon

Pronunciation: A(u)-be-ron

Auberon is from an Old French name of Old German origin. The meaning of the name Auberon is "noble", "royal bear". The name is possibly a variation of Aubrey or *Adalbero.*

Auberon is the king of the fairies in Shakespeare's, *A Midsummer Night's Dream* (1605).

August

Pronunciation: AW-gust

August is of Latin origin. The meaning of the name August is "great", "magnificent". The Latin version, Augustus is more commonly used in English-speaking countries.

Augustine

Pronunciation: AW-gus-tin

Augustine is of Latin origin. The meaning of Augustine is "great", "magnificent". Borne by perhaps the greatest of fathers of the Christian church, Saint Augustine of Hippo (354-430). Saint Augustine (sixth century) was the first Archbishop's of Canterbury, recognised for the frank "confessions", in which he speaks, "Oh God, make me chaste – but not yet". Augustine is diminutive of August, the English form of the Latin name *Augustinus.*

Augustus

Pronunciation: AW-gust-us

Augustus is of Latin origin. The meaning of Augustus is "great", "magnificent". It was given by the Senate to the Roman emperor Octavian in 27BC. Subsequently the name Augustus was used by his successors. The name was popular in the 18th century after German princely families brought the name to Britain.

Austin

Pronunciation: AW-sten

The name Austin is of French and Latin origin. The name is a variation of Augustine. The meaning of the name is "great", "magnificent". The name was popular in England during the 17th Century. Saint Augustine (seventh century) was occasionally called Austin.

Axel

Pronunciation: AX-el

Axel is of Hebrew origin. The meaning of the name Axel is "father is peace". Scandinavian variant of Absalom.

Aydan

Pronunciation: AY-dan

Aydan is a variant of the Gaelic name, Aidan, an anglicised form of the ancient Gaelic name Aedan. The meaning of the name Aydan is "fire".

B

Barnabas

Pronunciation: BAR-na-bus

The name Barnabas is of Greek and Aramaic origin. The meaning of Barnabas is "son of consolation". A biblical name; borne in the New Testament by Apostle who accompanied St Paul on his missionary journeys. Saint Barnabas's feast day is 11th June.

Barnaby

Pronunciation: BAR-naby

Barnaby is a medieval dialect form of the Greek, Aramaic name Barnabas. Charles Dickens popularized the name during the mid-19th century with his novel, 'Barnaby Rudge' (1841).

Baron

Pronunciation: BARE-an

The name Baron is of Old German and Old English Origin. The meaning of the name Baron is "young warrior". It is an adopted surname which was first used during the post-Conquest period to mean a vassal of a nobel. A baron was the lowest rank of a hereditary peerage that entitles the holder to serve in the House of Lords in England.

Barrett

Pronunciation: BARE-et

The name Barrett is possibly from Middle English *baret*, which means "dispute", "argument", or from the Old French word, *Barrette* meaning *"cap"*. The adopted surname was a given name used mostly in the 19th century.

Barry

Pronunciation: BARE-ee

Barry is of Irish and Gaelic origin, derive from the Old Irish name, Bairre. The meaning of the name Barry is "fair-haired". Saint *Bairre* (seventh century) founded a monastery that became the city of Cork in Ireland.

Bartholomew

Pronunciation: bar-THAWL-oh-myoo

Bartholomew is of Aramaic origin. The meaning of Bartholomew is "son of Talmai". Talmai being another name for Nathaniel, the apostle. Biblical; by name of one of the twelve apostles, Nathanael, who was known as the patron saint of tanners and vintners.

Bartholomew was a common boys name in the Middle Ages.

Basil

Pronunciation: BAZ-el

The name Basil is of Greek origin. The meaning of Basil is "royal", "kingly". From the Greek name Basileios, which is derived from "basileus". Saint Basil (fourth century) of Caesarea was called "Saint Basil the Great", he was regarded as one of the Fathers of the Eastern Church. Basil is also the name of several early saints martyred in the East. The name was common in the eastern Mediterranean and was brought to England by the Crusaders. Basil is also the name of a common herb.

Beau

Pronunciation: boh

The name Beau is of French origin, and the meaning of Beau is "handsome", "sweetheart". The novel "*Beau Geste*"(1924) was a bestseller and a popular movie. Beau is also the name of Ashley and Melanie Wilkes child in Margaret Mitchell's legendary "Gone with the Wind" (1936).

Benedict

Pronunciation: BEN-a-dikt

Benedict is of Latin origin from the Latin word, Benedictus. The meaning of Benedict is "blessed". Saint Benedict founded the Christian monastic order, the Benedictines. The name is popular with Roman Catholics and there have been 16 popes who shared the name Benedict.

Benjamin

Pronunciation: BEN-ja-men

Benjamin is of Hebrew origin, from the Hebrew name Benyamin. The meaning of Benjamin is "son of the right hand", "son of my old age". A biblical name; borne by the youngest and most beloved son of the patriarch Jacob and Rachel, who died giving birth to him. He was originally named Benoni.

Bennett

Pronunciation: BEN-et

Bennett is of French and Latin origin. The adopted surname has been used for both girl's and boy's names. Taken from the medieval vernacular form of Benedict.

Benson

Pronunciation: BEN-son

The adopted surname has been used as a given name since the 19th century. The meaning of the name Benson is "son of Ben". The name is also connected to a place name, Benson (formerly Bensington) in Oxfordshire.

Bentley

Pronunciation: BENT-lee

The name Bentley is of Old English origin. The meaning of the name Bentley is "bent grass meadow". The adopted surname is used more commonly as a boy's name, however it is also used as a girl's name. Bentley is also a place name for many places in England.

Bernard

Pronunciation: ber-NARD

The name Bernard is of Old French and Old German origin. The meaning of the name is "strong", "brave bear". The name was brought to England by the Norman Conquest.

Three famous medieval saints bore the name. An 11th century Saint Bernard of Menthon is revered as the patron saint of mountaineers. Saint Bernard of Clairvaux (1090-1153), a founder of a monastic order, and a scholastic philosopher.

Blaise

Pronunciation: blayz

The name Blaise is of French and Latin origin. From Latin Blasius, and derived from "*blaesus*". The meaning of the name is "lisping", "stammering". Saint Blaise, a 4th-century Armenian bishop is supposedly endowed with miraculous healing power. He is regarded as the patron of those suffering from sore throats.

Blake

Pronunciation: blayk

Blake is of Old English origin. The meaning of the name Blake is "black", "pale". The adopted surname is used as both a boy's name and a girl's name. Blake was originally used as a nickname for someone with skin or hair that was either very dark ("blaec") or very light ("blac").

Boaz

Pronunciation: boa-Z

Boaz is of Hebrew origin. A biblical name; Boaz is the name of several characters. The name was revived by the Puritans, it was occasionally used in England during the 17th and 18th centuries. The meaning of the name is "swiftness", "strength".

Boris

Pronunciation: BOR-iss

Boris is of Russian and Slavic origin. Originally from the Tartar nickname, *Bogoris*. The meaning of the name is "small", "battle glory". Borne by a 9th-century ruler of Bulgaria who converted his Kingston to Christianity. A 10th-century Russian saint also known as Romanus, Saint Boris is known as the patron saint of Moscow.

Bowen

Pronunciation: BOH-en

The name Bowen is of Welsh origin. The meaning of the name Bowen is "son of Owen", "son of the young one".

Boyd

Pronunciation: boyd

Boyd is of Gaelic and Scottish origin. Boyd is an adopted Irish and Scottish surname. The name was first used as a surname in Scotland in the 13th century, it has been in regular use as a first name since the early 20th century. Scottish Gaelic, from the word *buidhe*, which means "yellow", "blonde".

Braden

Pronunciation: BRAY-den

The name Braden is of Irish and Gaelic origin. The meaning of the name is "descendant of bradán". Bradán is a personal name that means "salmon". Braden is an adoptive Irish surname.

Bradley

Pronunciation: BRAD-lee

Bradley is of Old English origin. The meaning of Bradley is "broad meadow", "broad wood". Bradley is an adopted surname and also a place name. Bradley has been used as a given first name since the mid-19th century.

Brady

Pronunciation: BRAY-dee

The name Brady is of Irish and Gaelic origin. The meaning of the name is "descendant of Brádach". The name is used as both a boy's name and as a girl's names.

Brandon

Pronunciation: BRAN-den

Brandon is of Old English origin. The meaning of the name Brandon is "broom", "hill". Brandon is an adopted surname and an English Place name.

Braxton
Pronunciation: b-rax-ton
Braxton is of Old English origin. The meaning of Braxton is "Brock's town". Brock is an informal word used for "badger". Braxton is an adopted surname and a place name.

Brendan
Pronunciation: BREN-den
Brendan is of Celtic, Irish and Gaelic origin. The meaning of the name Brandan is "Prince". From an old Irish Gaelic name *Bréanainn*. The name was borne by a legendary 6th-century Irish abbot and saint. Saint Brendan of Ireland is renowned for his adventurous traveling and scholarship. He was known as "the Voyager" after a seven-year voyage, possibly to North America.

Brennan
Pronunciation: BREN-an
Brennan is of Irish and Gaelic origin. The meaning of the name Brennan is "teardrop". Brennan is used as

both a boy's name and as a girl's name. The name is also a variant of Brendan.

Brent

Pronunciation: brent

The name Brent is of Old English and Celtic origin. The meaning of the name is "hill", "mount". The name might also have been used to refer to criminals branded or burned as punishment. Brent is an adopted surname.

Brenton

Pronunciation: BREN-ton

Brenton is of Old English origin. The meaning of Brenton is "Bryni's settlement". Brenton is also an adopted surname and a place name.

Brett

Pronunciation: bret

The name Brett is of Latin origin. The meaning of the name is "from Britany", "from Britain". Brett is an adopted surname which originated in the Middle Ages, as an ethnic name for a native of Brittany.

Brian

Pronunciation: BRY-en

The name Brian is of Celtic, Irish and Gaelic origin. The meaning of the name Brian is "high", "noble". The name was possibly introduced to England by Norman invaders; however the name was born by a great Irish chieftain, Brian Boroimhe. He was a warrior who became high king of Ireland and one of its greatest national heroes. After he defeated a Viking invasion and liberated the country from the Danes in 1014.

Broderick
Pronunciation: BRAH-der-ik
Broderick is a transferred use of the surname, which is derived from the Welsh personal name Rhydderch. The name could possibly be of Old German and mean, "famous power".

Brody
Pronunciation: BROH-dee
The name Brody is of Irish and Gaelic origin. The meaning of Brody is "ditch". Brody is also a place name, there is a Castle Brodie in Scotland. It could also possibly be related to "brathair" which means, "brother" in Irish.

Brooks
Pronunciation: brux

Brooks is of Old English and Old German origin. The meaning of Brooks is "water", "small stream". Brooks is used as both a boy's name and a girl's name.

Bruce
Pronunciation: brooce

Bruce is of Norman-French origin, introduced to Britain by the Norman Conquest. Adopted Scottish surname, originally a Norman baronial name and place name.

Bruno
Pronunciation: BROO-noh

The name Bruno is of Old German origin. From Old German *brun*, the meaning of the name Bruno is "brown". Bruno was used as a name in the ruling families of Germany during the Middle Ages. Saint Bruno was a 10th-century German saint who founded an order of Carthusian monks, whom the German town of Brunswicl is named.

Bryn
Pronunciation: br-yn

The name Bryn is of Welsh origin. The meaning of the name Bryn is "hill". The name is also a short form of

Brynmor. Bryn is used as both a boy's name and girl's name.

Bryce
Pronunciation: Bryce
The name Bruce is of Scottish origin. The meaning of Bryce is "of Britain". Bryce is a variant of Brice which originated as a transferred use of the Scottish surname, derived from the medieval given name.

Buddy
Pronunciation: bud-DEE
Buddy is a variant of the English word Bud. The meaning of Buddy is "brother", and it has been used as a nickname since the medieval times.

Byron
Pronunciation: BYE-ron
Byron is an adopted surname and English place name derived from *byre*, "barn", "cowshed". The name is of Old English origin. The meaning of Byron is "at the byres".
The name was popular in the 19th century. Lord Byron was a poet renowned for his wildness and debauchery.

C

Caddis

Pronunciation: CAD-is

The name Caddis is of Old English origin. The meaning of Caddis is "worsted fabric".

Cade

Pronunciation: kayd

The name Cade is of Old English and Old French origin. The meaning of the name Cade is "round", "gentle cask". The adopted surname was originally used as a nickname. Cade was also the name of a character in Margaret Mitchell's, "Gone with the Wind" (1936).

Caden

Pronunciation: KAY-den

Caden is of Scottish origin, taken from the Scottish surname McCadden. The meaning of the name is "son of Cadán".

Cadogan

Pronunciation: ca-do-gan

Cadogan is of Welsh origin. Anglicised form of Cadwgan or cadwgawn, derived from *cad*, meaning "battle", *gwogann*, meaning "glory". The meaning of the name Cadogan is "battle glory". It is the name of several Welsh princes from the early Middle Ages. Borne by two characters in *Mabinogian*, the collection of Welsh legends.

Caesar

Pronunciation: SEE-zer

The name Caesar is of Latin origin. The meaning of Caesar is "head of hair". A famous bearer of the name was Julius Caesar (104-44BC). Due to his success and power, the name Caesar then became the title of the Roman emperors with the meaning "ruler".

Caius

Pronunciation: keys

The name Caius is of Latin origin. The meaning of Caius is "happy". The name is a common Roman form of the name Gaius.

Caiden

Pronunciation: KAY-den

The name Caiden is of Arabic origin. The name may also refer to an Old English word meaning "round". The name Caiden means "companion". It also a variant of the name Kaden.

Cain

Pronunciation: KA-yn

The name Cain is of Hebrew origin. The meaning of Cain is "acquired, spear". A Biblical name; Cain was Adam and Eve's first born son. He killed his brother in anger and jealousy, and he spent the rest of his life as a wanderer in exile.

Cairo

Pronunciation: KIE-ro

Cairo is of Arabic origin. The meaning of the name is "victorious". Cairo is also a place name, the capital of Egypt.

Caesar

Pronunciation: SEE-zer

The name Caesar is of Latin origin. The meaning of Caesar is "hair". From the family name of the legendary Roman emperor Gaius Julius Caesar, which was traditionally said to be derived from *caesus*, 'cut'. Cut from his dead mother's womb, Caesar was the first baby to have been delivered by Caesarean section.

Caleb
Pronunciation: KAY-leb
Caleb is of Hebrew origin. The meaning of the name Caleb is "faith, whole-hearted". A biblical name; a companion of Moses and Joshua. Caleb was noted for his fearlessness and his devotion to God. The name was popular among the Puritans.

Callan
Pronunciation: KAL-an
The name Callan is of Gaelic and Scottish origin. The meaning of Callan is "battle, rock". Callan is originally a surname.

Callum
Pronunciation: KAL-um
Callum is of Scottish Gaelic origin. The name is a variant of Calum. Derived from the Latin first name Columba, meaning 'dove'. Borne by an early Celtic saint (521-597).

Calvin

Pronunciation: KAL-vin

The name Calvin is of French origin. The meaning of Calvin is "little bald one". An adopted French surname, from Old French *chauve*, 'bald'. Given at first in honor of the French theologian Jean Calvin (1509-1564).

Camden

Pronunciation: KAM-den

The name Camden is of Scottish and Gaelic origin. The meaning of the name Camden is "winding valley." Camden is also a place name.

Cameron

Pronunciation: KAM-er-en

Cameron is of Scottish and Gaelic origin. The meaning of Cameron is "crooked nose, crooked stream". Cameron is used as both a boy's name and a girl's name. The adopted Scottish surname was borne by a prominent Highland clan. The name was rarely used outside of Scotland before the 1950's.

Camilo

Pronunciation: ka-MEE-loh

Camilo is of Latin origin. The meaning of the name

Camilo is "helper to the priest". The name is a masculine variation of the name Camilla.

Campbell

Pronunciation: CAM-bel

Campbell is of Scottish and Gaelic origin. An adopted Scottish surname, from *cam beaul*. The meaning of the name Campbell is "crooked mouth". A family name of the Dukes of Argyll. The name has been in use since the mid-20th century.

Carl

Pronunciation: karl

The name Carl is of Old German origin. The name Carl is an old fashioned variation of Karl, the German form of Charles.

Carlos

Pronunciation: KAR-lohs

Carlos is of Spanish origin. The meaning of the name Carlos is "free man". The name is a variant of the name Charles.

Carlton

Pronunciation: KARL-ten

The name Carlton is of Old English origin. The

meaning of Carlton is "free peasant settlement".
Adopted surname and common English place name,
from Old English carl.

Carson

Pronunciation: KAR-sen

Carson is of Scottish and Old English origin. The
meaning of the name Cason is "son of the marsh
dwellers". Carson is an adopted Scottish surname,
possibly taken from the medieval name de Carsan. The
first known bearer was Robert de Carsan in the 13th
century.

Carter

Pronunciation: KAR-ter

Carter is of Old English origin. The meaning of the
name Carter is "one who transports goods". Originally
a surname and a given occupational name.

Casey

Pronunciation: KAY-see

The name Casey is of Irish and Gaelic origin. The
meaning of Casey is "alert, watchful". The name Casey
is used as both a boy's name, and as a girl's name.
Casey is from the male Gaelic name *Cathasaigh*.

Cassius

Pronunciation: KASH-us

Cassius is of Latin origin. The meaning of the name Cassius is "empty, hollow". The name is an old Roman family clan name.

Cecil

Pronunciation: SESS-ul

The name Cecil is of Latin origin. The meaning of Cecil is "blind". An adopted surname from the Roman family name Caecilius, derived from Latin Caecus, 'blind'. The name was popular during the late 19th century.

Cedric

Pronunciation: SED-rik

The name Cedric is of Old English origin. The meaning of Cedric is "kind, loved". Possibly an altered form of the name Cerdic, a 6th-century king of Wessex. The name Cedric was invented by Sir Walter Scott for the character Cedric of Rotherwood for his book, *Ivanhoe* (1819).

Cesar

Pronunciation: sez-ZAR

Cesar is of Latin origin. The meaning of the name Cesar is "head of hair".

Chance

Pronunciation: chans

The name Chance is of Middle English origin. The meaning of Chance is "good fortune". Originally a surname. Chance is also a variant of the name Chauncey.

Chandler

Pronunciation: CHAND-ler

Chandler is of Middle English and Old French origin. The meaning of the name Chandler is "candle maker". The adopted surname was also an occupational name from 'chandele' meaning 'candle'. Chandler is used as both a boy's name and as a girl's name.

Charles

Pronunciation: charlz

Charles is of Old German origin. The meaning of the name Charles is "free man". Charles the Great (742-814) was also known as Charlemagne, was a powerful German leader who created a more ordered society out of the chaos that followed the fall of Rome. Charles became king of the Franks in 771, he was the first Holy Roman Emperor in 800. He united France and much of central Europe. He was said to have been eight feet tall and extremely strong. His widespread fame gave rise to many forms of his name. Charles and its variant forms have been favored by royalty of several different countries. Diminutives: Charley, Charlie, Chas, Chay, Chuck.

Chester

Pronunciation: CHES-ter

Chester if of Old English and Latin origin. The meaning of the name Chester is "camp of soldiers". Chester is an adopted surname and English place name that is derived from Latin castra, 'camp'.

Chris

Pronunciation: kris

The name Chris is of Greek origin. The meaning of Chris is "bearing Christ". Chris is a short form of the names Christopher and Christian.

Christian

Pronunciation: KRIS-chen

Christian is of Latin origin. The meaning of the name Christian is "follower of Christ". According to the Bible the term was first used at Antioch (Acts 11:26); 'And when he had found him, he brought him unto Antioch. And the disciples were called Christians first in Antioch'. The name Christian comes from the Latin girls name, Christianus. It may have become a popular male name due to the success of John Bunyan's 'Pilgrim's Progress' (1678), whose hero is called Christian. Diminutives: Chris, Christie, Christy.

Christopher

Pronunciation: KRIS-toh-fer

Christopher is of Greek origin. The meaning of the name Christopher is "bearing Christ". From the Greek name Khristophoros, from Khristos. The name was popular among early Christians. The symbolic legend of giant Saint Christopher, 'the bearer of Christ', carried the Christ child safely across a river. Saint Christopher is considered the patron saint of travelers. The name has been in constant use since the 15th century. Diminutives: Chris, Kris, Christie, Kester, Christy.

Cian

Pronunciation: KEE-an

The name Cian is of Irish and Gaelic origin. The meaning of Cian is "ancient". Borne by the name of Brian Boru's son in law, who played a major role in the battle of Clontarf in the 11th century.

Clarence

Pronunciation: KLARE-ence

Clarence is of Latin origin. The meaning of Clarence is "one who lives near the river Clare". Clarence was first used as a given name since the mid-19th century.

Clark

Pronunciation: klark

The name Clark is of Latin origin. The meaning of Clark is "clerk, cleric". An adopted surname, originally an occupational name for a clerk or cleric. The name was popularized in the 20th century by the actor Clark Gable (1901-1960). The name was also made famous by the fictional character Clark Kent, otherwise known as Superman.

Clay

Pronunciation: KLAY

Clay is of Old English origin. Originally an occupational or place name which involved clay. Clay was a valued natural resource in earlier times. Clay can be used as a short form of the name Clayton.

Clayton

Pronunciation: KLAYT-en

The name Clayton is of Old English origin. The meaning of Clayton is "clay settlement". The name is an adopted surname and English place name derived from Clay. Its use as a first name dates back to the beginning of the 19th century.

Clement
Pronunciation: KLEM-ent

Clement is of Latin origin. The meaning of the name Clement is "merciful". Borne by several early saints, including Clement of Alexandria (c.150-c215). A disciple of St Paul who became the first of thirteen popes bearing the name. The name was popular during the Middle Ages.

Clifford
Pronunciation: KLIF-erd

The name Clifford is of Old English origin. The meaning of Clifford is "cliff-side ford". Originally a surname used as given name from the seventh-century. Diminutive; Cliff.

Clifton
Pronunciation: KLIF-ten

The name Clifton is of Old English Origin. The meaning of Clifton is "town by the cliff". Originally a surname used as given name.

Clinton
Pronunciation: KLIN-ten

Clinton is of Old English origin. The meaning of Clinton is "fenced settlement". Clinton is both a surname and a place name from *Glympton*, in Oxfordshire.

Clive
Pronunciation: kleeve

The name Clive is of Old English origin. The meaning of Clive is "cliff, slope". Clive is an adopted surname and place name from Old English Clif. The name was made popular in honour of Robert Clive, a famous English soldier known as Clive of India.

Clyde
Pronunciation: klyd

The name Clyde is of Scottish origin. Clyde is also a place name, the River Clyde in Scotland. Clyde Barrow was a notorious outlaw, who made the name well known during The Great Depression with his partner Bonnie.

Cody

Pronunciation: KO-dee

The name Cody is of Irish and Gaelic origin. The meaning of the name Cody is "helper". Cody is used as both a boy's name, and as a girl's name.

Cole

Pronunciation: kohl

Cole is of Middle English and Old French origin. The meaning of Cole is "charcoal". Originally a surname that was derived from a medieval given name. Cole is used as both a boy's name and as a girl's name.

Colin

Pronunciation: KOH-lin

Colin is of Irish and Scottish Gaelic origin. The meaning of the name is "young creature". The name has been used as an Anglicized form of Cailean. Collin is a diminutive form of the medieval name Colle, which is a short form of the Greek name Nicholas.

Conan

Pronunciation: KOH-nan

Conan is of English, Irish and Scottish Gaelic origin. The meaning of Conan is "hound, high". The name was taken to Ireland after the Norman Conquest.

Borne in Irish legend, Conan was a warrior who fought under Finn mac Fumhail (Finn McCool). Also the name of a seventh-century saint who was an Irish missionary on the Isle of Man.

Connor

Pronunciation: KAH-ner

Connor is of Irish and Gaelic origin. Anglicised form of the Irish Gaelic name Conchobhar, Borne in Irish legend by the son of Nessa, who became a legendary king of Ulster. As an old man, he lusted after the young Deirdre and forced her to marry him. The meaning of Connor is "hound lover".

Conrad

Pronunciation: KAHN-rad

Conrad is of Old German origin. The meaning of Conrad is "brave, counsel". The name of 10th-century bishop of Constance, it was reintroduced to the English-speaking world in the 19th century. Conrad is also the name of nine saints and several German kings during the Middle Ages.

Constantine

Pronunciation: KAHN-stan-teen

Constantine is of Latin origin. The meaning of Constantine is "constant". Constantine the Great (c.

288-337) was the first Cristian emperor, who left Rome to found Constantinople. The name was popular among the Puritans as virtue name. Constantine was also the name of 11 Byzantine emperors and a royal name in Greece. Borne by three Scottish kings.

Cooper

Pronunciation: KOO-per

The name Cooper is of Old English origin. The meaning of Cooper is "barrel maker". The name may also be the English form of a German surname which means "coppersmith".

Corey

Pronunciation: KOR-ee

The name Corey is an English surname derived from an Old Norse personal name Kori. Corey is used as both a boy's name, and as a girl's name. The meaning of the name may mean "God, peace".

Cornelius

Pronunciation: kor-NEEL-yus

The name Cornelius is of Latin origin. The Roman family name may be derived from cornu. The meaning of Cornelius is "horn". Cornelius is a famous Latin clan name. A biblical name: borne by a Roman centurion converted by St Peter. Cornelius is also the name of a third-century pope who is venerated as a saint.

Cortez

Pronunciation: kor-TEZ

Cortez is of Spanish origin. The meaning of the name Cortez is "courteous". The name is also a variant of Curtis. Cortez was the surname of the 16th-century Spanish explorer Hernando Cortes. His small expeditionary force conquered the Aztec civilization of Mexico.

Courtney

Pronunciation: COURT-ney

Courtney is of Old French origin. The meaning of Courtney is "domain of Curtis". The name is both a surname and a place name. Courtney is a Norman baronial name from places in Northern France called Courtenay. Courtney is used as both a boy's name and a girl's name.

Craig

Pronunciation: krayg

Craig is of Scottish and Gaelic origin. The meaning of Craig is "rocky". The name is derived from the word "crag". Originally Craig was used as a Scottish surname.

Cruz

Pronunciation: Krooz

Cruz is of Spanish and Portuguese origin. The meaning of the name Cruz is "cross."

Curtis

Pronunciation: KERT-iss

The name Curtis is of English and Old French origin. The meaning of Curtis is "Courteous, polite". Originally used as a nickname in the Middle Ages, for courteous person. Curtis is also used as a surname. Curtis was originally used as a first name in the 19th century.

Cyrus

Pronunciation: SY-russ

Cyrus is of Greek origin. The meaning of Cyrus is "lord". Derived from Kyros of the name of several kings of Persia. A biblical name; Cyrus is named in the book of Isaiah, as the one who would overthrow Babylon and liberate the Israelites. In the fifth century BC, Cyrus the Great conquered Babylon at the height of its powers and founded the Persian Empire.

D

Dace

Pronunciation: dayce

The name Dace is of French origin. The meaning of Dace is "of the nobility". The name may also be used as a form of Dasius and Datius.

Dacey

Pronunciation: DAY-cee

Dacey is of Irish, Gaelic and Latin origin. The meaning of Dacey is "from the South". The name is used as both a boy's name and as a girl's name.

Dag

Pronunciation: dag

Dag is of Scandinavian origin. The meaning of the name Dag is "daylight". Borne in mythology; Dag was the son of Night who brought the daylight as he rode his horse around the earth.

Dagan

Pronunciation: DAY-gan

The name Dagan is of Hebrew origin. The meaning of Dagan is "the earth".

Dagobert
Pronunciation: DAG-o-bert
The name Dagobert is of Old German origin. The meaning of Dagobert is "bright day".

Dahy
Pronunciation: DA-hy
Dahy is of Irish and Gaelic origin. The meaning of the name of Dahy is "quick footed".

Dailey
Pronunciation: DAY-lee
The name Dailey is of Irish and Gaelic origin. The meaning of Dailey is "assembly".

Dainard
Pronunciation: DAYN-ard
Dainard is of Old English origin. The meaning of Dainard is "bold Dane".

Dakota
Pronunciation: da-KOH-tah

Dakota is of Native American Indian origin. The meaning of the name Dakota is "friend". Originally a tribal and place name.

Dale

Pronunciation: dayl

The name Dale is of Old English origin. The meaning of Dale is "Valley". Originally a surname, Dale is also a place name.

Dalton

Pronunciation: DOLL-ton

The name Dalton is of Old English origin. The meaning of Dalton is "from the valley town". Dalton is also a place name.

Damian

Pronunciation: DAY-mee-en

Damian is of Greek origin. The meaning of the name Damian is "to tame". Anglicised from the Greek name Damianos, from *daman*, 'to tame'. Saint Damian, a 4th-century Greek martyr is known as the patron saint of doctors. The Belgian priest Father Damien is honored for giving his life to the lepers of Molokai in Hawaii.

Damon

Pronunciation: DAY-mon

The name Damon is of Greek origin. The meaning of Damon is "one who Tames". From Greek demos, 'land' or 'people'. The name is a variant of Damian.

Dane

Pronunciation: dayn

Dane is of English origin. The meaning of the name Dane is "from Denmark". Originally a surname that indicated Danish ancestry.

Daniel

Pronunciation: DAN-yel

The name Daniel is of Hebrew origin. The meaning of Daniel is "God has judged". A biblical name; borne in the Old Testament by a prophet and writer, his story is told in the book of Daniel. He is probably most known for being thrown into a den of lions and surviving (Daniel 6:16). Diminutives: Dan, Dannie, Danny

Danny

Pronunciation: DANN-ee

Danny is of Hebrew origin. The meaning of the name Danny is "God has judged". Danny is a variant of the name Daniel.

Dante

Pronunciation: DAHN-tay

Dante is of Spanish, Latin and Italian origin. The meaning of the name Dante is "lasting, enduring". Poet, Dante Alighieri was best known for Dante's Inferno, his graphic description of the medieval version of Hell.

Danyal

Pronunciation: DAN-yal

The name Danyal is of Hebrew origin. The meaning of Danyal is "God has judged". Danyal is a variant of the name Daniel.

Darcy

Pronunciation: DAR-cee

The name Darcy is of Irish and Gaelic origin. The meaning of Darcy is "dark". An adopted Norman baronial surname (D'Arcy). The name was introduced to Britain during the Norman Conquest. Darcy is used as both a boy's name, and as a girl's name. Darcy is also a Norman place name.

Dargan

Pronunciation: DAR-gan

The name Dargan is of Irish origin. The meaning of Dargan is "black haired". The name is a variant of Deegan.

Darius

Pronunciation: DARE-ee-us

The name Darius is of Greek and Persian origin. The meaning of Darius is "maintains possessions well". From the Greek name Dareios, derived from Old Persian *darayavush*, from *daraya*, 'posses', and *vahu*, 'well'. A biblical name; born in the Old Testament by Darius the Great. He was the governor of Persia, who became king in 521BC (Ezra 4:5). Darius is also the name of a saint, who was martyred at Nicaea.

Darrell

Pronunciation: DARR-ell

The name Darrell is of Old English and Old French origin. The meaning of Darrell is "open". An adopted surname and originally a French place name, Arielle in the northern region of Calvados. Darrell is also a variant of the name Darryl.

Darren

Pronunciation: DAR-en

Darren is of Irish and Gaelic origin. The meaning of the name Darren is "great". Originally an adopted Irish surname, first used as a given name in the 20th century. The name became popular during the 1960's.

Dave

Pronunciation: DAY-ve

The name Dave is of Hebrew origin. The meaning of Dave is "beloved; son of David". Dave is a variant of the name David.

David

Pronunciation: DAY-vid

The name David is of Hebrew origin. The meaning of David is "beloved". From Hebrew *dawid*, which means 'beloved'. A biblical name; borne in the Old Testament by the youngest son of Jesse. David was a shepherd, poet, musician, soldier, king and a prophet. He slew the giant Goliath and found favor with Saul with his talented harp playing. He is the only David mentioned in the Bible. The 6th-century saint, St David is regarded as patron saint of Wales. Diminutives: Dave, Davey, Davy.

Dawson

Pronunciation: DAW-sun

The name Dawson is of Old English origin. The meaning of Dawson is "son of David". Originally a form of the medieval surname.

Deacon

Pronunciation: DEE-ken

Deacon is of Greek origin. The meaning of the name Deacon is "dusty one; messenger". A deacon is a ministerial assistant in a Christian congregation.

Dean

Pronunciation: deen

Dean if of Old English origin. The meaning of the name Dean is "Valley". An adopted surname, derived from the Old English *denu*, meaning 'valley'. Dean is also a place name.

Declan

Pronunciation: DECK-lan

The name Declan is of Irish origin. The meaning of Declan is unknown. Anglicised form of the Irish Gaelic name Deaglán. Borne by a 5th century Irish bishop of Ardmore.

Dennis

Pronunciation: DEN-iss

Dennis is of English and Greek origin. The meaning of the name Dennis is "follower of Dionysius". The name is a variant of Dionysius. A biblical name; borne by a judge of Athens who was converted to Christianity by the apostle Paul. A 3rd-century evangelist missionary to Gaul and a traditional patron saint of France was said to have been beheaded in Paris in 272. He was then supposed to have walked for two miles carrying his own head, before placing it down on the site which is now where the Cathedral of Saint Denis stands. Diminutives: Dennie, Denny.

Denzil

Pronunciation: DEN-zil

The name Denzil is of Old English origin. The meaning of Denzil is unknown. An adopted surname, from Denzell, in Cornwall. It was first adopted by the Holles family, when it became connected to them by marriage.

Derek

Pronunciation: DARE-ik

The name Derek is of Old German origin. The meaning of Derek is "people's ruler". The name is

German form of Theodoric. Derek was introduced to Britain in the late Middle Ages by immigrant Flemish weavers and merchants.

Desmond

Pronunciation: DEZ-mund

The name Desmond is of Gaelic and Irish origin. The meaning of Desmond is "from South Munster". Originally an adopted surname and Irish place name referring to Munster which is one of the five regions of ancient Ireland. From Irish Gaelic Deas Mumhain, which means 'South Munster'. The name was first used in Ireland in the mid-19th century.

Devon

Pronunciation: DEV-en

Devon is of English origin. The meaning of the name Devon is uncertain. Devon is originally an adopted surname, English county name, and the name of several towns in America. The name is used as both a boy's name and as a girl's name.

Dexter

Pronunciation: DEKS-ter

The name Dexter is of Old English and Latin origin. The meaning of Dexter is "right handed, fortunate".

Originally derived from Greek *dexi*, meaning '
worship'. Dexter is an Old English occupational name.

Diego
Pronunciation: dee-AY-go
Diego is of Spanish origin. The meaning of the name
Diego is "he who supplants". Borne by a Mexican
peasant to whom the Virgin of Guadalupe appeared
was called Juan Diego.

Digby
Pronunciation: DIG-bee
The name Digby is of Old Norse origin. The meaning
of Digby is "town by the ditch". Digby is also a place
name.

Dillan
Pronunciation: DILL-an
The name Dillan is of Irish and Gaelic origin. The
meaning of Dillan is "like a lion, loyal". The name is a
variant of Dillon. Dillan is used as both a boy's name
and as a girl's name.

Dion
Pronunciation: DEE-on

Dion is of Greek origin. The meaning of the name
Dion is unknown. Dion is a short form of the
Dionysius.

Dirk

Pronunciation: derk

The name Dirk is of Dutch origin. The meaning of the
Dirk is "the people's ruler". The name is a variation of
Derek. The name was made popular by a Scottish born
actor and writer, Dirk Bogarde. Dirk is also a Scottish
term for a small, sharp knife.

Dominic

Pronunciation: DAH-ma-nik

Dominic is of Latin origin. The meaning of the name
Dominic is "Lord". From Latin *Dominicus*, which
means 'of the Lord'. St Dominic (1170-1221) founded
the Dominican order of the monks. The name became
popular throughout the Christian world. Diminutive:
Dom.

Donald

Pronunciation: DAHN-ald

Donald is of Gaelic and Scottish origin. The meaning
of Donald is "great chief". Anglicised form of the
Scottish Gaelic name Domhall (*doe-nall*). From Old

Celtic *dubno*, meaning 'world', and *val*, 'rule'. Donald is one of the clan names of Scotland. Borne by several early kings of Scotland. Diminutives: Don, Donny.

Donovan

Pronunciation: DAH-na-vun

The name Donovan is of Irish and Gaelic origin. The meaning of Donovan is "dark haired chieftain".

Doran

Pronunciation: DOR-an

The name Doran is of Irish and Gaelic origin. The meaning of Doan is "stranger, exile".

Dorian

Pronunciation: DOR-ee-en

The name Dorian is of Greek origin. The meaning of Dorian is "Descendant of Dorus". Borne by an ancient Greek people and meaning 'from Doris' (an area of northern Greece). The name was popularised by Oscar Wilde's novel, *The Picture of Dorian Gray* (1891).

Dougal

Pronunciation: DOO-gal

The name Dougal is of Celtic origin. The meaning of Dougal is "dark stranger". Anglicised of the Irish

Gaelic name Dubhghall, meaning 'dark stranger'. The name was given by the Irish to invading Vikings in the 9th century. Diminutives: Dough, Dougie.

Douglas

Pronunciation: DUG-las

The name Douglas is of Gaelic and Scottish origin. The meaning of Douglas is "black river". Initially derived from the River Douglas, the name is also a place name. The name was adopted by a powerful clan and used as a first name in the 16th century. The river name and surname is also found in Ireland, Scotland and in the Isle of Man. Diminutives: Doug, Dougie.

Dudley

Pronunciation: DUD-lee

Dudley is of Old English origin. The meaning of the name Dudley is "people's field". Dudley is an adopted surname and English place name. An aristocratic family name of the Earls of Leicester. Dudley has been used as a given name since the 19th century.

Duncan

Pronunciation: DUN-kin

The name Duncan is of Gaelic and Scottish origin. The meaning of Duncan is "dark warrior". Borne by a 7th-century abbot of Iona and two medieval kings of Scotland, including Duncan I who was murdered by Macbeth in 1040. Shakespeare immortalised him in his play, *Macbeth* (1606).

Dunstan

Pronunciation: DUN-sten

Dunstan is of Old English origin. The meaning of Dunstan is "brown hill". From Old English *dun*, 'hill', and *stan* meaning, 'stone'. St Dunstan was a renowned 10th century Archbishop of Canterbury, who restored the monastery system in England. Dunstan is also a place name.

Dylan

Pronunciation: DIL-an

The name Dylan is of Welsh origin. The meaning of Dylan is "son of the sea". Borne in a Welsh legend by the son of a sea god. Welsh poet Dylan Thomas (1914-1953), and American singer Bob Dylan (1941) popularised the name.

E

Eamon

Pronunciation: AY-mon

Eamon is of Irish and Gaelic origin. The meaning of the name Eamon is "wealthy protector". The name is a variant of Edmund.

Earl

Pronunciation: erl

The name Earl is of Old English origin. The meaning of Earl is "nobleman, warrior". From Old English *eorl*. The name was originally based on the English title, and used as a nickname for people who worked for the aristocratic household of Earl.

Earland

Pronunciation: erl-AND

The name Earland is of Old English origin. The meaning of Earland is "earl's land". Earland is also a place name.

Earlston

Pronunciation: erl-ST-on

The name Earlston is of Old English origin. The meaning of Earlston is "earl's settlement".

Early

Pronunciation: erl-EE

Early is of Old English origin. The meaning of the name Early is "eagle wood". Possibly derived from the Old English term *eorlic*, or from the English word 'early'.

Earvin

Pronunciation: EAR-vin

The name Earvin is of Gaelic origin. The meaning of Earvin is "green, freshwater". The name is a variant of Irvin. The name was made famous by American basketball legend Earvin 'Magic' Johnson.

Eastman

Pronunciation: EES-tman

The name Eastman is of Old English origin. The meaning of Eastman is "man from the East".

Easton

Pronunciation: EES-tun

Easton is of Old English origin. The meaning of the name Easton is "East settlement". The name may possibly have been derived from an Old English phrase meaning, 'island of stones'.

Eben

Pronunciation: EBB-an

The name Eben is of Hebrew origin. The meaning of Eben is "stone". The name is also used as a nickname for Ebenezer.

Ebenezer

Pronunciation: EBB-an-ee-zer

The name Ebenezer is of Hebrew origin. The meaning of Ebenezer is "stone of help". A biblical name; Ebenezer was the name of a memorial stone set up by the prophet Samuel in order to mark a critical battle and victory in Jewish history. The name was first used as a given first name in the 17th century by the Puritans. Charles Dicken's popularised the name in his novel, *A Christmas Carol* (1843).

Edan

Pronunciation: EE-dan

The name Edan is of Irish, Gaelic and Scottish origin. The meaning of Edan is "fire". The name is a variant of Aidan. Edan is also a saint's name.

Edbert
Pronunciation: ED-bert
The name Edbert is of Old English origin. The meaning of Edbert is "bright".

Eddie
Pronunciation: ED-ee
Eddie is of English origin. The meaning of the name Eddie is unknown. The name is used as a nickname for Edgar, Edmund, Edward and Edwin. Eddie is used as both a boy's name and as a girl's name.

Edel
Pronunciation: ED-el
Edel is of Old German origin. The meaning of the name Edel is "noble".

Edgar
Pronunciation: ED-gar
Edgar is of Old English origin. The meaning of the name Edgar is "spear". From the Old English name Eadgar, from *ead*, 'riches' or 'prosperous', and *gar*,

'spear'. A royal name in Anglo-Saxon England. Borne by a 10th-century king of England. Edgar is one of few early Anglo-Saxon names to have survived the Norman Conquest. Shakespeare used the name for the son of the Duke of Gloucester in *King Lear* (1605). Diminutives: Ed, Eddy, Eddie

Edmund

Pronunciation: ED-mund

The name Edmund is of Old English origin. The meaning of Edmund is "wealthy protector". From the Old English name Eadmund, from *ead*, 'rich', and *mund*, 'protection'. Edmund is the name of several early royal and saintly figures. The name was one of few early Anglo-Saxon names to have survived the Norman Conquest. Diminutives: Ed, Eddy, Eddie, Ned, Neddie, Neddy, Ted, Teddy, Teddie.

Edward

Pronunciation: ED-werd

Edward is of Old English origin. The meaning of the name Edward is "wealthy guard". From the Old English name Eadweard, from *ead*, 'rich', and *weard*, 'guardian'. Edward is one of the few Anglo-Saxon names to have survived the Norman Conquest. Borne by three Anglo-Saxon kings and eight kings of England since the Norman Conquest. King Edward the Confessor, 1042-1066 was also a saint. Edward is a consistently popular name. Diminutives: Ed, Eddie, Eddy, Ned, Neddy, Neddie, Ted, Teddy, Teddie.

Edwin

Pronunciation: ED-win

The name Edwin is of Old English origin. The meaning of Edwin is "wealthy friend". From the Old English name Eadwine, from *ead,* 'rich', and *wine,* 'friend'. Borne by a 7th -century king of Northumberland who converted to Christianity. Edwin is one of the few Anglo-Saxon names to have survived the Norman Conquest. The name was revived in the 19th century. Diminutives: Ed, Eddie.

Eli

Pronunciation: EE-lye

The name Eli is of Hebrew origin. The meaning of Eli is "high". The Hebrew meaning is, "height, elevation". A biblical name; borne in the Old Testament by a high priest who brought up the prophet Samuel. The holy name was popular among Puritans in the 17th century.

Elias

Pronunciation: ee-LYE-us

Elias is of Greek and Hebrew origin. The meaning of the name Elias is "Jehovah is God". A biblical name; borne in the New Testament, from the Greek form of Elijah.

Eliot

Pronunciation: EL-i-ot

The name Eliot is of Greek and Hebrew origin. The meaning of Eliot is "Jehovah is God". The name is a variant of the biblical name, Elias. An adopted surname, diminutive of Elie. Also the Old French form of Elias.

Elroy

Pronunciation: EL-roy

Elroy is of French origin. The meaning of the name Elroy is "the king". The name is a variation of Leroy. Possibly influenced by the Spanish *el*, 'the'.

Elwin

Pronunciation: EL-win

The name Elwin is of Old English origin. The meaning of Elwin is "elf, fair brow". From Old English *aethel*, 'nobel', and *wine*, 'friend'. Variant of Elvin.

Elwyn

Pronunciation: EL-win

Elwyn is of Gaelic and Welsh origin. The meaning of the name Elwyn is, "white, blessed, holy". Influenced by Welsh *(g)wyn*. A variant of the name Alan. Elwyn is also a form of the name of a 6th-century Irish saint.

Emil

Pronunciation: AY-mul

The name Emil is of Latin origin. The meaning of Emil is "rival, eager". The German name is derived from the Latin *Aemilius*, meaning 'eager'.

Emile

Pronunciation: AY-mile

Emile is of Latin origin. The meaning of the name Emile is "rival, eager". The name is a variant of Emil. From the Roman surname *Aesmilius*. The name was made popular by the French writer Emile Zola (1840-1902).

Emanuel

Pronunciation: ee-MAN-yo-el

Emanuel is of Hebrew origin. The meaning of the name Emanuel is "God is with us". A biblical name;

borne in the Old Testament to the child whose birth Isaiah foretold. The name was applied to the New Testament, to the coming Messiah. Diminutive: Manny.

Emmanuel

Pronunciation: ee-MAN-yoo-el

Emmanual is of Hebrew origin. The meaning of the name Emmanuel is "God is with us". The Hebrew for of Immanuel. A biblical name; borne in the Old Testament. The name was applied to the New Testament, a name title for the coming Messiah. Diminutive: Manny.

Eric

Pronunciation: AIR-ik

The name Eric is of Old Norse origin. The meaning of Eric is "complete ruler". Old Norse, from *ei*, 'always', and *ric*, 'ruler'. The name was introduced to Britain during the 9th century by Scandinavian settlers. The original form is Erik, borne by nine Danish kings. The name was revived in the 19th century. Eric is also used as a nickname for Frederic. Diminutives: Rick, Ricky.

Ernest

Pronunciation: ERN-ist

Ernest is of Old German origin. The meaning of the name Ernest is "seriousness". From the Old German name Ernst, meaning 'earnestness', or 'seriousness'. The Hanoverians introduced the name to Britain during the 18th century. The name became more popular due to Oscar Wilde's play, *The Importance of Being Ernest* (1899). Diminutives: Ern, Ernie, Erny.

Esmond

Pronunciation: EZ-mund

Esmund is of Old English origin. The meaning of Esmond is "ease of protection". From an Old English name, Eastmund, from *east*, 'grace', and *mund*, 'protection'. The name is an adopted surname in modern times, due to the success of Thackeray's *History of Henry Esmond* (1852).

Ethan

Pronunciation: EE-than

Ethan is of Hebrew origin. The meaning of the name Ethan is "firmness". A biblical name; Ethan the Ezrahite was mentioned in the Old Testament. Known for his wisdom, Solomon was superior in wisdom. Ethan Allen (1738-1789) made the name more popular in America after he played an important role in the

American War of Independence.

Eugene
Pronunciation: you-JEEN
The name Eugene is of Greek origin. The meaning of
Eugene is "noble aristocrat". From the Old French
form of a Greek name, derived from *eugenios.* 'noble'.
Borne by several saints, two bishops and four popes.
Variations: Eoan, Euan, Ewan, Ewen.

Evan
Pronunciation: EV-an
The name Evan is of Hebrew, Scottish and Welsh
origin. The meaning of Evan is "God is gracious".
Anglicisation of Ieuan, Evan is the Welsh form of John.
Scotland also uses Evan as an anglicised form of
Eoghan. The Hebrew meaning of Evan means "rock".

Evelyn
Pronunciation: EV-e-lyn
Evelyn is of Norman origin. Anglicised form of the
Norman French feminine name Aveline. Evelyn is
used as both a boy's name, and as a girl's name. The
named was adopted as a boy's name in the 17th
century. Originally a surname and used as a given
name.

Everard

Pronunciation: EV-er-ard

Everard is of Old English and Old German origin. The meaning of the name Everard is " brave, boar". Taken from an Old English name, from *eofor*, 'boar', and *heard*, 'strong'. The Norman invaders used an Old German version. The Norman name has been used as a given name since the 19th century.

Ezra

Pronunciation: AIRZ-rah

The name Ezra is of Hebrew origin. The meaning of Ezra is "help". A biblical name; borne by prophet and author of the fifteenth book of the Bible. Ezra is one of the Old Testament names used by the Puritans.

F

Fabian

Pronunciation: FAY-bee-en

Fabian is of Latin origin. The meaning of the name Fabian is "bean". From the Roman family name Fabius. Borne of 16 saints and a 3rd-century pope. The socialist Fabian Society, founded in 1884, was named after a Roman general who resisted Hannibal's 3rd-century advance on Rome.

Farran

Pronunciation: FA-rran

The name Farran is of Old English and Old French origin. The meaning of Farran is "handsome servant". The name is a variant of the Old English name, Farren.

Felix

Pronunciation: FEEL-iks

The name Felix is of Latin origin. The meaning of Felix is "happy, lucky". From Felicitas, Roman goddess of good fortune and happiness. The name was borne by several saints and three popes. Felix was a popular name for early Christians.

Fergus

Pronunciation: FER-gus

Fergus is of Irish, Gaelic and Scottish origin. The meaning of the name Fergus is "vigorous man". Irish, anglicised form of Gaelic name Fearghas, from *fear*, 'man', and *gus*, 'vigour'. The name was borne in Irish legend by Fergus mac Roich. Saint Fergus (8th century) was a missionary to Scotland.

Diminutive: Fergie

Fenton

Pronunciation: FEN-ton

The name Fenton is of Old English origin. The meaning of Fenton is "marsh settlement". Fenton is also a place name from *fenn tûn*.

Finbar

Pronunciation: FIN-bar

Finbar is of Gaelic and Irish origin. The meaning of the name Finbar is "white, fair head". Irish, anglicised form of the Gaelic name Fionnbharr, from *fionn*, 'white, fair', and *barr*, 'head'. Finbar is a fairy king in

Irish mythology. Finbar was a 6th-century bishop of Cork, said to have crossed the Irish Sea on horseback. Diminutives: Finn, Bairre, Barry.

Fingal

Pronunciation: FIN-gal

The name Fingal is of Gaelic and Scottish origin. The meaning of Fingal is "fair, white stranger". Borne in Gaelic legend by the heroic father of Ossian. The name was originally used by the Irish for Norse settlers in Ireland. James Macpherson's poem Fingal (1762).

Finlay

Pronunciation: FIN-lay

Finlay is of Scottish and Gaelic origin. The meaning of the name Finlay is "fair, white warrior". Scottish, anglicised form of the Gaelic name Fionnlagh, from *fionn*, 'white, fair' and *laogh*, 'Warrior'.

Finn

Pronunciation: FIN

The name Finn of Irish, Gaelic and Old German origin. The meaning of Finn is "white, fair". Irish, anglicised form of *fionn*, 'fair, white'. Finn mac Cumhaill is a legendary hero of Irish mythology.

Fletcher

Pronunciation: FLECH-er

Fletcher is of Old French origin. The meaning of the name Fletcher is "arrow maker". The adopted surname is originally an occupational name for an arrow maker. From Old French *fleche*, 'arrow'. Fletcher Christian was the famous leader of the mutiny on the Bounty in 1789.

Florian

Pronunciation: FLOR-ee-an

The name Florian is of Latin origin. The meaning of Florian is "Flower". Derived from the Latin word flos, 'flower'. From a Roman clan name. Saint Florian was a 3rd century Roman soldier.

Floyd

Pronunciation: F-lo-yd

The name Floyd is of Welsh origin. The meaning of Floyd is "grey haired". The adopted Welsh surname, is a derivative of Lloyd, from the Welsh *llwyd*, 'grey'.

Flyn

Pronunciation: FL-yn

Flyn is of Irish and Gaelic origin. The meaning of the name Flyn is "descendant of Flann". The name is a variant of Flynn.

Francesco

Pronunciation: FRAN-ches-CO

Francesco is of Latin origin. The meaning of the name Francesco is "Frenchman". Francesco is a variant of the Latin name, Francis.

Francis

Pronunciation: FRAN-sis

The name Francis is of Latin origin. The meaning of Francis if "Frenchman". Anglicised form of the Italian name Francisco, derived from the Latin Franciscus which means 'French'. France was originally the kingdom of the Franks. The name was assumed by Saint Francis of Assisi (1181-1226), he is known as the gentle giant and associated with nature after preaching birds. Frances is the feminine form. Diminutives: Frank, Frankie

Franklin

Pronunciation: FRANK-lin

The name Franklin is of Old English origin. The meaning of Franklin is "freeman". The adopted surname is taken from Old English *francoleyn,* which means 'a freeman', specifically a landowner, not of noble birth, typically a prosperous farmer.
Diminutives: Frank, Frankie.

Frederick

Pronunciation: FRED-er-ik

The name Frederick is of Old French and Old German origin. The meaning of Frederick is "peaceful ruler". The Old English name Freodhoric was superceded by the Old German, Frithuric, derived from *frithu,* 'peace', and *ric,* 'ruler'. The Hanoverians brought the name to Britain in the 18th century.

G

Gabriel

Pronunciation: GAY-bree-el

The name Gabriel is of Hebrew origin. The meaning of Gabriel is "Hero of God". A biblical name; borne by the name Archangel Gabriel, one of God's chief messengers, and sometimes regarded as the angel of death. In the New Testament, he appeared to Mary and told her that she was to be the mother of Christ. Diminutive: Gabe.

Gareth

Pronunciation: GARE-eth

Gareth is of Welsh origin. The meaning of the name Gareth is "gentle". The name first appeared in Sir Thomas Malory's 15th-century account of the legendary Round Table, *Morte D'Arthur*. Sir Gareth was well known for his modesty and bravery. Diminutives: Garth, Gary, Garry.

Garfield

Pronunciation: GARF-ield

The name Garfield is of Old English origin. The meaning of Garfield is "spear field". The adopted surname was most likely used as a first name in honour of J A Garfield (1831-1881), a 20th-century president of the U.S,

Garry

Pronunciation: GAR-ee

The name Garry is of Old English origin. The meaning of Garry is "spear". The name is a diminutive of Gareth. Gary Cooper popularised the name during the 1930's, he had taken the name from his hometown Gary, Indiana.

Gavin

Pronunciation: GAV-en

Gavin is of Welsh origin. The meaning of the name Gavin is "white falcon". The name is a variation of the medieval name Gawain.

Gawain

Pronunciation: GA-wain

The name Gawain is of Welsh and Scottish origin. The meaning of Gawain is "white falcon". The name is a variant of Gavin.

Geoffrey

Pronunciation: JEF-ree

Geoffrey is of Old German origin. The meaning of the name Geoffrey is "peace". The name was introduced to Britain during the Norman Conquest. Geoffrey was a popular name during the medieval era.

George

Pronunciation: JORJ

The name George is of Greek origin. The meaning of George is "farmer". From Greek *georgos*, meaning 'farmer'. The name was influenced by Old Latin and Old French. Borne by several early saints, including St George, a knight who became the patron saint of England. He achieved legendary status through the medieval story of him slaying a fire breathing dragon. The legend is a symbolic tale of good triumphing evil, with the dragon being the devil. The name is a royal name, borne by six kings of England.

Gerald

Pronunciation: JARE-ald

The name Gerald is of Old German origin. The meaning of Gerald is "spear ruler". The name was popular during the medieval era and was later revived in the 19th century. Diminutives: Ged, Der, Gerry. Jed, Jerry,

Gerrard
Pronunciation: JARE-ard
The name Gerrard is of Old German origin. The meaning of Gerrard is "spear ruler". The name is a variant of Gerald. The name was popular during the medieval era, and later revived during the 19th century. Diminutives: Gerry, Jerry.

Gilbert
Pronunciation: GIL-bert
Gilbert is of Old French origin. The meaning of the name Gilbert is "bright promise". It was a Norman introduction to Britain. Diminutives: Gil, Gilly, Gillie.

Giles
Pronunciation: jiles
The name Giles if of Greek origin. The meaning of Giles is "small goat". The name is an altered version of the Latin name Aegidius, from the Greek name Aigidios. The name refers to the goat skin that ancient

shields were made of. St Giles is regarded as the patron saint of cripples, beggars, and blacksmiths. Churches that are dedicated to him are typically located outside of city centers, where cripples were condemned to live.

Glen

Pronunciation: glen

Glen is of Irish and Gaelic origin. The meaning of Glen is "glen". The adopted surname is from Gaelic *gleann*, meaning 'valley'. A Glen is a narrow valley between hills. The name is also a place name.

Glyn

Pronunciation: glin

The name Glyn is of Irish and Gaelic origin. The meaning of Glyn is "valley of water". Glyn is a place name. The name is also a variant of Glen. Glyn is used as both a boy's name and as girl's name.

Goldwin

Pronunciation: GOLD-win

The name Goldwin is of Old English origin. The meaning of Goldwin is "golden friend". From the Old English name Goldwine.

Gordon

Pronunciation: GORD-en

Gordon is of Old English and Gaelic origin. The meaning of the name Gordon is "large fortification". An adopted Scottish surname, derived from a place name. The name was first adopted as a first name in honour of Charles Gordon (1833-1885), a British general who was killed at Khartoum.

Graham

Pronunciation: GRAY-em

The name Graham is of Old English origin. The meaning of Graham is "gravel area". The name was derived from the Lincolnshire town of Grantham. The adopted surname, was taken to Scotland in the 12th century by Sir William de Graham.

Grant

Pronunciation: GRAN-t

The name Grant is of English and Gaelic origin. The meaning of Grant is "tall, big". An adopted surname derived from French *le grand* and given to tall men. The name first became popular as a first name in Scotland and America.

Granville

Pronunciation: GRAN-vill

The name Granville of Old French origin. The meaning of Granville is "big town". Originally a place name. Granville is also an adopted French surname, derived from *grande ville*, which means 'large town'.

Gregory

Pronunciation: GREG-er-ee

Gregory is of Greek origin. The meaning of the name Gregory is "watchful, vigilant". Gregory the great (c. 540-604) was the first of sixteen popes of that name and one of the eleven Doctors of the Western Church. He founded monasteries and remodeled the church liturgy, and developed the Gregorian chants.

Greville

Pronunciation: GREV-vill

The name Greville is of Old French origin. The meaning of Greville is unknown. As adopted surname, from the French name for one from Greville.

Griffin

Pronunciation: GRIF-en

Griffin is of Latin origin. The meaning of Griffin is "hooked nose". Borne in Greek mythology and medieval legend; the Gryphon was a fierce creature with foreparts of an eagle and the hindquarters of a lion.

Guy

Pronunciation: gye

The name Guy is of Old German origin. The meaning of Guy is "wood". From the Old French name Guido, derived from the Old German name Wildo, from *witu*, meaning 'wood'. Guy was the French name of the early Christian martyr St Vitus. Guy Warwick, a medieval figure of romance and a hero of the Crusades, popularised the name. The name remained popular until it became associated with the leader of the Gunpowder Plot (1605), Guy Fawkes.

Gwyn

Pronunciation: GW-in

The name Gwyn is of Welsh origin. The meaning of Gwyn is "fair, blessed, holy, white". The name is used as both a boy's name, and as a girl's name.

H

Hadrian

Pronunciation: HAY-dree-en

Hadrian is of Latin origin. The meaning of the name Hadrian is "from Hadria". The name is a variation of Adrian. Hadria was a north Italian city.

Haydn

Pronunciation: HAY-den

The name Hayden is of Old English origin. The meaning of Hayden is "hedged valley". The name is conjectured to be a Welsh variant of Aidan.

Hamish

Pronunciation: HA-mish

The name Hamish is of Scottish origin. The meaning of Hamish is "he who supplants". The name is a Scottish form of James.

Harald

Pronunciation: HA-ra-ld

Harald is of Old Norse origin. The meaning of Harald is "army ruler". From Haraldr, an Old Norse form of Harold. The name is a variant of Harold.

Hardy
Pronunciation: HAR-dee
Hardy is of Old German origin. The meaning of Hardy is "bold, brave". Originally from the surname meaning, 'bold'.

Harley
Pronunciation: HAR-lee
The name Harley is of Old English origin. The meaning of Harley is "hare meadow, harewood".

Harold
Pronunciation: HARE-uld
The name Harold is Old English origin. The meaning of Harold is "army ruler". Old English from *here*, meaning 'army', and *weald*, 'power'. The name was influenced by the Old Norse name Haraldr.
Diminutive: Harry

Harrison
Pronunciation: HARE-ee-sun

The name Harrison is of Old English origin. The meaning of Harrison is "son of Harry". Harrison is an adopted surname.

Harry

Pronunciation: HARE-ee

The name Harry is of Old German origin. The meaning of Harry is "home leader". The name is a diminutive of Henry or Harold.

Hartley

Pronunciation: HART-lee

Hartley is of Old English origin. The meaning of the name Hartley is "stag meadow". Hartley is an adopted surname from Old English place name.

Harvey

Pronunciation: HAR-vee

The name Harvey is of Old English and Old French origin. The meaning of Harvey is "eager for battle". The name is a variant of the French name Herve.

Hasan

Pronunciation: HAS-an

The name Hasan if of Arabic origin. The meaning of Hasan is "beautiful, good-looking". The name is a variant of Hassan. Al Hasan was the Prophets grandson, the son of Fatima and Haidar. Hasan and his brother, Husayn are regarded as the rightful successors of Muhammad by the Shiites.

Hector
Pronunciation: HEK-tor
The name Hector is of Greek origin. The meaning of Hector is "to restrain". Greek meaning, 'holding fast'. Borne as the Prince of Troy, Hector was the Trojan hero who was killed by being lashed to his chariot and dragged around the walls of Troy, by Achilles.
Diminutives: Heck, Heckie.

Hedley
Pronunciation: HED-lee
The name Hedley is of Old English origin. The meaning of Hedley is "heathered meadow". The name is an adopted surname, derived from an English place name.

Henry
Pronunciation: HEN-ree
Henry is of Old German origin. The meaning of the name Henry is "home ruler". From Old German *haim*, meaning 'home', and *ric*, 'ruler'. The name was

adopted by the Normans and brought to Britain. The name is borne by eight English Kings. Diminutives: Hal, Hank, Harry, Hen.

Herbert
Pronunciation: HER-bert
The name Herbert is of Old German origin. The meaning of Herbert is "illustrious warrior". The name was brought to Britain by the Normans and died out by the Middle Ages. The name was later revived in the 19th century. Herbert is most notably the family name of the Earls of Pembroke.

Herman
Pronunciation: HER-man
Herman is of Old German origin. The meaning of Herman is "soldier". From the Old German name Hariman, from *here,* meaning 'army'. The Normans brought the name to Britain, where it died out in the Middle Ages. The name was later revived in the 19th-century. St Herman from the 11th-century, wrote hymn "Salve Regina".

Horace
Pronunciation: HOR-ess

The name Horace is of Latin origin. The meaning of Horace is unknown. From the Roman family name Horatius. Borne by Roman lyrical poet, Quintus Horatius Flaccus (65-8BC).

Howard
Pronunciation: HOW-erd
The name Howard is of Old English origin. The meaning of Howard is "noble watchman". An adopted aristocratic and occupational surname. Howard is the family name of the Dukes of Norfolk. The name was used as a given first name during the 19th century.

Howell
Pronunciation: HOWE-ll
The name Howell is of Welsh origin. The meaning of Howell is "eminent, remarkable". Anglicised form of the Welsh name Hywel. Howell is also an adopted surname.

Hugh
Pronunciation: HEW
Hugh is of Old German origin. The meaning of Hugh is "soul, heart, intellect". The name was introduced to Britain by the Normans and became popular during

the Middle Ages. St Hugh of Lincoln was a 14th-century bishop of Lincoln.

Humbert

Pronunciation: HUM-bert

The name Humbert is of Old German origin. The meaning of Humbert is "famous warrior". Old French name from Old German *hun*, meaning 'warrior' and *berht*, 'bright'. The name was introduced to Britain by the Normans.

Humphrey

Pronunciation: HUM-free

Humphrey is of Old German origin. The meaning of Humphrey is "peaceful warrior". The name was made popular by Hollywood actor, Humphrey Bogart (1899-1957). Diminutive: Humph

I

Iago

Pronunciation: I-ago

The name Iago is of Spanish and Welsh origin. The meaning of Iago is "he who supplants". The name is a variation of the name Jacob. Iago is also a Hebrew variant of the name James. Shakespeare gave the name to his villain in *Othello* (1604).

Ian

Pronunciation: EE-an

Ian is of Gaelic and Scottish origin. The meaning of the name Ian is "God is gracious". Ian is a Scottish variant of the name John. The name was anglicised to Ian. Iain is the Gaelic spelling.

Ibrahim

Pronunciation: ee-bra-HEEM

The name Ibrahim is of Arabic origin. The meaning of Ibrahim is "father of many". The name is variant of the Hebrew name Abraham.

Idan

Pronunciation: EE-dan

Idan is of Hebrew origin. The meaning of the name Idan is "era, time".

Idris

Pronunciation: E-dris

The name Idris is of Arabic and Welsh origin. The meaning of Idris is "fiery leader, Prophet". Borne in Welsh legend by a giant magician, astronomer and prince whose observatory was on Cader Idris. Described in the Koran, the Arabic name was borne by a man described as 'a true man' and 'a prophet', he was also the founder of the first Shiite dynasty (788-974). The name is used as both a boy's name and as a girl's name.

Ignatius

Pronunciation: eeg-NAH-see-ers

Ignatius is of Latin origin. The meaning of Ignatius is "fire, burning". From a Roman family name, Egnatius. Borne by several saints, including the Spanish-born Saint Ignatius. Loyola (1491-1556). He founded the Society of Jesus, the Jesuits.

Igor

Pronunciation: EE-gor

The name Igor is of Russian origin. The meaning of Igor is "watchfulness of Ing". The name is a Russian form of the Scandinavian name Ingvarr.

Immanuel

Pronunciation: ih-Man-yoo-el

The name Immanuel is of Hebrew origin. The meaning of Immanuel is "God is with us". The name is a variant of Emmanuel.

Ingram

Pronunciation: IN-gram

The name Ingram is of Old English and Scandinavian origin. The meaning of Ingram is "raven of peace".

Inigo

Pronunciation: I-ni-go

The name Inigo is of Spanish origin. Inigo is a Medieval Spanish variation of Ignatius. St Ignatius Loyola was born Inigo Lopez de Recalde. The name is often associated with the great English architect, Inigo Jones.

Ira

Pronunciation: EYE-rah

Ira is of Hebrew origin. The meaning of the name Ira is "full grown, watchful". From Hebrew, meaning, 'watchful'. A biblical name; borne in the Old Testament, the name of a priest of King David.

Irvine

Pronunciation: EYE-van

Irvine is of Gaelic and Scottish origin. The meaning of the name Irvine is "fresh water". Originally a Scottish surname that derived from a Celtic river. Irvin is a variation of Irvine or Irving. Irvine is also a place name of a town in Ayrshire.

Isaac

Pronunciation: EYE-zik

The name Isaac is of Hebrew origin. The meaning of Isaac is "laughter". Hebrew derived from the verb 'to laugh'. A biblical name; borne in the Old Testament he was the only son of Abraham and Sarah. God tested Abraham's faith when Isaac was a young boy, he asked him to sacrifice his own son. God relented and provided him with a Ram as a substitute, whilst Abraham prepared to kill his son. The name was introduced to Britain by the Normans. Izaak is a variation of the name. Diminutives: Ike, Zak, Zack.

Isaiah

Pronunciation: eye-ZY-ah

Isaiah is of Hebrew origin. The meaning of the name Isaiah is "God is salvation". Hebrew, meaning 'the Lord is generous'. A biblical name; borne by one of the major prophets in the Old Testament. He wrote the book of Isaiah and was best known for foretelling the coming of the Messiah. The name was popular in the 17th century with the Puritans.

Ivan

Pronunciation: EYE-van

The name Ivan is of Hebrew and Russia origin. The meaning of Ivan is "God is gracious". Ivan is the Russin form of the name John. Ivan IV of Russia was famously known as Ivan the Terrible (1533-1584).

Ivor

Pronunciation: EYE-vor

Ivor if of Old Norse and Scandinavian origin. The meaning of the name Ivor is "yew, army". Scandinavian, from Old Norse *yr*, 'yew' and *herr*, 'army'. In Welsh, the name is used as a form of *Ifor*, meaning 'lord'. The name is also used as an anglicised form of the Scottish Gaelic name Lomhar.

J

Jabez

Pronunciation: j(a)-bez

The name Jabez is of Hebrew origin. The meaning of Jabez is "borne in pain". A biblical name; borne in the Old Testament, Jabez is well-respected man whose prayer to God for blessing was answered (4:9-11).

Jabin

Pronunciation: j(a)-bin

Jabin is of Hebrew origin. The meaning of the name Jabin is "God had built". A biblical name; meaning 'discerner', or 'the wise'.

Jabir

Pronunciation: j(a)bir

The name Jabir is of Arabic origin. The meaning of Jabir is "consolation".

Jacan

Pronunciation: JA-can

The name Jacan is of Hebrew origin. The meaning of Jacan is "trouble". A biblical name; he is mentioned as a family leader of the tribe of Gad (5:13).

Jace

Pronunciation: jayce

Jace is of English origin. The meaning of the name Jayce is "the Lord is my salvation". The name is a short form of the Hebrew name Jason.

Jachin

Pronunciation: j(a)-chin

The name Jachin is of Hebrew origin. The meaning of Jachin is "he establishes". A biblical name; Jachin and Boaz were the names given by their craftsman to two large cast bronze pillars, that stood on either side of the entrance to the Temple in Jerusalem. Built by King Solomon according to God's instructions.

Jacinto

Pronunciation: ha-CEEN-toh

Jacinto is of Spanish and Greek origin. The meaning of Jacinto is unknown. Jacinto is a masculine form of the Greek flower name, Hyacinth.

Jack

Pronunciation: jak

Jack is of Old English origin. The meaning of the name Jack is "God is gracious". Jack is a diminutive of John. The name was popular during the Middle Ages and has recently undergone a new surge in popularity.

Jacob

Pronunciation: JAY-kub

The name Jacob is of Hebrew origin. The meaning of Jacob is "he who supplants". An anglicised form of the Hebrew name Yaakov. A biblical name; borne by the greatest patriarch of the Old Testament, the son of Isaac and Rebekah. He was the father of the twelve tribes of Israel. After wrestling with an angel, he was given the name Israel and became the ancestors of the nation of Israel.

Jamil

Pronunciation: JA-mil

The name Jamil if of Arabic origin. The meaning of Jamil is "handsome, graceful". The name is a variant of Jamal.

James

Pronunciation: jayms

The name James is of Hebrew origin. The meaning of James is "he who supplants". The name is a variation of Jacob, derived from the Latin form, Jacomus. A biblical name; borne in the New Testament by one of the twelve apostles of Jesus. He was a relative of Jesus, possibly a brother or a cousin. The name spread to Britain and became popular during the 13th century. The name became associated with the royal house Stuart. Diminutives: Jamie, Jem, Jim, Jimmy, Jemmy.

Jared

Pronunciation: JARE-ed

The name Jared is of Hebrew origin. The meaning Jared is "descending, rose". A biblical name; borne in the Old Testament by the father of Enoch. Jared was a pre-Flood ancestor of Jesus. The Puritan adoption underwent a revival in the 1960's. This was possibly due to the TV Western *Big Valley* (1965-1969), with its character Jarrod.

Jason

Pronunciation: JAY-sun

The name Jason is of Greek and Hebrew origin. The meaning of Jason is "healer; the Lord is salvation". The name is a variant of Joshua. A biblical name; borne by an early Christian associate of Paul. Jason is an anglicised form of a Greek name, borne in Greek mythology. Jason was the leader of Argonauts who sailed his ship to *Argos* in search of the Golden Fleece.

Jasper
Pronunciation: JAS-per
Jasper is of Greek origin. The meaning of the name Jasper is "treasure holder". English form of the French name, Gasper, and the German name, Caspar. In medieval tradition, the name was given to one of the three Magi. Jasper is also the name of a gemstone.

Jeremiah
Pronunciation: jare-ah-MYE-ah
The name Jeremiah is of Hebrew origin. The meaning of Jeremiah is "appointed by God". A biblical name; borne by one of the major 7th century BC Hebrew Prophets. The scholar was the author of the Book of Lamentations and the Book of Jeremiah. The name was popular among the Puritans. Diminutive: Jerry.

Jerome
Pronunciation: jer-OME
The name Jerome is of Greek origin. The meaning of Jerome is "sacred name". From Greek, meaning 'holy name'. Saint Jeroma (c. 342-420), was a biblical scholar

who translated the Vulgate Bible into Latin, for the Western Church. He is often portrayed with a lion beside him, whilst he is writing or studying in cardinal's dress. His feast day is 30th September. Diminutive: Jerry.

Jesse

Pronunciation: JESS-ee

Jesse is of Hebrew origin. The meaning of the name Jesse is "God exists". A biblical name; borne in the Old Testament by the shepherd father of King David, from whom the ancestry of Christ can be traced. Jesse was adopted by the Puritans. The name was revived in the 20th century.

Jethro

Pronunciation: JETH-roh

The name Jethro is of Hebrew origin. The meaning of Jethro is "pre-eminence, eminent". A biblical name; borne by in the Old Testament by Moses's father in law. The name was common among Puritans.

Jocelyn

Pronunciation: JOS-e-lyn

The name Jocelyn is of Old German origin. The meaning of Jocelyn is "one of the Goths". The name was introduced to Britain by the Normans. Jocelyn is used as both a boy's name, and as a girl's name. Diminutive: Joss.

Joel

Pronunciation: JOH-ul

The name Joel is of Hebrew origin. The meaning of Joel is "Jehovah is the Lord". A biblical name: borne by a prophet of the 8th century BC, he was also the author of the Old Testament Book of Joel.

John

Pronunciation: JO-hn

John is of Hebrew origin. The meaning of the name John is "God is gracious". A biblical name; borne by several figures, including the longest-lived of the twelve apostles. St John the Baptist, who was the relative and forerunner of Christ. He was sent 'to prepare the way of the Lord', and baptized Christ in the Jordan River. The name is possibly the most popular name in history, borne by numerous saints, popes and kings. Diminutives: Hank, Jack, Jock, Johnnie, Johnny.

Johnathan

Pronunciation: JOHN-a-thun

The name Johnathan is of Hebrew origin. The meaning of Johnathan is "gift of God. The name is a variant of Jonathan. Diminutives: Johnnie, Johnny, John, Jon.

Jonathan

Pronunciation: JAHN-a-thun

Jonathan is of Hebrew origin. The meaning of the name Jonathan is "gift of God, God has given". A biblical name; borne in the Old Testament by son of King Saul, Jonathan was renowned for his manliness and generosity. He was also a great friend of King David, he later saved his life from Saul. Jonathan was eventually killed in battle. The name was adopted by the Puritans. Diminutives: Johnnie, Johnny, Jon.

Jordan

Pronunciation: JOR-dan

Jordan is of Hebrew origin. The meaning of the name Jordan is "down-flowing". From the name of the river in the Middle East where Christ was baptized by John the Baptist. The name has been used as a first name since the Crusades. The name underwent a popular revival in the 1980's. Jordan is used as both a boy's name, and as a girl's name.

Joseph

Pronunciation: JOH-sef

The name Joseph is of Hebrew origin. The meaning of Joseph is "Jehovah increases, God will add". A biblical name; borne by three major figures. The son of Jacob and Rachel, Joseph was sold into slavery by his jealous brothers. He later became an important advisor to the Pharaoh and a supreme power in Egypt. St Joseph the husband of Virgin Mary and the earthly father of Jesus. He is the patron saint of carpenters, and his feast day is 19th March. St Joseph of Arimathea was a rich Jew who would not declare his faith publicly. He was the one who brought Christ down from the cross and buried him in a private tomb. Diminutives: Jo, Joe.

Joshua

Pronunciation: JOSH-yoo-ah

Joshua is of Hebrew origin. The meaning of the name Joshua is "God is salvation". A biblical name; Joshua was an attendant to Moses, and later succeeded him as the leader of the Israelites. Joshua is also known for leading the defeat of the city of Jericho by the blowing of trumpets. Diminutive: Josh.

Jude

Pronunciation: JU-de

The name Jude is of Greek origin. The meaning of Jude is "praised". The name is a variation of Judas. A biblical name; the apostle St Jude was the author of the New Testament epistle of Jude. He is regarded as the patron saint of hopeless causes. Thomas Hardy popularised the name during the 19th century with his novel, *Jude the Obscure* (1895).

Julian

Pronunciation: JOO-lee-en

The name Julian is of Greek origin. The meaning of Julian is "Jove's child". From the Roman family name Julius. Julian is borne by several saints. The name was brought to Britain during the Middle Ages.

Julius

Pronunciation: JU-li-us

Julius is of Greek origin. The meaning of the name Julius is "Jove's child". A Roman family name of several of the most powerful Roman emperors, including Emperor Gaius Julius Caesar.

Justin

Pronunciation: JUS-tin

The name Justin of Latin origin. The meaning of Justin is "just, righteous".

From the Latin name Justinius, derived from *justus*, meaning 'just'. Borne by four saints, St Justin (2nd century) was a Greek philosopher who wrote of the moral values of Christianity. The name was also borne by Byzantine emperors. Justin was revived in the 20th century.

K

Kacey

Pronunciation: KAY-see

The name Kacey is a variant of Casey. Kacey is used as both a boy's name, and as a girl's name

Kade

Pronunciation: kayd

Kade if of Scottish origin. The meaning of the name Kade is "from the wetlands". The name is also a variant of Cade.

Kaden

Pronunciation: KAYD-en

The name Kaden is of Arabic origin. The meaning of Kaden is "Companion". Kaden is also an Old German place name.

Kamal

Pronunciation: KA-mal

Kamal is of Arabic origin. The meaning of Kamal is "perfection". The name is also found in India, where its origin is from Sanskrit.

Kane
Pronunciation: KAYN
The name Kane is of Gaelic and Irish origin. The meaning of Kane is "battle". Anglicised form of the Irish Gaelic name *Cathán,* derived from *cath,* 'battle'.

Kareem
Pronunciation: kah-REEM
Kareem is of Arabic origin. The meaning of the name Kareem is "generous, noble".

Karl
Pronunciation: karl
The name Karl is of Old German origin. The meaning of Karl is "free man". Karl is the German form of Charles.

Kavanagh
Pronunciation: KAV-a-nagh

The name Kavanagh is of Irish and Gaelic origin. The meaning of Kavanagh is "follower of Kevin". Originally an Irish surname.

Kay

Pronunciation: KAY

The name Kay is of Latin and Old Welsh origin. The meaning of Kay is "happy". An ancient name borne in the legend by a knight of the Round Table. Kay is used as both a boy's name and as a girl's name.

Keanu

Pronunciation: kee-AH-noo

Keanu is of Hawaiian origin. The meaning of the name Keanu is "cool breeze from the mountains".

Keegan

Pronunciation: KEE-gan

The name Keegan is of Irish and Gaelic origin. The meaning of Keegan is "little fiery one".

Keir

Pronunciation: KEE-er

The name Keir is of Gaelic origin. The meaning of Keir is "dusky, dark haired". The name may have been adopted in honour of the first Labour MP, James Keir Hardie (1856-1915). Actor Keir Dullea also made the name popular during the 1970's.

Kelvin

Pronunciation: KEL-vin
The name Kelvin is of English origin. The meaning of Kelvin is "friend of ships". Kelvin is also a place name referring to a Scottish river.

Kendall

Pronunciation: KEN-dal
The name Kendall is of Old English origin. The meaning of the Kendall is "the Kent River Valley". An adopted surname, from a Cumbrian place name, Kendal. The name is used as both a boy's name, and as a girl's name. Kendal has been used as a given name since the 19th century.

Kendrick

Pronunciation: KEN-drik
Kendrick if of Welsh origin. The meaning of the name Kendrick is "greatest champion". An adopted Welsh

surname, derived from an early first name, Cywrig.
The name is also possibly from Old Welsh *cyne*,
'royal', and *ric*, 'ruler'.

Kenneth

Pronunciation: KEN-eth

Kenneth is of Irish and Gaelic origin. The meaning of
the name Kenneth is "handsome". Anglicisation of the
Gaelic name Cainnech, which means 'handsome'.
Diminutives: Ken, Kenny.

Kent

Pronunciation: KENT

Kent is of Old English origin. The meaning of the
name Kent is "edge". The adopted surname is also a
place name derived from the English county.

Kenton

Pronunciation: KENT-on

The name Kenton is of Old English origin. The
meaning of Kenton is "the royal settlement". An
adopted surname and English place name.

Kester

Pronunciation: KES-ter

Kester is of Greek and Gaelic origin. The meaning of the name Kester is "bearing Christ". Kester is a Medieval diminutive of Christopher.

Kevin

Pronunciation: KEV-in

The name Kevin is of Irish and Gaelic origin. The meaning of Kevin is "handsome beloved".

Anglicization of the Irish Gaelic name Caoimnin, from *caomh*, 'handsome'. Borne by an Irish hermit saint of the 7th century, he was the patron saint of Dublin. The name was rarely used outside of Ireland until the 20th century, when it became hugely popular. Diminutive: Kev.

Kieran

Pronunciation: KEER-en

Kieran is of Irish and Gaelic origin. The meaning of the name Kieran is "black". Anglicization of the Irish Gaelic name Ciaran, which means 'dark'. Borne by two Celtic saints of the 5th and 6th century. The name was revived and became popular during the 20th century.

Kim

Pronunciation: KIM

The name Kim is of English origin. The meaning of Kim is "gold". Originally a diminutive of Kimball or Kimberley. The name is used as both a boy's name and as a girl's name.

Kingsley

Pronunciation: KINGS-lee

The name Kingsley is of Old English origin. The meaning of Kingsley is "king's meadow". The adopted surname is also a place name, from the Old English name Cyningesleah, which means 'king's wood'. Writer Charles Kingsley (1817-1875) made the name more popular in the 19th century.

Kingston

Pronunciation: KING-ston

The name Kingston is of Old English origin. The meaning of Kingston is "King's settlement". Kingston is also a place name.

Konrad

Pronunciation: KAHN-rad

The name Konrad is of Polish and German origin. The meaning of Konrad is "bold advisor". The name is a variant of the Old German name Conrad. From German *rad* 'counsel' and *conja*, meaning 'bold'.

Kumar

Pronunciation: KU-mar

The name Kumar is of Hindi and Sanskrit origin. The meaning of Kumar is "male child".

Kurt

Pronunciation: KURT

Kurt is of German origin. The meaning of the name Kurt is "courageous advice". The name is a variant of the Old German name Conrad.

Kyle

Pronunciation: KYL

The name Kyle is of Gaelic origin. The meaning of Kyle is "straight". An adopted Scottish place name, from the Scottish term *kyle*, which means 'straight', or 'channel'. Derived from the Gaelic *caol*, 'narrow'. Kyle is the name of the central district of Ayrshire in western Strathclyde.

L

Lachlan

Pronunciation: LOCH-lan

The name Lachlan is of Irish and Gaelic origin. The meaning of Lachlan is "from the land of lakes". From the Scottish name Lachlann, the Gaelic word for Norway. Diminutive: Lockie.

Lambert

Pronunciation: LAMB-bert

Lambert is of Scandinavian origin. The meaning of the name Lambert is "land brilliant". Old German from *landa*. St Lambert popularised the name in medieval Belgium and Netherlands. He was a 7th-century bishop of Maastricht. The name spread to Britain in the Middle Ages.

Lance

Pronunciation: LANCE

The name Lance is of French origin. The meaning of Lance is "land". French from the Old German name

Lanzo. Diminutives: Lancelot, Launcelot.

Lancelot
Pronunciation: LANS-e-lot
The name Lancelot is of Old French origin. The meaning of Lancelot is "servant". Borne in Arthurian legend by the most famous knight of the Round Table, Lancelot du Lac. His seduction of Queen Guinevere, started a war that resulted in the destruction of the Round Table, and the death of King Author.

Laurence
Pronunciation: LAUR-ence
The name Laurence is of French origin. The meaning of Laurence is "from Laurentium", an ancient Italian town of olive groves. Laurence is a variant of the Latin name Lawrence. Borne by a 3rd-century deacon of Roman, he was martyred in 258 by being roasted on a gridiron. He is considered the patron saint of curriers and his feast day is 10th August. Diminutives: Lanty, Larry, Laurie, Lawri.

Lee
Pronunciation: LEE
Lee is of Old English origin. The meaning of the name Lee is "wood, meadow, clearing". An adopted surname

and place name. Lee was first used as a first name in the 19th century, probably in honour of the Confederate general Robert E. Lee (1807-1870). The name is used as both a boy's name and as a girl's name.

Leighton

Pronunciation: LAY-ton

The name Leighton is of Old English origin. The meaning of Leighton is "meadow settlement". The adopted surname was derived from the place name, from Old England *leac*. Leighton has been used as a first name since the 19th century.

Lennox

Pronunciation: LEN-iks

The name Lennox is of Gaelic and Scottish origin. The meaning of Lennox is "with many elm trees". An adopted Scottish surname, from the Levenach. The name also appears in Shakespeare's *Macbeth* (1606).

Leo

Pronunciation: LEE-oh

The name Leo is of Latin origin. The meaning of Leo is "Lion". From Latin *leo*. The name was popular in Roman times. Leo is the fifth sign of the zodiac. The name was borne by thirteen popes, including Leo the Great (5th century) and four saints.

Leon

Pronunciation: LEE-ahn

Leon is of Greek origin. The meaning of the name Leon is "Lion". Lion is a variant of Leo.

Leonard

Pronunciation: LEN-ard

The name Leonard is of Old German origin. The meaning of Leonard is "lion strength". From the Old German name Leonhard. The name was popularised in the 6th century by St Leonard, he was a Frank at the court of Clovis. He is the patron saint of prisoners, and his feast day is 6th November. Diminutives: Len, Lennie, Lenny, Leo.

Leslie

Pronunciation: LEZ-lee

The name Leslie is of Gaelic and Scottish origin. The meaning of Leslie is "Holly garden". An adopted Scottish surname, derived from the place name Lesslyn. It was used as a first name in the 19th century. Diminutive: Les.

Lester

Pronunciation: LES-ter

The name Lester is of Old English origin. The meaning of Lester is "from Leicester". The adopted surname was adopted in the 19th century.

Lewis

Pronunciation: LOO-iss

The name Lewis is of Old German origin. The meaning of Lewis is "famous warrior". An anglicised form of the name Louis.

Liam

Pronunciation: LEE-am

Liam is of Old German origin. The meaning of the name Liam is "determined protector". The name is originally a diminutive of Uilliam, an Irish variation of William. The name became popular in its own right.

Lincoln

Pronunciation: LINK-en

The name Lincoln is of Old English origin. The meaning of Lincoln is "lake colony". An adopted surname and English place name, originally used to indicate 'the Roman colony at the lake'. Abraham Lincoln (1809-1865) popularised the name as a first name. He was the 16th president of the US whose presidency won the Civil War, and abolished slavery.

Lindsay

Pronunciation: LIN-d-say

Lindsay is of Old English origin. The meaning of the name Lindsay is "Lincoln's marsh". Sir Walter de Lindesay brought the name to Scotland from Lindsey, Lincolnshire. The name is used as both a boy's name and as a girl's name.

Linford

Pronunciation: LIN-ford

The name Linford is of Old English origin. The meaning of Linford is "linden tree ford". An adopted surname and English place name.

Linus

Pronunciation: LYE-nus

The name Linus is of Greek origin. The meaning of Linus is "flax". The name is a Latin form of the Greek name Linos. A biblical name; borne by a Christian companion to Paul in Rome. In Greek mythology, Linus is the name of Hercules's music tutor.

Lionel

Pronunciation: LYE-a-nel

The name Lionel is of Latin origin. The meaning of Lionel is "Lion". The name is originally a medieval diminutive of Leon. The name was borne by a knight of King Author's Round Table.

Llewellyn, Llewelyn

Pronunciation: loo-ELL-en

The name Llewellyn is of Welsh origin. The meaning of Llewellyn is " like a lion, leader". Borne by two 13[t]-century Welsh princes, Llewelyn ap Iorwerth and Llywelyn ap Gruffydd.

Lloyd

Pronunciation: loyd

The name Lloyd is of Welsh origin. The meaning of Lloyd is "gray haired". An anglicised form of the Wlesh name Llwyd.

Louis

Pronunciation: LOO-iss

The name Louis is of French and Old German origin. The meaning of Louis is "famous warrior". From the Old German name Chlodovech. The name was borne

by nineteen kings of France and numerous saints.
Diminutive: Lou.

Lucas
Pronunciation: LOO-kas
Lucas is of Greek origin. The meaning of the name
Lucas is " man of Lucania", in southern Italy. The
name is a variation of Loukas. The name was
introduced to Britain in the 12th century.

Lucian
Pronunciation: LOO-shun
The name Lucian is of Latin origin. The meaning of
Lucian is "light". From the Roma clan name Lucianus.
St Lucian of Antioch was a 4th-century scholar.

Lucius
Pronunciation: LOU-cius
The name Lucius is of Latin origin. The meaning of
Lucius is "light". From Latin *lux*. Lucius was a popular
name in Ancient Rome. The name was borne by three
popes.

Luke
Pronunciation: LOO-k

The name Luke is of Greek origin. The meaning of Luke is "man of Lucania", a region in southern Italy. A biblical name; St Luke the Evangelist, apparently wrote the third gospel and the Acts of the Apostles. He is a patron saint of doctors and artists, and is described in the Bible as a physician (Colossians 4:14).

Lyall

Pronunciation: LYE-al

The name Lyall is of Old Norse origin. The meaning of Lyall is "Wolf". From an Old Norse name, Liulfr.

Lyle

Pronunciation: LYE-el

The name Lyle is of Old French origin. The meaning of Lyle is "the island". An adopted Scottish surname, from Old French *de lisle*, which means 'of the island'.

Lyndon

Pronunciation: LIN-dan

The name Lyndon is of Old English origin. The meaning of Lyndon is "linden tree hill". Lyndon is an adopted surname and place name. The name became popular in America after Lyndon Baines Johnson (1908-1978), who was the 36th president.

M

Mackenzie

Pronunciation: ma-KEN-zee

The name Mackenzie if of Gaelic and Irish origin. The meaning of Mackenzie is "son of the wise ruler". An adopted Scottish surname, from Gaelic Mac Coinnich. Mackenzie is used as both a boy's name, and as a girl's name.

Magnus

Pronunciation: MAG-ness

The name Magnus is of Latin origin. The meaning of Magnus is "great". The name was adopted by St Olaf of Norway, an admirer of Charlemagne. The name is borne by several Norwegian Kings and several Scandinavian saints. The name was introduced from Scandinavia to Scotland by one of the Saints, who visited the Scottish islands of Orkney and Shetland.

Malachi

Pronunciation: MAL-a-kye

Malachi is of Hebrew origin. The meaning of the name Malachi is "messenger of God". A biblical name; borne by the author of the last book of the Old Testament, and a prophet. His prophesies are focus mainly on the coming of Judgment Day. The name is believed to have come from the text itself: 'Behold, I will send my messenger, and he shall prepare the way before me' (Malachi 3:1).

Malachy

Pronunciation: MAL-a-key

The name Malachy is of Hebrew origin. The meaning of Malachy is "messenger of God". The name is a variant of Malachi. The name was first adopted in reference to an early Irish King, Maoileachlainn. The name was popularized in the 12th century by St Malachy (1095-1148), he was a bishop of Armagh.

Malcolm

Pronunciation: MAL-cum

Malcolm is of Gaelic and Scottish origin. The meaning of the name Malcolm is "devotee of Saint Columba". Anglicised from the Gaelic name Mael Coluim. The name was borne by four medieval Scottish kings. Malcolm is also the name of the prince of Scotland who became King of Scotland, after Macbeth murdered his father. Shakespeare immortalised the true story in his play, *Macbeth* (1606).

Mallory

Pronunciation: MALL-or-ee

The name Mallory is of Old French origin. The meaning of Mallory is "unfortunate". The name is used as both a boy's name and as a girl's name.

Manfred

Pronunciation: MAN-fred

The name Manfred is of Old German origin. The meaning of Manfred is "man of peace". From Old German *man*, meaning 'man', and *fred*, 'peace'. The name was introduced to Britain by the Normans and fell out of use after the Middle Ages. Manfred was later revived in the 19th century. Lord Byron used the name for his epic poem *Manfred* (1817).

Manley

Pronunciation: MAN-lee

The name Manley is of Old English origin. The meaning of Manley is "shared land, wood". Manley is also a place name.

Marius

Pronunciation: MAR-ee-us

Marius of Latin origin. The meaning of the name Marius is "dedicated to Mars". The name is an adoption of the Roman family name Marius, from Mars, Roman god of war. The name is also a variant of Mario.

Mark

Pronunciation: MAR-k

The name Mark is of Latin origin. The meaning of Mark is "dedicated to Mars". The name is an anglicised form of the Latin name, Marcus. A biblical name; borne in the New Testament by St Mark, author of the second Gospel who died in c. 68. His feast day is 25th April.

Marshall

Pronunciation: MAR-shal

The name Marshal is of Old French origin. The meaning of Marshall is "caretaker of horses". An adopted surname, originally derived from a Norman French occupational name for a groom, *mareshcal*. Marshall is also a law enforcement title and a military title. The name has been used as a first name since the early 19th century.

Martin

Pronunciation: MART-en

Martin is of Latin origin. The meaning of the name Martin is "dedicated to Mars". Martin is an anglicised form of the Latin name Martinus. The name originates with the Roman war god, Mars. St Martin of Tours (c. 316-97) popularised the name throughout medieval Europe. He was converted to Christianity while a soldier in Rome and later became bishop of Tours. He is best known for cutting his cloak in two and sharing it with a beggar. His feast day is 11th November. Civil rights activist Martin Luther King popularised the name in the 20t[h] century.

Matthew

Pronunciation: MATH-yoo

The name Matthew is of Hebrew origin. The meaning of Matthew is "gift of God". A biblical name; borne in the New Testament by one of Christ's twelve apostles. Also known as Levi, he wrote the first Gospel account of the life of Jesus. His feast day is 21st September. Matthew is the form of the Hebrew name, Mattathia. The name was introduced to Britain by the Norman's. Diminutives: Mat, Matt, Mattie.

Matthias

Pronunciation: ma-THYE-us

The name Mattias is of Greek, Hebrew and German origin. The meaning of Mattias is "gift of God". New Testament Greek form of the Hebrew name Mattathia. A biblical name; borne in the New Testament by the disciple who was selected to replace Judas as an apostle, 'the thirteenth apostle' (Acts 1:23-26).

Maurice

Pronunciation: maw-REESE

Maurice is of Latin origin. The meaning of the name Maurice is "Moorish".

From the Latin name Mauricius. Borne by a 3rd-century saint who was martyred in Switzerland. The Roman name was introduced to Britain by the Normans.

Maxim

Pronunciation: MAX-im

Maxim is of Latin origin. The meaning of the name Maxim is "greatest". The name is a variation of Maximus. The name was used by Daphne du Maurier in his novel, *Rebecca* (1940). Maxim is also the name of three Roman emperors and several early saints.

Maximilian

Pronunciation: MAX-i-mi-lian

The name Maximilian is of Latin origin. The meaning of Maximilian is "greatest". From the Latin name Maximilianus. Borne by a 3rd-century martyr. The name of three Roman emperors and several early saints.

Maxwell

Pronunciation: MAKS-wel

The name Maxwell is of Old English origin. The meaning of Maxwell is "Mack's stream". An adopted Scottish surname and place name. The name has been used in Scotland since the mid-19th century

Maynard

Pronunciation: MAY-nerd

The name Maynard is of Old German origin. The meaning of Maynard is "brave, strength". Maynard is an adopted surname, originally from Norman French *magin,* meaning 'strength'. The name was introduced to Britain by the Normans.

Melville

Pronunciation: MEL-ville

The name Melville is of Old French origin. The meaning of Melville is "bad settlement". Originally a Norman French baronial name derived from Malleville. The surname was adopted by those fleeing to Scotland from a poor settlement in northern France. Herman Melville (author of *Moby Dick)*, popularised the name during the 19th century. Diminutive: Mel.

Melvin

Pronunciation: MEL-vin

The name Melvin in of uncertain origins. Possibly a variation of Melville or a masculine form of Malvina. Diminutive: Mel.

Merlin

Pronunciation: MER-lin

Merlin is of Welsh origin. The meaning of the name Melvin is "sea fortress". From Latinate form, Merlinus, of the Old Welsh name Myrddin. Borne in Arthurian legend by magician Merlin Ambrosius. The name is used as both a boy's name and as a girl's name.

Merton

Pronunciation: MERT-on

Merton is of Old English origin. The meaning of the name Merton is "town by the lake". Merton is an adopted surname and English place name, from Old English *mere*, meaning 'lake', and *tun*, 'settlement'.

Michael
Pronunciation: MYE-kal
The name Michael is of Hebrew origin. The meaning of Michael is "who is like God?" A biblical name; borne by St Michael the Archangel who defeated the dragon. He was the leader of the seven archangels and leader of the celestial armies. Angels, Michael and Gabriel are given personal name in the canonical Bible. Several saints, Emperors and Kings have borne the name. Michael has been popular in the English-speaking world since the Middle Ages. Diminutives: Mick, Mickey, Micky, Mike, Mikey, Mischa, Misha, Mitch.

Miles
Pronunciation: myls
The name Miles if of Latin origin. The meaning of Miles is "soldier". Derived from Latin *miles*, meaning 'solider', owing to the military association of St Michael the Archangel.

Montgomery
Pronunciation: mon-GOH-mer-ree

The name Montgomery is of Old French origin. The meaning of Montgomery is "mountain of the powerful one". Montgomery is an adopted surname, and originally a Norman baronial name and place name, from Calvados. The Welsh county of Montgomeryshire was named after a Norman settler. Montgomery is the surname of English and Scottish earls.

Mordecai

Pronunciation: MOR-de-cai

Mordecai is of Hebrew origin. The meaning of the name Mordecai is "little man, follower of Marduk (a god of the Babylonians)".A biblical name; borne in the Old Testament by a cousin and guardian of Esther. Mordecai warned Esther of Haman's plans to massacre all Jews (Esther 4-7). The name was popular in the 17th and 18th century.

Morley

Pronunciation: MOOR-lee

The name Morley is of Old English origin. The meaning of Morley is "meadow on the moor". An adopted surname and English place name.

Mortimer

Pronunciation: MORT-im-er

Mortimer is of Old French origin. The meaning of the name Mortimer is "dead sea". Mortimer is an adopted aristocratic surname, itself derived from a Norman baronial name and place name, Mortimer in Normandy. The name has been used as a first name since the 19th century.

Morton

Pronunciation: MORT-on

The name Morton is of Old English origin. The meaning of Morton is "moor town, settlement on the moor'. An adopted surname and English place name. Morton has been used as a first name since the 19th century.

Moses

Pronunciation: MOH-ziz

Moses is of Hebrew and possibly Egyptian origin. The meaning of Moses is "saviour". Anglicised form of the Hebrew name Moshe. A biblical name; borne by the Hebrew baby who was found floating on the River Nile and adopted by an Egyptian Pharaoh's daughter. Moses was a patriarch who led the Israelites out of Egypt for the Promised Land. The name was popular in medieval Britain and was later revived by the Puritans after the Reformation.

Mostyn

Pronunciation: MOS-tyn

The name Mostyn is of Welsh origin. The meaning of Mostyn is "mossy settlement". An adopted Welsh surname and place name in Clywd, North Wales.

Muhammad

Pronunciation: mo-HAM-med

The name Muhammad is of Arabic origin. The meaning of Muhammad is "praiseworthy". Borne by the Prophet and founder of Islam, Abu al-Qasim Muhammad. He was borne at Mecca in c.570 and died at Medina in 632. Mohammad is one of the most popular Islamic boy's names.

Murray

Pronunciation: MUR-ee

The name Murray is of Gaelic origin. The meaning of Murray is "sea". Murray is an adopted Scottish surname, from Scottish Gaelic *muir*. Murray is the surname of an ancient Scottish clan. The name was adopted as a first name in the 19th century.

Myron

Pronunciation: MYE-an

The name Myron is of Greek origin. The meaning of Myron is "myrrh, fragrant oil". Borne by a Greek sculptor of the 5th century BC, he was renowned for his realistic statues of athletes, animals, and gods.

N

Naim

Pronunciation: NA-im

The name Naim is of Arabic origin. The meaning of Naim is "comfortable, tranquil". Variations: Naeem.

Nairn

Pronunciation: NA-ir-n

The name Nairn is of Scottish and Gaelic origin. The meaning of Nairn is "river with alder trees". Celtic dweller by the alder tree. Nairn is also a place name.

Nathan

Pronunciation: NAY-than

Nathan is of Hebrew origin. The meaning of the name Nathan is "God has given". Hebrew, meaning 'gift'. A biblical name: borne in the Old Testament, Nathan was God's prophet who advised King David to build the temple during the reigns of David and Solomon.

Nathaniel

Pronunciation: na-THAN-yel

The name Nathaniel is of Hebrew origin. The meaning of Nathaniel is "God has given". Hebrew, meaning 'gift of God'. A biblical name; borne in the New Testament by one of Christ's twelve apostles. He was also known as Bartholomew. Shakespeare used the name Nathaniel in *Love's Labour's Lost* (1594). Diminutives: Nat, Nath, Nathan.

Ned

Pronunciation: ned

The name Ned is of English origin. The meaning of Ned is "wealthy guard". Ned is used as a nickname for Edward.

Neil

Pronunciation: neel

Neil is of Irish and Gaelic origin. The meaning of Neil is "Champion". The name is a Scottish variation of Niall which dates back to the Middle Ages.

Nelson

Pronunciation: NEL-sun

The name Nelson is of Irish and Gaelic origin. The meaning of Nelson is unknown. The adopted surname was first used as a first name in the 19th century. Naval hero of Trafalgar, Admiral Lord Horatio Nelson (1758-1805) popularised the name.

Neville

Pronunciation: NEV-il

The name Neville is of Old French origin. The meaning of Neville is "new village". Neville is an adopted aristocratic surname and Old French place name. From Old French, *neuve,* meaning 'new', and *ville,* 'town'. It was introduced to Britain during the Norman Conquest.

Niall

Pronunciation: NYE-al

Niall is of Irish and Gaelic origin. The meaning of Niall is "Champion". Borne by a 5th-century Irish king, Niall of the Nine Hostages.

Nicholas

Pronunciation: NIK-oh-lus

Nicholas is of Greek origin. The meaning of the name Nicholas is "people of victory". Anglicised from the Greek name Nikolaos, from *nike,* meaning 'victory', and *laos,* 'people'. A biblical name: borne by one of seven qualified men in the first-century Christian congregation. The name is also borne by a 4th-century

bishop of Myra who is now considered patron saint of
Greece and Russia, as well as children, scholars, sailors
and pawnbrokers. St Nicholas in his Dutch
incarnation of Santa Claus is well known throughout
the Christian world for bringing Christmas presents.

Nigel
Pronunciation: NYE-jel
The name Nigel if of Gaelic and Irish origin. The
meaning of Nigel is "Champion". The name was
revived in the 19th century, during the craze for
medieval names.

Noel
Pronunciation: NOH-el
Noel is of French origin. The meaning of the name
Noel is "Christmas". An Old French, from *noel,* which
was derived from the Latin *dies natalis,* meaning
birthday. Referring directly to the birthday of Christ.
The name is used as both a boy's name and as a girl's
name.

Norman
Pronunciation: NOR-mahn
The name Norman is of Old German origin. The
meaning of Norman is "northerner". Derived from

Old German *nord*, 'north', and *man*, 'man'. The name was already in use in Britain before the Norman Conquest, however it was then reinforced and used to describe the Norman invaders and their descendants. The name was revived in the 19th century. Diminutive: Norm.

O

Odysseus

Pronunciation: OD-ys-seus

Odysseus is of Greek origin. The meaning of the name Odysseus is "angry man". Original Greek form of the hero of Homer's epic, the *Odyssey*.

Olaf

Pronunciation: OH-loff

The name Olaf is of Old Norse origin. The meaning of Olaf is "ancestor's relic". From the Old Norse name Anleifr, meaning 'relic of his ancestor's'. A royal name in Norway. It was borne by several Scandinavian kings, including St Olaf, patron saint of Norway.

Oliver

Pronunciation: AH-lih-ver

Oliver is of Latin origin. The meaning of the name Oliver is "olive tree". The name may be a variation of the Olaf. The name fell from favor after the death of Oliver Cromwell (1599-1658) but became popular again in the 19th century. Possibly due to the influence

of Charles Dickens's novel Oliver Twist (1838).
Diminutives: Noll, Ol, Ollie,

Omar

Pronunciation: OH-mar

The name Omar is of Arabic and Hebrew origin. The
meaning of Omar is "speaker, long-lived". The name is
a variation of Umar, or from Hebrew meaning
'eloquent'. A biblical name: the son of Esau, a sheik of
Edom. Omar Khayyam (12th century) was an
astronomer, a mathematician and also a poet.

Orlando

Pronunciation: or-LAHN-doh

Orlando is of Spanish origin. The name is an Italian
form of Roland (Old German). The name means
"renowned land".

Orson

Pronunciation: OR-sun

The name Orson is of Latin origin. The meaning of
Orson is "bear". Old French *ourson*, meaning 'little
bear'. A French medieval legend, the name was borne
by the twin brother of Valentine. The children were
sons of an exiled Byzantine Princess. Orson was
carried off by a bear as a baby and reared by bears in

the forest. Director and Actor Orson Welles (1915-1985) made the name popular.

Oscar
Pronunciation: OS-ker
Oscar is of Old English origin. The meaning of the name Oscar is "spear of the gods". The name was used by Scottish writer, James Macpherson (1736-17-96) for the son of Ossian In his Ossian poems. Napoleon Bonaparte, was a great admirer of Macpherson's work, and later gave the name to his godson. He ascended the throne of Sweden as Oscar I.

Oswald
Pronunciation: OZ-wild
The name Oswald is of Old German origin. The meaning of Oswald is "God's power". From an Old English name, from os, 'god', and weald, 'rule'. The Shropshire town of Oswestry is said to have been named after a 7th-century saint and king of Northumbria borne with the name. The name Oswald was popular during the Middle Ages. Diminutives: Oz, Ozzie, Ozzy.

Otto

Pronunciation: AW-toh

Otto is of Old German origin. The meaning of the name Otto is "wealth". A modification of a common element of Old German names, *od*, meaning 'prosperity'. Borne by four Holy Roman Emperors. The name became less popular in Britain after the Middle Ages.

Owen

Pronunciation: OH-en

The name Owen is of Scottish and Greek origin. The meaning of Own is "born of youth". The name is a variant of the Latin name Euenuis. Borne in Welsh legend by several important figures. One being, Owen Glendower (1359-1416). He fought unsuccessfully for Welsh independence from England. The name has huge popularity in Wales.

P

Pablo

Pronunciation: PAB-low

The name Pablo is of Spanish origin. The meaning of Pablo is "little". The name is a variant of Paul. Borne by artist Pablo Picasso (1881-1973).

Pacifico

Pronunciation: PAS-if-i-co

The name Pacifico is of Spanish and Latin origin. The meaning of Pacifico is "calm, tranquil".

Palmer

Pronunciation: PAHL-mer

The name Palmer is of Old English origin. The meaning of Palmer is "Pilgrim". Originally a surname used to refer to the palm branch carried by a Christian pilgrim, whilst they travelled to a holy shrine.

Paris

Pronunciation: PARE-iss

The name Paris is of Greek origin. In Greek mythology, Paris was the name of the young prince of Troy, whose love affair with Helen caused the Trojan war. Paris is used as both a boy's name and as a girl's name. The name was also an English given surname for immigrants from the capital of France.

Parker
Pronunciation: PAR-ker
Parker is of Old English origin. The meaning of Parker is "park keeper". Originally an occupational name, that was used as a surname. Parker became a popular given name in the 19th century.

Parry
Pronunciation: PAR-ry
The name Parry is of Old Welsh origin. The meaning of Parry is "son of Harry". The name is also an English variant of Perry.

Patrick
Pronunciation: PAT-rik
The name Patrick is of Latin origin. The meaning of Patrick is "patrician". St. Patrick (c. 389-461) was a Briton and a Roman citizen who travelled as a missionary to Ireland. After he arrived in Wicklow in

432, he is credited with converting almost the entire country to Christianity. St Patrick is also renowned for ridding Ireland of snakes and vermin. He is the patron saint of Ireland, his feast day is 17th March. The name spread outside of Ireland in the 18th century.

Paul

Pronunciation: pahl

Paul is of Latin origin. The meaning of the name Paul is "small". From the Roman family name Paulus, originally from *paulus*, 'small'. Borne by Saul of Tarsus (Acts 13:9), he was a Roman citizen and persecutor of Christians until his conversion. As St Paul, he is considered to be the co-founder of the Christian Church with St Peter.

Perceval

Pronunciation: PER-ce-val

The name Perceval is of Old French origin. The meaning of Perceval is "pierce the vale". From Old French *perce*, 'pierce', and *val*, 'valley'. Invented by a medieval poet, Chretien de Troyes in his 12th century accounts of Arthurian legend.

Percy

Pronunciation: PER-see

Percy is of Latin origin. The meaning of the name Percy is "to penetrate the hedge". Percy is an adopted aristocratic surname, born by the Duke of Northumberland. Derived from the Old French *perce*, 'piece', and *haie*, 'hedge'.

Peter
Pronunciation: PEE-tar

The name Peter is of Greek origin. The meaning of Peter is "rock". A biblical name: borne as one of the twelve apostles. The name was given to his apostle Simon by Jesus. Peter the fisherman was impulsive and had a strong faith. "Thou art Peter, and upon this rock I will build my church" (Matthew 16:18). St Peter is considered to be one of the co-founders of the Christian Church with St Paul. In the Catholic tradition the first Bishop of Rome and the first pope. Peter is considered the patron saint of fisherman, his feast day is 29th June. J M Barrie's play Peter Pan (1904) revived the name and made it more popular.

Philip
Pronunciation: FIL-ip

The name Philip is of Greek origin. The meaning of Philip is "horse lover". The Greek name *Philipos*, which means 'lover of horses'. A biblical name; borne by one of Christ's twelve apostles and several early saints. Philip has been in regular use since the early Christian times. St Philip the Apostle's feast day is 1st May.

Piers
Pronunciation: PEE-ers
The name Piers if of Greek origin. The meaning of Piers is "rock". French medieval vernacular form of the name Peter. The name was introduced to Britain by the Normans in the Middle Ages.

Plantagenet
Pronunciation: P-lanta-genet
Plantagenet is of Old French origin. The meaning of the name Plantagenet is "shoot of broom". The name was commonly given to the English royal line from Henry II to Richard III. Broom is an English flower.

Porter
Pronunciation: PORT-er
The name Porter is of English origin. The meaning of Porter is "gatekeeper". Originally an English occupational name and given surname. Porter is also a French name given to people who made their living

carrying loads. The French meaning of Porter is "to carry".

Presley

Pronunciation: PRES-ley

Presley is of Old English origin. The meaning of the name Presley is "priest's meadow". The name has been used since the Middle Ages. Presley is also a place name. The name was made famous by the single Elvis Presley.

Preston

Pronunciation: PRES-ten

The name Preston is of Old English origin. The meaning of Preston is "priest's settlement". Preston is also a place name.

Price

Pronunciation: PRI-ce

The name Price is of Old French origin. The meaning of Price is "prize".

Purvis

Pronunciation: PUR-vis

The name Purvis if of English and French origin. The meaning of Purvis is "purveyor". Originally a term for someone who provides food and provisions.

Q

Qasim

Pronunciation: KA-sim

The name Qasim is of Arabic origin. The meaning of Qasim is "charitable, generous".

Quade

Pronunciation: kwayde

The name Quade is of Gaelic origin. The meaning of Quade is unknown. The name is derived from a Scottish clan name McQuade.

Quanah

Pronunciation: KWAH-ne

The name Quanah is of Native American Indian origin. The meaning of Quanah is "sweet smelling". The name was borne by a 19th-century chief of the Comanche.

Quennell

Pronunciation: KWEN-el

The name Quennell is of Old French origin. The meaning of Quennell is "small oak". Originally a place name.

Quentin
Pronunciation: KWEN-tin
The name Quentin is of Latin origin. The meaning of Quentin is "fifth". Old French form of the Latin name Quintius, from *quintus*, 'fifth'. It was the name of a 3rd-century saint and missionary to Gaul.

Quigley
Pronunciation: KWIG-lee
The name Quigley is of Irish and Gaelic origin. The meaning of Quigley is "one with messy hair".

Quillan
Pronunciation: KWIL-an
The name Quillan is of Irish and Gaelic origin. The meaning of Quillan is "cub".

Quimby
Pronunciation: KWIM-bee
Quimby is of Old Norse origin. The meaning of Quimby is "estate of the woman". Quimby is also a place name.

Quincey

Pronunciation: KWIN-cey

Quincey is of Old French origin. The meaning of the name Quincey is "Estate of the fifth son". Adopted surname, originally a baronial name from Cuinchy in northern France. Quincey can be used as a both a boy's name, and as a girl's name.

Quinn

Pronunciation: KWIN

The name Quinn is of Irish and Gaelic origin. The meaning of Quinn is "counsel". An adopted Irish surname, from the Gaelic name O Cuinn, meaning 'decedent of Conn'. Quinn has been used a given name from very ancient times.

Quintin

Pronunciation: KWIN-tin

Quintin is of Old English origin. The meaning of the name Quintin is "fifth". The name is a variant of Quentin. Quintin is an adopted surname and a place name, from Old English cwen, 'queen' and tun, 'settlement'. Diminutive: Quent, Quint.

Quinton

Pronunciation: KWIN-ton

The name Quinton is od Old English origin. The meaning of Quinton is "queens settlement". Originally a place name.

Quintus
Pronunciation: KWIN-tus
The name Quintus is of Latin origin. The meaning of Quintus is "fifth". The Roman name was often given to the fifth born son, in the days of large families. Quintus is a variant of Quentin. Diminutive: Quent, Quint.

Quintrell
Pronunciation: kwin-TREL
The name Quintrell is of English origin. The meaning of Quintrell is "dashing, elegant".

R

Ralph

Pronunciation: RAL-f

The name Ralph is of French origin. The meaning of Ralph is "counsel". From the Norman French name Raulf.

Ramsey

Pronunciation: RAM-see

Ramsey is of Old English origin. The meaning of the name Ramsey is "raven island". An adopted Scottish surname, which was originally derived from the Huntingdonshire town of Ramsey. Earl of Huntington brought the name to Scotland in the 12th century.

Ranald

Pronunciation: RAN-ald

The name Ranald is of Scottish origin. The meaning of Ranald is unknown. The name is an anglicised form of Raghnall.

Randall

Pronunciation: RAN-dall

The name Randall is of Old English origin. The meaning of Randall is unknown. The name is a medieval form of Randolf. Diminutives: Ran, Randy.

Randolf

Pronunciation: RAN-dolf

The name Randolf is of Old Norse origin. The meaning of Randolf is "shield, wolf". From the Old Norse name Rannulfr. Diminutives: Ran, Randy.

Raoul

Pronunciation: RA-oul

The name Raoul is of French origin. The meaning of Raoul is "wolf counsel". The name is a French form of Ralph. The name was popular in medieval Britain.

Ravi

Pronunciation: RAV-ee

The name Ravi is of Indian origin. The meaning of Ravi is "sun". Ravi was the name of the sun god.

Raymond

Pronunciation: RAY-mund

The name Raymond is of Old German origin. The meaning of Raymond is "protecting hand". From the Old French name Raimund. The name was borne by a 11th-century Count who was a Crusader leader of the First Crusade. The name was introduced to Britain by the Normans. Diminutive: Ray.

Rayner
Pronunciation: RAY-ner
The name Rayner is of Old German origin. The meaning of Rayner is "judgment warrior". The name was introduced to Britain by the Normans.

Reuben
Pronunciation: ROO-ben
The name Reuben is of Hebrew origin. The meaning of Reuben is "Behold, a son". A biblical name: borne by the firstborn of Jacob's twelve sons.

Rex
Pronunciation: reks
The name Res is of Latin origin. The meaning of Res is "king". The name is also considered a diminutive of Reginald.

Rhys

Pronunciation: rees

Rhys is of Welsh origin. The meaning of the name Rhys is "passion, enthusiasm". Rhys is a native Welsh form of Reece. The name was borne by two medieval Welsh lords.

Richard

Pronunciation: RICH-erd

The name Richard is of Old German origin. The meaning of Richard is "powerful leader". From an Old German name Ricohard. Diminutives: Rick, Dickie, Dickon, Dicky, Rich, Richie, Rick, Ricky.

Ridley

Pronunciation: RID-lee

The name Ridley is of Old English origin. The meaning of Ridley is "reed meadow". Originally an adopted surname and place name, from Old English elements hreod.

River

Pronunciation: RIV-er

The name River is of English origin. The name was popular during the 1960's when people took names from nature. Hollywood actor, River Phoenix (1970-1993) popularised name.

Roald

Pronunciation: ROH-al

The name Roald is of Old Norse origin. The meaning of Roald is "famous ruler, famed power".

Robert

Pronunciation: RAH-bert

Robert is of Old German origin. The meaning of the name Robert is "bright fame". From the Old German name Hrodebert. The name was introduced to Britain by the Normans. Robert has been a popular boys name since the Middle Ages. King Robert the Bruce (1274-1329) popularised the name in Scotland. Diminutives: Bob, Bobbie, Bobby, Hob, Rab, Rabbie, Rob, Robbie, Robby.

Robin

Pronunciation: RAH-bin

The name Robin is of English origin. The meaning of Robin is unknown. Robyn is originally a diminutive of Robert. The name has been popular since the medieval days of Robin Hood.

Roderick

Pronunciation: RAH-der-ik

The name Roderick is of Old German origin. The meaning of Roderick is "famous power". The name was first introduced to Britain by the Norman invaders. The name was revived by Sir Walter Scott in his poem *The Vision of Don Roderigo* (1811). Diminutives: Rod, Rody.

Rodney

Pronunciation: RAHD-nee

Rodney is of Old English and Old German origin. The meaning of the name Rodney is "Roda's island". An adopted surname and place name. It was originally adopted in honour of Admiral Lord Rodney (1719-1792), who led the French Navy to defeat in 1759.Diminutives: Rod, Roddy.

Roger

Pronunciation: ROH-jer

The name Roger is of Old German origin. The meaning of Roger is "famous spearman". From from the Old French name Rogier, which is derived from Old German *hrod*. The name was introduced to Britain by the Normans. Roger was a popular name throughout the Middle Ages and in the 19th and 20th centuries.

Roland

Pronunciation: ROH-land

The name Roland is of Old German origin. The meaning of Roland is "renowned land". Roland is rejoiced in the 12th century French poetic sagas, *Chanson de Roland*, as a hero in the service of Charlemagne. He was the most famous of Charlemagne's soldiers, who died c. 778. Roland is also known as the Christian Theseus and the Achilles of the West. Roland is an anglicised form of the name Rowland. The name was introduced to Britain by the Normans. Diminutive: Roly.

Rollo

Pronunciation: ROH-llo

The name Rollo is of Latin origin. The meaning of Rollo is unknown. Rollo is Latin from of the name Roul. The name was borne by an ancestor of William the Conqueror and a Norman pirate (c. 860-932).

Roman

Pronunciation: roh-MAHN

The name Roman is of Latin origin. The meaning of Roman is "citizen of Rome". Roman is an anglicised form of the name Romeo. The name is also a variant of Romanus, the name of several saints and a pope.

Romeo
Pronunciation: ROAM-ee-ohh
Romeo is of Latin origin. The meaning of the name Romeo is "citizen of Rome". The name was made famous by Shakespeare's *Romeo and Juliet* (1595).

Ronald
Pronunciation: RAH-nald
The name Ronald is of Old Norse origin. The meaning of Ronald is "ruler's counselor". The name was revived in the 19th century. Diminutives: Ron, Ronnie.

Rory
Pronunciation: ROR-ee
The name Rory is of Irish and Gaelic origin. The meaning of Rory is "red king". The name is an anglicised form of the Irish Gaelic names *Ruaidhrí, Ruarí,* and Scottish Gaelic names, *Ruairidh, Ruaraidh.*

Ross

Pronunciation: ros

Ross is of Scottish and Gaelic origin. The meaning of the name Ross is "headland, cape". Derived from Scottish Gaelic *ros*, meaning 'headland'.

Ross is an adopted surname and place name.

Rowan

Pronunciation: RO-wan

The name Rowan is of Gaelic origin. The meaning of Rowan is "little red-haired one". An adopted Irish surname. Borne by a 6th-century saint who founded the monastery of Lothar.

Roy

Pronunciation: roy

The name Roy is of Irish and Gaelic origin. The meaning of Roy is "red". From Scottish Gaelic, *ruadh*. The name was also influenced by the Old French term *roi*, which means 'king'.

Rudolf

Pronunciation: ROO-dol-f

The name Rudolf is of Latin origin. The meaning of Rudolf is "famous wolf". From Rudolphus, the Latinate form of Hrodwulf. Diminutives: Rudi, Rudy.

Rufus

Pronunciation: ROO-fuss

The name Rufus is of Latin origin. The meaning of Rufus is "red-haired". Rufus was first used a first name during the 19th century. A biblical name; borne by the name of two 1st century Christians.

Rupert

Pronunciation: ROO-pert

The name Rupert is of Old German origin. The meaning of Rupert is unknown. From Rupprecht, a German form of Robert. The name was popularised throughout Britain by Prince Rupert of the Rhine (1618-1692). He was the nephew of Charles I. St Rupert of Salzburg of the 8th century was involved in the founding of Salzburg.

Russell

Pronunciation: RUSS-el

Russell is of Old French origin. The meaning of the name Russell is "little red". Russell is an adopted surname from Old French *roux*. The name was first used as a first name in the 19th century. Diminutives: Russ.

Ryan

Pronunciation: RYE-an

The name Ryan is of Gaelic origin. The meaning of Ryan is "king". From the Irish Gaelic surname O'Riain, which means 'a descendant of Rian'.

S

Saahdia

Pronunciation: sa(ah)-dia

The name Saahdia is of Aramaic origin. The meaning of Saahdia is "the Lord's help".

Saarik

Pronunciation: sa(a)-rik

The name Saarik is of Hindi origin. The meaning of Saarik is unknown. Saarik is also the name of a small songbird.

Saber

Pronunciation: S-(a)-ber

The name Saber is of French origin. The meaning of Saber is "sword". Saber is the name of a curved sword.

Sabino

Pronunciation: sa-BEE-noh

Sabino is of Latin origin. The meaning of the name Sabino is "Sabine". The Sabines were a tribe from Italy. Romulus arranged for the Sabine women to be kidnapped, and provided as wives for the citizens of Rome. Sabino is also a saint's name.

Sacha

Pronunciation: S(a)-cha

The name Sacha is of Greek and Russian origin. The meaning of Sacha is "man's defender". The name is used as both a boy's name and as a girl's name. Sacha is a diminutive of Alexander.

Sadiki

Pronunciation: S(a)-dee-kee

The name Sadiki is of Swahili origin. The meaning of Sadiki is "faithful, loyal".

Sadler

Pronunciation: SAD-ler

Sadler is of Old English origin. The meaning of the name Sadler is "harness maker". Originally a surname and occupational name. The name was first used as a first name in the 19th century.

Safford

Pronunciation: SAFF-ord

Safford is of Old English origin. The meaning of the name Safford is "willow river crossing". Originally a place name.

Saffron

Pronunciation: SAFF-ron

Saffron is the name of a plant. Saffron is used as bright orange/yellow spice. The name is used as both a boy's name and as a girl's name.

Sage

Pronunciation: sage

The name Sage is of Latin origin. The meaning of Sage is "healing herb". Sage is also the name of a plant. The name is used as both a boy's name and as a girl's name.

Sahil

Pronunciation: SA-hill

The name Sahil is of Hindi origin. The meaning of Sahil is "leader".

Salvador

Pronunciation: SAL-va-dor

The name Salvador is of Latin origin. The meaning of Salvador is "savior".

The name is a Spanish form of Salvator. Salvador is a place name in Latin America.

Samuel

Pronunciation: SAM-yoo-el

The name Samuel is of Hebrew origin. The meaning of Samuel is "God has heard". A biblical name; borne in the Old Testament as the prophet and judge who anointed Saul and David as kings of Israel (1 and 2 Samuel). The name was used by the Puritans. Samuel was a popular name throughout the 17th, 18th, and 19th centuries. The diminutive, Sam is one of the most popular boy's names in the English speaking world. Diminutives: Sam, Sammie, Sammy.

Scott

Pronunciation: skaht

Scott is of Old English origin. The meaning of the name Scott is "from Scotland, a Scotsman". An adopted Scottish surname, the name has been in regular use since the early 20th century. American writer, F Scott Fitzgerald (1896-1940) popularised the name.

Sean

Pronunciation: shon

The name Sean is of Irish and Hebrew origin. The meaning of Sean is "God is gracious". The name is an

Irish form of John, derived from the French form Jean. The name spread outside of Ireland in the 20th century.

Sebastian

Pronunciation: se-BASS-tian

Sebastian is of Greek origin. The meaning of the name Sebastian is "man of Sebastia". From the Latin name Sebastianus. The original form of the name referred to those from a particular city or region of Asia Minor. Borne by an early Roman soldier who converted to Christianity, his fellow officers tried to kill him with arrows. St Sebastian was a 3rd century martyred centurion who became the patron saint of soldiers. Shakespeare used the name for the twin brother of Viola in *Twelfth Night* (1601). Diminutives: Bastian, Bastien, Seb.

Seth

Pronunciation: seth

The name Seth is of Hebrew origin. The meaning of Seth is "set, appointed". A biblical name: borne in the Old Testament by the third son of Adam and Eve as a replacement for their dead son. Eve said Seth had been appointed to take the place of Abel, who had been killed by Cain. The name was popular with the Puritans of the 17th century.

Seymour

Pronunciation: SEE-mor

The name Seymour is of English origin. The meaning of Seymour is "Saint Maur". An adopted aristocratic surname and French place name from St Maur in France. The Norman French name Maur is derived from the Latin name Mauricius. The name has been in use as a first name since the 19th century.

Shane

Pronunciation: shayn

The name Shane is of Irish and Hebrew origin. The meaning of Shane is "God is gracious". The name is a variation of Sean. The name became more popular during the 1950's and 1960's due to the classic western film *Shane* (1953).

Sheldon

Pronunciation: SHEL-den

The name Sheldon is of Old English origin. The meaning of Sheldon is "steep valley". The adopted surname is derived from various English place names, including 'flat-topped hill'.

Sheridan

Pronunciation: SHARE-a-den

The name Sheridan is of Irish and Gaelic origin. The meaning of Sheridan is "seeker". An adopted Irish surname, from O Sirideain. The name was popularised by Irish playwright Richard Brinsley Sheridan (1751-1861). The name is used as both a boy's name and as a girl's name.

Sidney, Sydney

Pronunciation: SID-nee

Sidney is of Old English origin. The meaning of the name Sidney is "wide meadow". Sidney is an adopted surname and place name. The name has been used as a first name since the 17th century. Charles Dickens boosted the popularity of the name when he used it for his hero in *A Tale Of Two Cities* (1859). Australian city of Sydney was named in honour of Thomas Townshend. The name is used as both a boy's name and as a girl's name.

Silvester

Pronunciation: SIL-vest-er

The name Silvester is of Latin origin. The meaning of Silvester is "of the woods". The name was borne by an early Christian martyr and three popes.

Simon

Pronunciation: SYE-mun

The name Simon is of Hebrew origin. The meaning of Simon is "to hear, to be heard". The name is a variation of Simeon. A biblical name; borne in the New Testament by several characters. Simon was the name of two of the apostles, Simon Peter and Simon the Zealot. The name was popular from the Middle Ages through to the 18th century.

Sinclair

Pronunciation: sin-KLARE

Sinclair is of English origin. The meaning of the name Sinclair is "from Saint Clair". The name is an adopted Scottish surname, derived from a French baronial name and place name.

Sky

Pronunciation: SKY

The name Sky is of English origin. The meaning of Sky is unknown. The name is a variant of Skye. Sky is also used as a nickname for the Skyler variant. The name was popular during the 1960's when people took names from nature.

Solomon

Pronunciation: SAH-lah-mun

Solomon is of Hebrew origin. The meaning of the name Solomon is "peace". A biblical name; borne in the Old Testament by a king of Israel, the son of David and Bathsheba. He was known for his wisdom and justice, and wrote the Book of Proverbs. Solomon was a popular name during the Middle Ages, the name was revived in the 17th century.

Spencer

Pronunciation: SPEN-ser

The name Spencer is of Middle English origin. The meaning of Spencer is "dispenser of provisions". The adopted aristocratic surname, was originally an occupational name for a steward or butler. The name has been associated with the Churchill family, Dukes of Marlborough since the 18th century.

Stafford

Pronunciation: STAFF-ord

The name Stafford is of Old English origin. The meaning of Stafford is "Ford by a landing place". An adopted aristocratic surname and English place name. Stafford has been in occasional use as a first name since the mid-19th century.

Stanford

Pronunciation: STAN-ford

Stanford is of Old English origin. The meaning of the name Stanford is "stoney ford". Stanford is also a place name.

Stanley

Pronunciation: STAN-lee

The name Stanley is of Old English origin. The meaning of Stanley is "stony meadow". Stanley is an adopted surname and place name. The name was first used as a first name in the 19th century. Diminutive: Stan.

Stephen

Pronunciation: STEE-ven

The name Stephen is of Greek origin. The meaning of Stephen is "garland, crown". From Greek stephanos, which means 'crown'. St Stephen was the first person to be martyred for his Christian faith. Accused of blasphemy, he was stoned to death by the Jews (Acts 6-8). The name was borne by several saints and ten popes. The name was introduced to Britain by the Normans. Diminutives: Steve, Stevie.

Stewart

Pronunciation: STOO-ert

The name Stewart is of Old English origin. The meaning of Stewart is "steward". The name is an early variant of Stuart. Stewart was the family name of the royal house of Scotland from 1371 to 1714, and of England from 1603. Originally an occupational name, a medieval steward was charged with the care of the castle and estate affairs. Diminutives: Stew, Stu.

Stuart

Pronunciation: STU-art

Stuart is of Old English origin. The meaning of the name Stuart is "steward". Originally an occupational name, the steward administers a large feudal household. The name was introduced by Mary Queen of Scots. Stuart and Steward are clan names of the royal house of Scotland. Diminutives: Stew, Stu.

Sullivan

Pronunciation: SIL-IH-VUN

The name Sullivan is of Gaelic origin. The meaning of Sullivan is "dark eyes".

T

Tabor

Pronunciation: TAY-bor

The name Tabor is of Hebrew and Hungarian origin. The meaning of Tabor is "misfortune, bad luck". A biblical name; Mount Tabor a landmark mountain near Nazareth.

Tad

Pronunciation: tad

The name Tad is of English origin. The meaning of Tad is "heart". The name is a diminutive of Tadhg or Thaddeus. Tad is also used in American slang meaning, 'small'.

Tadhg

Pronunciation: teig

The name Tadhg is of Irish, Gaelic and Scottish origin. The meaning of Tadhg is "poet, philosopher".

Talfryn

Pronunciation: tal-(f)-ryn

The name Talfryn is of Welsh origin. The meaning of Talfryn is "high high".

Taliesin
Pronunciation: TAL-ie-sin
The name Taliesin is of Welsh origin. The meaning of Taliesin is "shining forehead". Borne by a 6th century Welsh poet.

Tam
Pronunciation: TAM
Tam is of Aramaic origin. The meaning of the name Tam is "twin". The name is a variant of Thomas. A biblical name: borne by one of the twelve apostles, he is also known as 'doubting Thomas'.

Tancred
Pronunciation: TAN-cred
The name Tancred is of Old German origin. The meaning of Tancred is "counsel, advice". Tancred was an 11th century Norman knight and Crusader, he was the son of Otho the Good and Emma Guiscard. He appears as one of the leading characters in the Italian Torquato Tasso's poem, *Jerusalem Delivered* (1581). He also inspired Rossini's opera *Tancredi* (1813) and

Disraeli's novel *Tancred (1847)*. The name was introduced to Britain by the Normans.

Terence

Pronunciation: TARE-ence

The name Terence is of Latin origin. The meaning of Terence is "one who initiates an idea". Latin from the Roman family name, Terentius. diminutives: Tel, Terry.

Theobald

Pronunciation: THEE-o-bald

The name Theobald is of Old German origin. The meaning of Theobald is "brave people". Diminutive: Theo.

Theodore

Pronunciation: THEE-a-dor

Theodore is of Greek origin. The meaning of name Theodore is "God's gift". Theodore is an early Christian name and a saint's name. The name became popular after a stuffed toy bead was named Teddy in hour of the US president, Theodore Roosevelt (1858-1919). Diminutives: Ted, Teddie, Teddy, Theo.

Theodoric

Pronunciation: THEE-o-dor-ic

The name Theodoric is of Old German origin. The meaning of Theodoric is "people's ruler, leader of the people". The name was borne by a king of the Ostrogoths (c. 454-526) who invade Italy. Diminutives: Derek, Derrick, Theo.

Thomas

Pronunciation: TAH-mas

Thomas is of Aramaic origin. The meaning of Thomas is "twin". A biblical name; borne by one of the twelve apostle also known as 'doubting Thomas'. The Apocrypha's Acts of Thomas tells of the apostle's missionary work in India. His feast day in 3rd July. Diminutives: Tom, Tommie, Tommy, Tam.

Thorley

Pronunciation: THOR-lee

The name Thorley is of Old English origin. The meaning of Thorley is "Thor's meadow, Thor's wood". Thorley is also a place name.

Thurston

Pronunciation: THER-sten

The name Thurston is of Old English origin. The meaning of Thurston is "Thor's stone".

Tierney

Pronunciation: TIE-r-ney

The name Tierney is of Irish and Gaelic origin. The meaning of Tierney is "Lord". An adopted surname from the Irish Galic name Ó Tighearnaigh.

Timothy

Pronunciation: TIM-oh-thee

Timothy is of Greek origin. The meaning of the name Timothy is "God's honor". A biblical name; born by a young Christian who was a companion of St Paul. Timothy is derived from the Greek name Timotheos. Charles Dickens popularised the name in the 19th century with his novel, *A Christmas Carol* (1843). Diminutives: Tim, Timmie, Timmy.

Tobias

Pronunciation: TOB-ias

The name Tobias is of Hebrew origin. The meaning of Tobias is "God is good". A biblical name; borne in the Old Testament Apocrypha's Book of Tobit, Tibias, was accompanied on a journey to Ecbatana by the

Archangel Raphael. The name was used by the Puritans and later revived in the 19th century.

Todd

Pronunciation: tahd

The name Todd is of Middle English origin. The meaning of Todd is "Fox". The name possibly used to refer to a fox hunter, or to indicate colouring, or cunning. Todd is an adopted surname.

Torquil

Pronunciation: TOR-quil

The name Torquil is of Gaelic and Scottish origin. The meaning of Torquil is "Thor's helmet". Scottish Gaelic, from *porketil*, por being a contraction of Thor (the Norse god of thunder). *Ketil* meaning, 'cauldron'. Thor's cauldron was an instrument used for sacrifices. The name was introduced to Britain by the Vikings.

Traherne

Pronunciation: TRA-herne

The name Traherne is of Welsh origin. The meaning of Traherne is "strength of iron, greatly akin to iron". The name is a variant form of Welsh Trahaearn.

Travers

Pronunciation: TRAV-ers

The name Travers is of Old French origin. The meaning of Travers is "to cross over". An adopted surname from Old French *travers*, meaning 'crossing'. Originally an occupational surname given to gatekeepers and others who collected tolls at bridges.

Travis

Pronunciation: TRAV-iss.

Travis is of Old French origin. The meaning of the name Travis is "to cross over". An adopted surname from Old French *travers*, meaning 'crossing'. Travis was an occupational surname given to gatekeepers and others who collected tolls at bridges.

Tremaine

Pronunciation: TRE-maine

Tremaine is of English origin. The meaning of Tremaine is "town built with stone". The name is a variant of Tremain. Tremaine is an adopted Cornish surname.

Trevor

Pronunciation: TREV-or

The name Trevor is of Welsh origin. The meaning of Trevor is "great settlement". Trevor is an adopted Welsh surname.

Tristan
Pronunciation: TRISS-tan
The name Tristan is of Celtic origin. The name is influenced by Old French *triste*, from Latin *tristis*, meaning 'sad'. Borne in Arthurian legend as a Knight of the Round Table and the tragic hero of the medieval tale, *Tristan and Isolde*. Tristan was a hero of Celtic legend and medieval romance.

Troy
Pronunciation: TR-oy
The name Troy is of Irish and Gaelic origin. The meaning of Troy is "descendant of the footsoldier". An adopted surname which was given to those who migrated to England from Troyes in France, after the Norman conquest of 1066. Troy is also associated with the ancient city In Asia Minor where the Trojan wars were fought. The name is used as both a boy's name and as a girl's name.

Tyrone
Pronunciation: TY-rohn

The name Tyrone is of Gaelic origin. The meaning of Tyrone is "land of Eoghan". An adopted surname, derived from the Northern Ireland county of Tyrone. Diminutive: Ty.

U

Ulises

Pronunciation: u-li-ses

Ulises is a variant of the Latin name Ulysses, a variant of the Greek name Odysseus, which means "wrathful".

Ulick

Pronunciation: u-li-ck

The name Ulick is of Irish and Gaelic origin. The meaning of the name Ulick is "little William".

Ulysses

Pronunciation: you-LISS-ees

Ulysses is of Latin origin, a variant of the Greek name Odysseus, which means "wrathful".

Ulysses was an intelligent and resourceful hero of Homer's epic Odyssey.

Umar

Pronunciation: u-mar

The name Umar is of Arabic origin. The meaning of

the name is "flourishing". Borne by a lifelong companion of the Prophet Muhammad.

Umberto

Pronunciation: um-ber-to

Umberto is of Italian origin. The name is a variant of the Old German name, Humbert which means "renowned hun". Umerto is a royal name in Italy.

Upton

Pronunciation: Up-ton

Upton is an adopted surname and a place name. The name is of Old English origin, from *up*, "higher" and *tun*, "settlement". The meaning of the name Upton is "upper settlement".

Urban

Pronunciation: ur-ban

Urban is of Latin origin, from urbanus which means, "citizen". The meaning of Urban is "from the city". A biblical name; borne by a character in the New Testament. Urban is also the name of eight popes.

Uriah

Pronunciation: yer-RY-ah

The name Uriah is of Hebrew origin. The meaning of the name Uriah is "my light is Jehovah". A biblical name; borne in the Old Testament one of King David's warriors. He was the husband of Bathsheba, who was sent to certain death in battle by David.

Uriel

Pronunciation: OOR-ee-el

Uriel is of Hebrew origin. The meaning of the name is "angel of light", "flame of God". In the Apocrypha, Uriel is one of the seven archangels.

Urijah

Pronunciation: u-ri-jah

Urijah is a variant of the Hebrew name Uriah. The meaning of the name Urijah is "my light is Jehovah". A biblical name; borne of one of King David's warriors, and the husband of Bathsheba.

Uziel

Pronunciation: u-ziel

The name Uziel is of Hebrew origin. The meaning of the name is "strength", "power".

V

Vachel

Pronunciation: VAY-chel

The name Vachel is of Old French origin. The meaning of Vachel is "small cow".

Vail

Pronunciation: VAY-el

The name Vail is of Old English origin. The meaning of Vail is "Valley". Originally a place name.

Valen

Pronunciation: VA-len

Valen is a variant of the Latin name Valentine. The meaning of the name is "strong", "healthy". Valen is used as a both a boy's name and a girl's name.

Valentine

Pronunciation: VAL-en-tyne

Valentine is of Latin origin. The meaning of Valentine is "strong", "healthy". Valentine is also a variant of Valentinus, which was the name of more than 50 saints and three Roman emperors.

Van

Pronunciation: van

The name Van is of Danish origin. The name is diminutive of Ewan and Ivan. It is also a nickname for Evan. The adopted surname was introduced as a given name by early immigrants in America.

Vance

Pronunciation: vance

The name Vance is of Old English origin. The meaning of the name Vance is "marshland".

Varun

Pronunciation: va-run

The name Varun is of Hindi origin. The meaning of Varun is "water god".

Vaughn

Pronunciation: von

The name Vaughn is of Welsh origin. The adopted surname was first used as a given first name in early 20th century. The meaning of the name Vaughn is "little" taken from *fychan*, meaning "small".

Vere

Pronunciation: v (e)-re

Vere is of French origin. Vere is an adopted surname and French Baronial name. It is also an upper-class surname in England. Derived from Old French *vern* which means, "alder".

Vernon
Pronunciation: VER-non
Vernon is of Old French origin. Derived from Old French *vern* which means, "alder". The meaning of the name is "alder grove". The aristocratic surname was brought to England the Norman conquest. Richard de Vernon arrived in Britain with William the Conqueror in 1066. Vernon is also a place name.

Vicente
Pronunciation: VICE-nte
Vicente is a variant of the Latin name Vincent. The meaning of the Vicente is "prevailing".

Victor
Pronunciation: VIK-tor
The name Victor is of Latin origin. The meaning of the name Victor is "Champion". Victor is a very popular saint's name, common in Christian Rome.

Vincent

Pronunciation: VIN-sent

Vincent is of Latin origin. The meaning of Vincent is "prevailing". Derived from Latin *vincens*, meaning " conquering". Borne by several early saints and steadily used since the early Christian days. Saint Vincent of Saragossa was a 4th-century Spanish martyr. Saint Vincent de Paul, a 17th-century priest. The name was popular during the Middle Ages and revived during the 19th century.

Virgil

Pronunciation: VER-jil

Virgil is of Latin origin from *vergilius.* Anglicized form of the name of the Roman poet and philosopher, Publius Vergilius Maro. Regarded as one of the greatest poets of ancient Rome, he was considered to have had magical powers and many medieval romances the poems tell of his exploits. His work has been used to study Roman history and the Latin language for the past two-thousand years.

Vitus

Pronunciation: VI-tus

Vitus is a variant of the Latin name Vito. The meaning of the name is "life-giving".

Vivian

Pronunciation: VIV-ian

The name Vivian is of Latin origin. Old French form of the Latin name Vivianus, from *vivus* which means "alive", "lively". The meaning of the name Vivian is "full of life" Vivian is used as both a boy's name and as a girl's name.

W

Wade

Pronunciation: wayde

Wade is of Old English and Scandinavian origin. The meaning of the name Wade is "river ford". Wade is also a medieval given name taken from Scandinavian mythology.

Wadham

Pronunciation: WAD-ham

The name Wadham is of Old English origin. The meaning of Wadham is "Ford village". Wadham is also a place name.

Wadley

Pronunciation: WAD-lee

The name Wadley is of Old English origin. The meaning of Wadley is "Ford meadow". Wadley is also a place name.

Wadsworth

Pronunciation: WADS-wor-th

The name Wadsworth is of Old English origin. The meaning of Wadsworth is "village near the ford". Wadsworth is also a place name.

Wagner

Pronunciation: WAG-ner

The name Wagner is of German origin. The meaning of Wagner is "wagon builder". Originally an occupational name.

Wahib

Pronunciation: WA-hib

The name Wahib is of Arabic origin. The meaning of Wahib is "donor". The name is one of Allah's 99 attributes.

Wainwright

Pronunciation: WAYN-ri-ght

The name Wainwright is of Old English origin. The meaning of Wainwright is "wagon builder".

Waite

Pronunciation: WAY-te

The name Waite is of Middle English origin. The meaning of Waite is "guard, watchman". Originally an occupational name. Christmas carolers were known as 'waits'.

Wakeley
Pronunciation: VIV-ian
Wakeley is of Old English origin. The meaning of the name Wakeley is "damp meadow". Wakeley is also a place name.

Walcott
Pronunciation: WALL-cot
The name Walcott is of Old English origin. The meaning of Walcott is "cottage by the wall".

Waldemar
Pronunciation: WALD-e-mar
Waldemar is of Old German origin. The meaning of the name Waldemar is "renowned ruler".

Walden
Pronunciation: WALD-en
The name Walden is of Old English origin. The meaning of Walden is "wooden valley". Walden is also a place name.

Waldo

Pronunciation: WAL-DOH

The name Waldo is of Old German origin. The meaning of the name Waldo is "rule". Derived from a Latinized form of the Old German *wald*, which means "to rule". Waldo is a short form and diminutive of several Old German names such as Oswald.

Walker

Pronunciation: WAHL-ker

The name Walker is Old English origin. The meaning of the name is "cloth washer", "walker". Walker is an occupational name from the medieval era, were workers trod on fabric to cleanse of any impurities.

Wallace

Pronunciation: WAL-iss

The name Wallace is of Old French origin. The meaning of the name is "Welshman". Wallace is originally a Scottish surname which refers to foreigners. Use as a first name probably began in honor of a 13th-century Scottish hero, William Wallace. He was a Scottish patriot who struggled against King Edward 1.

Walter

Pronunciation: WAL-ter

Walter is of Old German origin. The meaning of the name Walter is "commander of the army". From the Old German *wald*, which means "power". It was introduced to Britain by the Normans.

Warren

Pronunciation: war-ren

The name Warren is of Old English origin. The meaning of Warren is "watchman". The name is also possibly from the Norman French *warrene*, which means "stockyard".

Wayne

Pronunciation: wayne

Wayne is an adopted surname of Old English origin. The name was originally given to cart makers or drivers. The meaning of the name Wayne is "wagon builder", "driver". The name was made famous by actor John Wayne (1907-1979).

Wentworth

Pronunciation: WEN-two-rth

The name Wentworth is an adopted surname that is of Old English origin. Wentworth is also a place name from Old English winter, "Winter" and the word, "enclosure". Used as a reference to settlements that was used only during the cold winter months. The meaning of the name is "pale man's settlement".

Wes

Pronunciation: wes

The name Wes is variant of the Old English name Wesley. It is also a variant of the English surname Westley. The meaning of the name Wes is "western meadow".

Wesley

Pronunciation: WES-lee

Wesley is of Old English origin. The meaning of Wesley is "western meadow". Wesley is also a place name and a variant of the English surname Westley. The adopted surname was used in honor of 18th-century brothers John and Charles Wesley, founders of the Methodism Church.

West

Pronunciation: we-ST

The name West is a variant of the Old English place name, Westbrook. The place names refers to the location of a person's dwelling. The meaning of the name West is "western stream".

Wilbur

Pronunciation: wil-BUR

Wilbur is an adopted surname from Old English *will*, meaning "desire" and burh, "fortress".

Wilder

Pronunciation: WILD-er

The name Wilder is of German origin. Originally an occupational name for someone who captures and kills wild animals. The meaning of the name is "Hunter".

Wiley

Pronunciation: WYE-lee

The name Wiley is of Old English origin. The meaning of the name Wiley is "crafty". The name is also possibly a place name of a village and a river in England, "water meadow".

Willard

Pronunciation: WIL-erd

Willard is of Old English origin. The meaning of the name is "strong desire" It is an adopted surname from *will*, "deserve", and heard, "brave".

William

Pronunciation: WIL-yum

The name William is of Old German origin. From *wil* meaning "desire" and *helm*, "helmet". The meaning of the name William is "desiring of protection", "determined protector". The name was brought to Britain by Norman invader William the Conqueror. Three out of four English boys were given some form of the conquerors name, William. It was probably the first name to enjoy popularity on a mass scale. William became the most popular name in Britain within a century of the Norman Conquest. The name was also borne by four kings of England and has remained a royal name in Britain for nearly one thousand years.

Willie

Pronunciation: WIL-ee

The name Willie is of English origin. Willie is used as both a boy's name and also as a girl's name.

Wilmer

Pronunciation: WIL-mer

Wilmer is of Old German origin. The meaning of the name Wilmer is "strong desire".

Windsor

Pronunciation: WIND-sor

Windsor is an adopted surname of Old English origin. The meaning of the name is "riverbank with a winch". From the Old English name Windels-ora, meaning "landing place with a winch". Windsor is also a place name of a town and castle in England. Windsor is the surname of the British royal family.

Winston

Pronunciation: WIN-stun

The name Winston is Old English origin. The meaning of the name Winston is "joyful stone". Winston is an adopted surname and English place name. From the Old English name Wynn, and *tun*, "settlement", which means "Wynn's place". Former British prime minister, Sir Winston Churchill was given the name from his families connections to the region.

Wolfgang

Pronunciation: WOLF-gang

Wolfgang is of Old German origin. The meaning of the name is "traveling wolf". Famous composer, Wolfgang Amadeus Mozart made the name famous in the English-speaking world.

Wyatt

Pronunciation: WY-ut

The name Wyatt is of Old English origin. The meaning of Wyatt is "war strength". Wyatt is an adopted surname from Old English *wig* meaning, "war" and *heard*, "hardy".

Wynne

Pronunciation: WYN-ne

The name Wynne comes from the Welsh word, *Gwen*, which means "fair, holy, blessed, white". The meaning of the name Wynne is "friend". Wynne is also a variant of the name Wynn. Wynne is used as both a boy's name and as a girl's name.

Wyndham

Pronunciation: WYND-ham

Wyndham is of Old English origin. The meaning of the name is "Wyman's hamlet", "hamlet near the winding way". Wyndham is an adopted surname and also a place name, it is a contracted form of the Norfolk town Wymondham.

X

Xavi

Pronunciation: X-avi

Xavi is a variant of the name Xavier. The meaning of the name is "name house".

Xander

Pronunciation: ZAN-der

The name Xander is of Greek origin. The meaning of the name Xander is "man's defender". The name is also a short form of Alexander.

Xavier

Pronunciation: ecks-ZAY-vee-er

Xavier is of Basque origin. The meaning of the name is "new house". Saint Francis Xavier (1506-52) was a Jesuit missionary, who took Christianity to the Japan and the East Indies. The name is especially popular in Roman Catholic families.

Xenophon

Pronunciation: X-(e)-no-phon

The name Xenophon is of Greek origin. The meaning of Xenophon is "foreign voice". The name was borne by a 4th-century Greek historian.

Xenos
Pronunciation: X-(e)-nos
The name Xenos is of Greek origin. The meaning of Xenos is "hospitality".

Xerxes
Pronunciation: ZURK-seez, Z-uh-rk-sihs
The name Xerxes is of Persian origin. The meaning of the name is "King", "monarch". Several Persian rulers bore the name Xerxes. One of the rulers from the fifth century BC started a war on the Greeks.

Xidorn
Pronunciation: X-(i)-do-rn
The name Xenophon is of American origin. The meaning of Xidorn is "truth seeker".

Xiomar
Pronunciation: zhoh-MAR
Xiomar is of Spanish origin. The meaning of the name Xiomar is "famous in battle". The name is a variant of Geomar.

Y

Yael

Pronunciation: yael

The name Yael is variant of the Hebrew name Jael. The meaning of the name Yael is "mountain goat", "fertile moor". The name is also a variant of the Old English name Yale.

Yannick

Pronunciation: ya-nni-CK

Yannick is a variant of Yann(French, Hebrew). The meaning of the name Yannick is "God is gracious". Yannick is used as both **a boy's name and as a girl's name.**

Yasser

Pronunciation: YAS-ser

Yasser is of Arabic origin. The name is a variant of the Arabic name Yasir. The meaning of the name Yasser is "wealthy", "well to do".

Yehudi

Pronunciation: yehu-di, ye-hudi

Yehudi is of Hebrew origin. The meaning of the name is "Judah", "praise".

Yoel

Pronunciation: yoel

Yoel is a variant of the Hebrew name Joel. The meaning of the name Yoel is "Jehovah is the Lord". A biblical name; borne as a prophet and writer of the Book of Joel.

Yorick

Pronunciation: yo-ri-ck

The name Yorick is a variation of Jorck, a Danish form of George. Yorick is of Old English origin, and the meaning of the name is "farmer". Shakespeare used the name for the court jester in Hamlet (1601).

Yosef

Pronunciation: YO-sef

Yosef is a variant of the name Yusuf. The meaning of the name Yosef is "the Lord increases".

Yousef

Pronunciation: you-sef

Yousef is a variant of the Hebrew name Joseph. A biblical name; borne of the son of Jacob, he was sold by his brothers into slavery, and become a supreme power in Egypt. The meaning of the name Yousef is "Jehovah increases".

Yusuf

Pronunciation: yu-suf

Yusuf is variant of the Hebrew name Joseph. The meaning of the name is "the Lord increases".

Yves

Pronunciation: eve

The name Eve is of French origin. The meaning of the name is "yew". The name is a French variation of Ivo, which is drawn from Old German, *Ivo.* Saint Yves (14th century) was a French lawyer and a priest. The name is also possibly an occupational name.

Z

Zachariah

Pronunciation: zak-a-RYE-ah

Zachariah is of Hebrew origin. The meaning of Zachariah is "the Lord recalled". Zachariah is a variation of the name Zechariah. A biblical name; Zachariah was an Old Testament king of Israel.

Zachary

Pronunciation: ZAK-a-ree

The name Zachary is of Hebrew origin. The meaning of the name Zachary is "the Lord recalled". Zachary is variation of the name Zachariah. A biblical name; Zachary is one of several names from the Old Testament.

Zach

Pronunciation: ZAK

The name Zack is diminutive of the several forms of Zachariah and Isaac.

Zachary

Pronunciation: ZAK-a-ree

The name Zachary is of Hebrew origin. The meaning of the name is "the Lord recalled". Zachary is a variant of the name Zachariah. A biblical name; Zachary is one of several names from the Old Testament.

Zahir

Pronunciation: ZA-hir

The name Zahir is of Arabic origin. The meaning of the name Zahir is "blossoming", "flourishing".

Zain

Pronunciation: zain

Zain is a variant of the Hebrew name Zane. It is also possibly a variant of the Hebrew name John. The meaning of the name Zain is "God is gracious".

Zander

Pronunciation: ZAN-der

Zander is of Greek and Slavic origin. The meaning of the name Zander is "man's defender". Zander is a short form of the name Alexander.

Zephaniah

Pronunciation: ze-pha-niah

The name Zephaniah is of Hebrew origin. The meaning of the name is "hidden by God". A biblical name; borne as a minor prophet.

Zeus

Pronunciation: ZOO-SE

Zeus is of Greek origin. The meaning of Zeus is "living". Zeus is the name of the chief of the Olympian gods, and father of the gods and goddesses.

Zion

Pronunciation: ZI-on

The name Zion is of Hebrew origin. The meaning of the name is "highest point". In the Christian religion, Zion is the name for heaven.

A-Z

Baby Girl

Names

For 2015

A

Abigail

Pronunciation: AB-ih-gayl

The name Abigail is of Hebrew origin. The meaning of Abigail is "father's rejoicing". A biblical name; borne in the Old Testament by the wife of King David (1 Samuel). Abigail was described as 'good in discretion and beautiful in form'. Abigail referred to herself as David's handmaiden so often that the name became a popular term for a lady's maid. The name was introduced to Britain in the 16th century. Diminutives: Abbey, Abbie, Abby, Abi, Gail, Gale, Gayle.

Ada

Pronunciation: AY-dah

The name Ada is of Old German origin. The meaning of Ada is "noble". The name possibly derives from the Old German Names Eda or Etta. Ada is also used as a short form of the names Adele and Adelaide. The name was borne by a 7th-century abbess of Saint Julien Des Près at Le Mans. The name was introduced to Britain in the 18th century.

Adela

Pronunciation: a-DELL-ah

Adela is of Old German origin. The meaning of the name Adela is "noble". Derived from Old German, athal. The name was introduced to Britain by the Norman invaders. Adela was the name of William the Conqueror's youngest daughter. The name died out during the Middle Ages and was later revived in the 19th century. Diminutives: Addie, Addy, Della.

Adelaide

Pronunciation: AD-a-layd

The name Adelaide is of Old German origin. The meaning of Adelaide is "noble kind". The name is a Norman French version of the Old German name, Adelheid. The name was borne by the wife of Otto The Great (10th century), Holy Roman Emperor. Queen Adelaide, wife of William IV popularised the name in the 19th century. The city of Adelaide in Australia is named after her. Diminutives; Addie, Addy.

Adrienne

Pronunciation: AY-dree-en

Adrienne is of Latin origin. The meaning of the name Adrienne is "from Hadria". The name is a French feminine form of Adrian.

Africa

Pronunciation: AF-ree-ca

The name Africa is of Irish Gaelic origin. The meaning of Africa is "pleasant". The name is an Irish Gaelic version of Aifric. Africa is also a place name for the continent.

Agatha

Pronunciation: AG-a-thah

The name Agatha is of Greek origin. The meaning of Agatha is "good". The name is a Latin form of the Greek name, Agathe. Borne by a 3rd-century martyr and saint. She was tortured and murdered at Catania in Sicily after she refused to marry a Roman consul. She is the patron saint of bell ringers. Her feast day is 5th February. The name underwent a popular revival in the 19th century. The name was also made famous by renowned writer, Agatha Christie (1890-1976).

Agnes

Pronunciation: AG-ness

Agnes is of Greek origin. The meaning of the name Agnes is "chaste, holy". The name is a Latin form of the Greek *hagnos*. Borne by a young Roman girl who was martyred at the age of thirteen on the orders of Diocletian in c. 304. Agnes had refused several offers of marriage, as she declared herself to be devoted to Christ. She is now regarded as the patron saint of virgins, Her feast day is 21st January. Diminutives: Aggie, Aggy, Ness, Nessa, Nesta.

Ailsa

Pronunciation: a(i)-LIS-ah

Ailsa is of Old Norse origin. The meaning of the name Ailsa is "island of Alfsigr". Ailsa is also a place name, Ailsa Craig in the estuary of the River Clyde. Diminutive: Ailie.

Aimee

Pronunciation: ay-MEE

The name Aimee is of Old French and Latin origin. The meaning of Aimee is "to love, beloved". The name has been used as a first name since the Middle Ages.

Aisha

Pronunciation: ah-EE-shah

Aisha is of Arabic origin. The meaning of the name Aisha is "alive, thriving". Borne by the third wife of Prophet Muhammad. H Rider Haggard popularised the name in his novel *She* (1887).

Alannah

Pronunciation: ah-LAH-nah

Alannah is of Irish Gaelic origin. The meaning of the name Alannah is "O my child". From Irish Gaelic, Oleanbh.

Alberta

Pronunciation: al-BER-tah

The name Alberta is of Old English origin. The meaning of Alberta is "noble, bright". The name is a feminine form of the masculine name Albert. Alberta is also the name of Canadian province, which was named after Princess Louise Alberta.

Alexandra

Pronunciation: al-eks-AHN-dra

The name Alexandra is of Greek origin. The meaning of Alexandra is "man's defender". The name is a feminine form of the masculine name Alexander. The name was popularised in the 19th century when Edward VII married the Danish Princess Alexandra in 1863. Diminutives: Alex, Alexa, Alix, Lex, Lexie, Lexy, Sandie, Sandra, Sandy, Tiggy, Zandra.

Alexis

Pronunciation: a-LEX-iss

Alexis is of Greek origin. The meaning of the name Alexis is "defender". Derived from Greek, *alexios,* which means 'to defend'. The name is often used a shortened variation of the name Alexander. Although Alexis is traditionally a male name, it is now also used for girls in the modern world. Saint Alexis was a popular saint of Edessa, admired as a 'man of God.'

Alice
Pronunciation: AL-iss
The name Alice is of Old German origin. The meaning of Alice is "noble, exalted". Originally a common adaptation of the name Adelaide, Alice became recognized as a first name in its own right. Lewis Carroll popularised the name with his books, *Alice's Adventures in Wonderland* (1865), and *Through the Looking Glass* (1872). The main character was based on his childhood friend Alice Lidell.

Amalia
Pronunciation: a-ma-LIA
Amalia is of Latin and Old German origin. The meaning of the name Amalia is "work". The name is a variation of Amelia.

Amanda
Pronunciation: ah-MAN-dah

The name Amanda is of Latin origin. The meaning of
Amanda is "loveable". From Latin *Amanda*, the female
form of *amare*. The name first appeared as first name
on a 1212 birth record from Warwickshire, England.
The name was popularised in the 17th century by the
playwright and poet, Colley Cibber (1671-1757).
Diminutives: Manda, Mandi, Mandie, Mandy.

Amelia

Pronunciation: a-MEEL-yah
Amelia is of Latin and Old German origin. The
meaning of the name Amelia is "eager worker, labour".
From Old German *amal*, and influenced by the Latin
name Aemelia. Princess Amelia brought the name to
Britain in the 18th century. Diminutives: Emily, Millie,
Milly.

Amina

Pronunciation: ah-MEEN-ah
The name Amina is of Arabic origin. The meaning of
Amina is "honest, peaceful". Amina bint-Wahab was
the mother of the Prophet Muhammad.

Amy

Pronunciation: AY-mee

The name Amy is of Old French and Latin origin. The meaning of Amy is "beloved". Amy is an anglicised form of the name Aimèe. Originally used as a nickname for the Latin name Amata. The name was popularised by characters in Louisa M Alcott's *Little Women* (1868).

Anastasia

Pronunciation: ahn-a-STAH-shah

Anastasia is of Greek origin. The meaning of the name Anastasia is "Resurrection". From the Greek word *anastasis*, which means 'rising up'. Borne by a Roman saint and matron, she was said to have buried the bodies of Saint Peter and Saint Paul with Saint Basilissa. The name is popular in Eastern Europe in honour of a 4th century Dalmation martyr. Anastasia was made famous in the 20th century by the daughter of Tzar Nicholas II, the last Russian czar. In 1920, a woman claiming to be Anastasia said that she had survived the massacre of the royal family in 1917, thus generating worldwide publicity.

Andrea

Pronunciation: AN-dree-ah

The name Andrea is of Greek origin. The meaning of Andrea is "manly, virile". The name is a feminine form of the masculine names Andreas and Andrew. The name is also used as a nickname for Alexandra. The name dates back to the 17th century.

Angela

Pronunciation: AN-je-lah

The name Angela is of Greek origin. The meaning of Angela is "angel, messenger of God". The name is a feminine form of Angel and Angelus. The name became popular in Britain from the 18th century. Diminutive: Angie.

Angelica

Pronunciation: an-JEL-ih-kah

Angelica is of Latin origin. The meaning of the name Angelica is "angelic". From the Latin *Angelicus.* Borne by the heroine of Matteo Boiardo's *Orlando Innamorato* (1487), Angelica was the beautiful daughter of the king of Cataio. Orlando's passionate love for Angelica ended up driving him mad. Diminutive: Angie.

Angelina, Angeline

Pronunciation: an-JEL-ih-na

The name Angelina is of Italian origin. The meaning of Angelina is "angel, messenger of God".. The name

Angeline is of French origin. Both Angelina and Angeline are variations of the Greek name Angela. Diminutive: Angie.

Angharad
Pronunciation: an-HAR-ad
The name Angharad is of Welsh origin. The meaning of Angharad is "beloved, much loved". Angharad is a character in the Welsh folk tales *Mabinogian*.

Anita
Pronunciation: a-NEE-tah
The name Anita is of Spanish origin. The meaning of Anita is unknown. Anita is originally a Spanish diminutive of Ann. The name was made famous by the Swedish film actress, Anita Ekberg.

Ann, Anne
Pronunciation: ANN-e
The name Anne is of English and Latin origin. The meaning of Anne is "God has favoured me". Anne is the English form of the biblical name Hannah.

Anna
Pronunciation: AN-ah

Anna is of Hebrew origin. The meaning of the name Anna is "God has favoured me". Anna is a Latinate variant of the name Hannah. In classical legend, Anna was the sister of Dido, Queen of Carthage. A biblical name; borne in the New Testament by an elderly prophetess (Luke 2:36-38).

Annabel

Pronunciation: AN-a-BELL

The name Annable is of Latin origin. The meaning of Annabel is "loveable". The name is a variation of Amabel. The name has been a popular first name in Scotland since the 12th century.

Anneka

Pronunciation: AN-ee-ka

Anneka is of Swedish origin. The meaning of the name Anneka is "sweet-faced". Anneka is a Swedish form of the name Ann(e).

Anneliese

Pronunciation: AN-ee-lee-se

Anneliese is of German origin. The meaning of the name Anneliese is "graced with God's bounty". Anneliese is a variant of the Latin name Annalisa. The

German name is a compound of Anna and Liese (Elizabeth).

Annette
Pronunciation: an-NET
The name Annette is of French origin. The meaning of Annette is unknown. Annette is feminine diminutive form of Antoine. Diminutive: Net, Nettie, Netty, Toinette, Toni.

Antoinette
Pronunciation: ann-twa-NET
The name Antoinette is of French origin. The meaning of Antoinette is unknown. Antoinette is a feminine diminutive form of the name Antoine. The name was made famous by the French Queen Marie Antoinette (1755-1793). Diminutives: Net, Nettie, Netty, Toinette, Toni.

Antonia
Pronunciation: ann-TONE-yah
Antonia is of Latin origin. The meaning of the name Antonia is unknown. Antonia is a feminine form of the masculine name Anthony. The name was a common Roman feminine family name. Diminutive: Toni, Tony, Tonia, Tonya.

Anya

Pronunciation: AN-ya

The meaning of Anya is "resurrection, God had favoured me". Anya is a variant of the Greek name Anastasia. The name is an anglicised spelling of the Spanish form of Ann(e).

Aphra

Pronunciation: AFF-rah

The name Aphra is of Hebrew origin. The meaning of Aphra is "young deer". The name is either derived from Hebrew *aphrah*, which means 'dust' or possibly a variation of the Latin name Afra.

Aoife

Pronunciation: EE-fra

The name Aoife if of Irish, Gaelic and Scottish origin. The meaning of Aoife is "beautiful". From Irish Gaelic *aoibh*, which means 'beauty'. The name is borne by numerous heroines in ancient Irish legend. Eva is the anglicized form of the name.

April

Pronunciation: AY-prill

The name April is of Latin origin. The meaning of April is "to open". April is also the name of the fourth month of the year. The name may have been influenced by the French equivalent, Avril.

Arabella
Pronunciation: AIR-a-bell-ah
The name Arabella is of Latin origin. The meaning of Arabella is "prayerful". The name might possibly be a variation of the Annabel. The name has been popular in Scotland since the 14th century and spread to England in the 18th century.

Areta
Pronunciation: A-re-ta
The name Areta is of Greek origin. The meaning of Areta is "virtue, excellence". Areta is related to the name Arethusa. The name is also a variant of the Greek name Aretha.

Ariadne
Pronunciation: ar-ee-AHD-nee
The name Ariadne is of Greek origin. The meaning of Ariadne is "most holy". Borne mythology; Ariadne was the daughter of King Minos of Crete. She helped Theseus to escape by giving him a ball of wool so that he could find his way out of the Labyrinth after he had

killed the Minotaur. Saint Ariadne is a 2nd century saint and Christian martyr.

Arianwen

Pronunciation: a-ree-AN-win

The name Arianwen is of Welsh origin. The meaning of Arianwen is "white, holy silver, fair". Borne in the 5th by a daughter of Brychan, a legendary Welsh chieftain.

Artemis

Pronunciation: AR-te-miss

The name Artemis is of Greek origin. The meaning of Artemis is unknown. Borne in Greek mythology; Artemis was a Greek goddess of the moon, hunting, and of chastity, equivalent to the Roman goddess Diana. Artemis is used as both a boy's name and as a girl's name.

Astrid

Pronunciation: AS-trid

The name Astrid is of Old Norse origin. The meaning of Astrid is "beautiful goddess". From Old Norse elements *áss*, which means 'god', and *fríor*, 'beautiful'.

Athene

Pronunciation: a-THEE-nee

The name Athene is of Greek origin. The meaning of Athene is "immortal". Borne in Greek mythology; Athene was the virgin goddess of arts, wisdom and war. She was supposedly born fully armed, from the head of Zeus. Athene was patron of the city of Athens.

Audrey

Pronunciation: AW-dree

The name Audrey is of Old English origin. The meaning of Audrey is "noble strength". Derived from the informal pronunciation of the name of Saint Etheldreda, 7th-century abbess of Ely.

Aurora

Pronunciation: aw-ROHR-ah

The name Aurora is of Latin origin. The meaning of Aurora is "dawn". Borne in mythology; Aurora was the goddess of sunrise. In various versions of the 'Sleeping Beauty' fairytale, the princess's name is Aurora.

Ava

Pronunciation: AY-vah

The name Ava is of uncertain origin. The meaning of Ava is also unknown. The name is possibly a medieval Germanic diminutive for names that begin with AV-. The name may possibly be a variation of Eva. Hollywood actress Ava Gardner (1922-1990) popularised the name.

Aveline
Pronunciation: AY-v-e-line
Aveline is of Norman origin. The meaning of the name Aveline is unknown. The name is a Latinate form of the Norman French name Eveline.

Avril
Pronunciation: AV-ril
The name Avril is of Latin origin. The meaning of Avril is "to open". From French *Avril*, which means 'April'. The name may also be a nickname for Averil.

B

Barbara

Pronunciation: BAR-bra

The name Barbara is of Greek and Latin origin. The meaning of Barbra is "strange, foreign woman". The name was originally an onomatopoeic word describing the babbling sound of an unintelligible foreign tongue. The name was applied to anyone who did not speak Greek. Saint Barbara is invoked as a protector against fire and lighting, she is the patron saint of architects, stonemasons, and fortifications. Her father was about to cut off her head when he was struck by lightning. Her actual existence is disputed. Diminutives: Bab, Babs, Barbie, Baubie, Bobby.

Bea

Pronunciation: bea

Bea is a diminutive of the names, Beatrice and Beatrix.

Beatrice, Beatrix

Pronunciation: BEE-a-triss

The name Beatrice is of Latin origin. The meaning of Beatrice is "bringer of joy". The name is mentioned in the Domesday book. Shakespeare used the name in Much Ado About Nothing (1598). The name was revived in the 19th century, possibly after Queen Victoria named one of her daughters Beatrice. Beatrice is also the name of the heroine of Dante's, *Divine Comedy* (c. 1309-02).

Belinda

Pronunciation: ba-LIN-dah

The name Belinda is of Old German origin. The meaning of Belinda is "snake". From the Old German name Betlindis. Diminutives: Bel, Bell, Belle, Linda, Lundy.

Bella

Pronunciation: BELL-ah

Bella is of Italian and Latin origin. The meaning of the name Bella is "beautiful". The name is also a diminutive of names incorporating the element –bella, such as Isabella.

Bennett

Pronunciation: BEN-et

Bennett is of French and Latin origin. The adopted surname has been used for both girl's and boy's names. Taken from the medieval vernacular form of Benedict.

Bentley
Pronunciation: BENT-lee
The name Bentley is of Old English origin. The meaning of the name Bentley is "bent grass meadow". The adopted surname is used more commonly as a boy's name, however it is also used as a girl's name. Bentley is also a place name for many places in England.

Bernadette
Pronunciation: ber-na-DET
The name Bernadette is of French and Old German. The meaning of Bernadette is "strong, brave bear". Bernadette is a French feminine form of the masculine name Bernard. Saint Bernadette Soubirous popularised the name during the 19th century. She was a French peasant girl who had visions of the Virgin Mary and uncovered a spring near Lourdes where miraculous cures are sought. Diminutives: Bernie, Berny.

Berta
Pronunciation: BERT-ah

The name Berta is of Old German origin. The meaning of Berta is "bright". The name was borne by the mother of Charlemagne. The name was introduced to Britain by the Normans.

Beryl

Pronunciation: BEHR-el

The name Beryl is of Greek origin. The meaning of Beryl is "light green semi-precious gemstone". From Old French *beril*, which was derived from Greek *berullos*, denoting a precious pale green stone with light blue, yellow and white lights. The name was popular during the 19th century.

Beth

Pronunciation: beth

The name Beth is of Hebrew origin. The meaning of Beth is "house". Beth is also a diminutive of the name Elizabeth. The name dates back to the 19th century. Louisa M Alcott popularised the name in her novel, *Little Women* (1868).

Bethany

Pronunciation: BETH-a-nee

The name Bethany is of Hebrew origin. The meaning of Bethany is "house of figs". A biblical name, Bethany is the name of the village near Jerusalem. Diminutive: Beth.

Bethia
Pronunciation: BE-thia
The name Bethia is of Hebrew origin. The meaning of Bethia is "daughter of God".

Betsy
Pronunciation: BET-see
The name Betsy is of Hebrew origin. The meaning of Betsy is "God is my oath". Betsy is a diminutive of the name Elizabeth.

Bette
Pronunciation: BET-ee
The name Bette is of Hebrew and French origin. The meaning of Bette is "God is my oath". Bette is a French diminutive of the name Elizabeth. The name was popularised by Hollywood actress Bette Davis (1908-1989).

Betty
Pronunciation: BET-ee

The name Betty is of Hebrew origin. The meaning of Betty is "God is my oath". The name was popular during the 20th century.

Beulah

Pronunciation: bea-u-LAH

The name Beulah is of Hebrew origin. The meaning of Beulah is "married". A biblical name for the land of Israel (Isaiah 62).

Beverly, Beverley

Pronunciation: BEV-er-lee

The name Beverly is of Old English origin. The meaning of Beverly is "beaver". Beverly is an adopted surname and place name, from Old English *beofor*. The name was first used as a masculine name in the 19th century. The name is now given to females.

Bianca

Pronunciation: bee-AHNK-ah

The name Bianca is of Italian origin. The meaning of Bianca is "pure, white". The name was used by Shakespeare in *The Taming of the Shrew* (1593). Bianca was the gentle sister of Katharina, 'the Shrew'. Shakespeare also used the name is Othello (1604).

Billie

Pronunciation: BILL-ee

The name Billie is of Old English origin. The meaning of Billie is unknown. Billie is a diminutive of the names Wilhelmina and William.

Birgit

Pronunciation: ber-GEET

Birgit is of Norwegian origin. The meaning of the name Birgit is "exalted one". Birgit is a variant of the name Bridget. Diminutives: Birgit, Brita, Britt.

Blake

Pronunciation: blayk

Blake is of Old English origin. The meaning of the name Blake is "black", "pale". The adopted surname is used as both a boy's name and a girl's name. Blake was originally used as a nickname for someone with skin or hair that was either very dark ("blaec") or very light ("blac").

Blanche

Pronunciation: BLAN-che

The name Blanche is of Old French and Old German origin. The meaning of Blanche is "white, pure".

Blanche of Lancaster brought the name to Britain in the 14th century.

Blodwen

Pronunciation: B-lod-wen

The name Blodwen is of Welsh origin. The meaning of Blodwen is "holy flower, white flower". The name was popular in the Middle Ages.

Blossom

Pronunciation: BLOSS-om

Blossom is of Old English origin. The meaning of the name Blossom is "flower-like". The name is a direct adoption of the English vocabulary, denoting a mass of flowers on a fruit tree. Blossom was first used as a first name in the 19th century.

Blythe

Pronunciation: bleeth

The name Blythe is of Old English origin. The meaning of Blythe is "blithe, cheerful". Originally an adopted surname.

Bobbie, Bobby

Pronunciation: BOB-ee

The name Bobbie is of Latin origin. The meaning of Bobbie is "foreign woman". Bobby is a variant of the Latin name Barbara. The name is also a diminutive of the name Roberta.

Bonita
Pronunciation: boh-NEE-tah
The name Bonita is of Spanish origin. The meaning of Bonita is "pretty". Diminutives: Bonni, Bonny.

Brady
Pronunciation: BRAY-dee
The name Brady is of Irish and Gaelic origin. The meaning of the name is "descendant of Brádach". The name is used as both a boy's name and as a girl's names.

Branwen
Pronunciation: BRAN-wen
The name Branwen is of Welsh origin. The meaning of Branwen is "raven, fair". Borne in Welsh legend by the heroine of one of the tales of the *Mabinogian*.

Brenda
Pronunciation: BREN-dah

The name Brenda is of Old Norse origin. The meaning of Brenda is "sword, torch". The name is sometimes considered to be a feminine form of Brendan.

Brennan

Pronunciation: BREN-an

Brennan is of Irish and Gaelic origin. The meaning of the name Brennan is "teardrop". Brennan is used as both a boy's name and as a girl's name. The name is also a variant of Brendan.

Bride

Pronunciation: BRI-de

Bride is of Gaelic origin. The meaning of the name Brid is "exalted one". Bride is a variation of the Gaelic name Bridget.

Bridie

Pronunciation: BRID-ee

Bridie is of Gaelic origin. The meaning of the name Bridie is "exalted one". Bridie is a variation of the Gaelic name Bridget.

Bridget

Pronunciation: BRIH-jet

Bridget is of Gaelic origin. The meaning of the name Bridget is "exalted one". Bridget is an anglicized version of the Irish name Brighid. Borne in mythology; Saint Brigid of Kildare (c. 450-525) is the second patron saint of Ireland, after Saint Patrick. Her feast day is 1st February. Diminutives: Biddy, Bridie.

Bridgid
Pronunciation: BRID-gid
The name Bridgid is of Gaelic origin. The meaning of Bridgid is "exalted one". Bridgid is a variation of the name Bridget.

Briony, Bryony
Pronunciation: BRI-on-ee
Briony is of Greek origin. The meaning of the name Briony is "luxurious growth". The name was adopted in the 19th century, when botanical names became fashionable.

Brooks
Pronunciation: brux
Brooks is of Old English and Old German origin. The meaning of Brooks is "water", "small stream". Brooks is used as both a boy's name and a girl's name.

Bronwen

Pronunciation: BRON-wen

The name Bronwen is of Welsh origin. The meaning of Bronwen is "white breast, blessed breast". Diminutive: Bron.

Bryn

Pronunciation: br-yn

The name Bryn is of Welsh origin. The meaning of the name Bryn is "hill". The name is also a short form of Brynmor. Bryn is used as both a boy's name and girl's name.

C

Caitlín

Pronunciation: KATE-lin

Caitlín is of Old French and Greek origin. The meaning of the name Caitlín is "pure". Caitlín is the Irish Gaelic form of the name Catherine.

Cameron

Pronunciation: KAM-ren

The name Cameron is of Scottish and Gaelic origin. The meaning of Cameron is "crooked nose". Cameron is a Scottish Highlands clan surname. Cameron is used as both a girl's name and as a boy's name.

Camilla

Pronunciation: ka-MEEL-ah

The name Camilla is of Latin origin. The meaning of Camilla is "helper to the priest". Camilla is a feminine form of the Roman family name Camilus. Fanny Burney popularised the name with her novel, Camilla (1796). Diminutives: Millie, Milly.

Candida

Pronunciation: kan-DEE-dah

The name Candida is of Latin origin. The meaning of Candida is "white". The name is borne by several early saints. Diminutive: Candy.

Carina

Pronunciation: ka-REEN-ah

The name Carina is of Latin origin. The meaning of Carina is "beloved, dear". Carina is a diminutive feminine form deriving from Italian *caro*.

Carla

Pronunciation: kar-LAH

Carla is of Old German origin. The meaning of the name Carla is "free man". Carla is a feminine form of the masculine name Carl. The name was popular throughout the late 20th century.

Carly

Pronunciation: KAR-lee

The name Carly is of Latin origin. The meaning of Carly is "free man". Carly is a diminutive of the names Carla, Carlotta and Caroline.

Carmel

Pronunciation: kar-MEL

Carmel is of Hebrew origin. The meaning of the name Carmel is "garden, orchard". A biblical name; Mount Carmel was where Elijah summoned Israel to choose between God and Baal (I King 18). In the 12th century, a monastery was founded dedicated to the Virgin Mary.

Carmela

Pronunciation: kar-MEL-ah

The name Carmela is of Italian origin. The meaning of Carmela is "garden, orchard". Carmela is an Italian variant of the name Carmel.

Carmen

Pronunciation: KAR-men

The name Carmen is of Spanish origin. The meaning of Carmen is "song, charm". The name is originally a Spanish form of the name Carmel, influenced by the Latin word, *carmen*. The name was popularised in the 19th century by Bizet's opera, *Carmen* (1875).

Carol

Pronunciation: KARE-ol

The name Carol is of Old German origin. The meaning of Carol is "free man". Carol is a feminine form of the names Charles, originated from the Latin name Carolus. Originally used as a boy's name, the name is now generally used for girls.

Caroline

Pronunciation: KARE-a-line

The name Caroline is of Old German origin. The meaning of Caroline is "free man". Caroline is a feminine form of the names Charles, originated from the Latin name Carolus. The German-born wife of King George II, Caroline of Ansbach, introduced the name to Britain. Diminutives: Carly, Caro, Carrie.

Carolyn

Pronunciation: KARE-a-lyn

The name Carolyn is of Old German origin. The meaning of Carolyn is "free man". Carolyn is a variant of the name Caroline, dating back to the 20th century.

Carys

Pronunciation: CHAR-is

Carys is of Welsh origin. The meaning of the name Carys is "love".

Casey

Pronunciation: KAY-see

The name Casey is of Irish and Gaelic origin. The meaning of Casey is "alert, watchful". The name Casey is used as both a boy's name, and as a girl's name. Casey is from the male Gaelic name *Cathasaigh.*

Cassandra

Pronunciation: ka-SAN-dra

Cassandra is of Greek origin. The meaning of Cassandra is "shining upon man". Cassandra is possibly a variation of the name Alexander. The name is borne in Greek mythology by a Trojan princess. She was blessed with the gift of prophecy and foretold the fall of Troy. However after turning down Apollo's advances, he was so angry that he arranged for her never to be believed. The name was revived in the 18th century. Diminutives: Cas, Cassie, Sandra.

Catherine

Pronunciation: KATH-rin

The name Catherine is of Greek origin. The meaning of Catherine is "pure". Borne by several early saints, saint Catherine Alexandria was a 4th-century martyr of noble birth. She was condemned to death on a spiked wheel however, the wheel mysteriously broke. This led to her being beheaded. Saint Catherine Alexandria is the patron saint of wheelwrights. Saint Catherine Siena is (1347-1380) is considered the patron saint of Italy. King Henry VIII had three wives names Catherine. Diminutives: Casey, Cate, Cath, Cathie, Cathy, Kate, Kay, Kit, Kitty.

Cathleen

Pronunciation: kath-LEEN

Cathleen is of Greek origin. The meaning of the name Cathleen is "pure". Cathleen is a variation of the name Catherine and was influenced by the Irish Gaelic name Caitlín.

Catrin

Pronunciation: CAT-rin

The name Catrin is of Greek origin. The meaning of Catrin is "pure". Catrin is a Welsh form of the name Catherine.

Catriona

Pronunciation: cat-REE-ona

Catriona is of Scottish Gaelic and Irish origin. The meaning of the name Catriona is "pure". Catriona is a variation of the name Catherine. Robert Louis

Stevenson popularised the name during the 19th century, with his novel *Catriona* (1893).

Cecilia

Pronunciation: sess-SEEL-yah

The name Cecilia is of Latin and Old Welsh origin. The meaning of Cecilia is "blind, sixth". Cecilia is a Latinate feminine form of the name Cecil. The name was borne in the 2nd century by a blind Roman martyr and saint. She is regarded as the patron saint of musicians and music. Her feast day is 22nd November. The name was popular during the Middle Ages. The name was later revived in the 18th century.

Diminutives: Cis, Ciss, Cissie, Cissy, Sissie, Sissy.

Cecilie

Pronunciation: sess-SEEL-e

The name Cecilie is of Latin and French origin. The meaning of Cecilie is "blind, sixth". Cecilie is a French feminine form of the name Cecil. Cecilie is also a variant of the names Cecilia and Cecily.

Ceinwen

Pronunciation: KAYN-wen

The name Ceinwen is of Welsh origin. The meaning of Ceinwen is "beautiful; gems".

Celeste

Pronunciation: she-LEST

The name Celeste is of Latin origin. The meaning of Celeste is "heavenly". The name was popular among early Christians. Celeste is a masculine form of the name Celestin.

Celine

Pronunciation: SEL-ine

The name Celine is of Latin origin. The meaning of Celine is "heaven". Derived from Latin *caelum*, which means 'sky'. The French name is spelled Cèline. The name was popularised by singer Celine Dion.

Ceridwen

Pronunciation: ke-RID-wen

The name Ceridwen is of Welsh origin. The meaning of Ceridwen is "fair, holy, blessed poetry. Borne in Celtic mythology by the Welsh goddess of poetic inspiration.

Chandler

Pronunciation: CHAND-ler

Chandler is of Middle English and Old French origin. The meaning of the name Chandler is "candle maker". The adopted surname was also an occupational name from 'chandele' meaning 'candle'. Chandler is used as both a boy's name and as a girl's name.

Chandra
Pronunciation: SHAN-drah
Chandra is of Hindi and Sanskrit origin. The meaning of the name Chandra is "moon shining". The greatest Hindu goddess Devi is also known as Chandra.

Chanel
Pronunciation: sha-NELL
Chanel is of Old French origin. The meaning of the name Chanel is "wine, amphora". The name was influenced by the legendary fashion designer Gabrielle 'Coco' Chanel (1883-1971). Chanel is also the name of the 14th-century French missionary saint.

Chantal
Pronunciation: shanh-TAL
Chantal is of Old French origin. The meaning of Chantal is "stone". An adopted surname and place name, after Chantal in Saóne-et-Loire. The name was originally given in honor of Saint Jeanne-Françoise de Chantal (1572-1641). She lived a strict religious life and founded an order of nuns, the Vistandines.

Charlene

Pronunciation: shar-LEEN

The name Charlene is of Old German origin. The meaning of Charlene is "free man". Charlene is a feminine form of the masculine name Charles.

Charlotte

Pronunciation: SHAR-let

The name Charlotte is of Old German origin. The meaning of Charlotte is "free man". Charlotte is a French feminine diminutive of Charles. The name has been used in England since the 17th century. The name was popularised by King George III's wife, Charlotte Sophia (1744-1817). E.B White also popularised the name in *Charlotte's Web* (1952). Diminutives: Charley, Charlie, Chattie, Chatty, Lottie, Lotty, Totty.

Charmaine

Pronunciation: shar-MAYNE

The name Charmaine is of English origin. The meaning of Charmaine is "charm". A modern coinage, derived from the name Carminea. The name was first used by Maxwell Anderson and Laurence Stallings in the play, *What Price Glory?* (1924).

Chastity

Pronunciation: CHASS-ti-tee

The name Chastity is of Latin origin. The meaning of Chastity is "pure". The virtue name is from Latin *castus*.

Cherie

Pronunciation: sha-REE

The name Cherie is of French origin. The meaning of Cherie is "darling". From French chère.

Cherry

Pronunciation: CHARE-ee

The name Cherry is of English and Old French origin. The meaning of Cherry is "cherry, tree". Cherry is originally a diminutive of the name Charity. The name later became associated with the sweet fruit. Cherry is also used as a diminutive of Cherie.

Cheryl

Pronunciation: CHER-ell

The name Cheryl is of French and Greek origin. The meaning of Cheryl is "cherry fruit, green gemstone". The name is an early 20th-century variation of the name Cherry.

Chiara

Pronunciation: kee-AH-ra

The name Chiara is of Italian and Latin origin. The meaning of Chiara is "bright, famous". The name is an Italian form of Clara and Claire. The name is borne by several early Italian saints.

Chloe

Pronunciation: KHLOH-ee

Chloe is of Greek origin. The meaning of the name Chloe is "green shoot". The name is associated with the Greek goddess of agriculture and fertility, Demeter. The name was borne in Longus's Greek romance, *Daphnis and Chloe*. A biblical name; Chloe is briefly mentioned by Saint Paul in the New Testament (1 Corinthians 1:11). The name was popular with the Puritans during the 17th century.

Christabel

Pronunciation: KRIS-ta-bell

The name Christabel is of Latin and French origin. The meaning of Christabel is "beautiful Christian". The name is a medieval coinage from the name Christ with –bel, from Latin *bella*. Samuel Taylor Coleridge popularised the name in his poem Christabel (1816).

Christabel Pankhurst (1880-1958) was a pioneer suffragette.

Christiana
Pronunciation: kris-TEEN-iah
Christiana is of Latin origin. The meaning of the name Christiana is "follower of Christ". The name is a medieval Latinate form of Christian. John Bunyan used the name for the wife of Christian in The Pilgrims' Progress (1684). Diminutives: Chris, Christie, Christy.

Christina
Pronunciation: kris-TEEN-ah
Christina is of Latin origin. The meaning of the name Christina is "follower of Christ". Christina is a feminine form derived from the Latin name Christianus. Diminutives: Chris, Chrissie, Chrissy, Tina.

Christine
Pronunciation: kris-TEEN
The name Christine is of French and Latin origin. The meaning of Christine is "follower of Christ". Christine is a French form of the name Christina. The name was

introduced to Britain in the 19th century. Diminutives: Chris, Chrissie, Chrissy.

Ciara

Pronunciation: kee-AR-ah

The name Ciara is of Irish and Gaelic origin. The meaning of Ciara is "black". Ciara is a modern Irish feminine form of the name Ciaran.

Cindy

Pronunciation: SIN-dee

The name Cindy is of English and Greek origin. The meaning of Cindy is "from Mount Kynthos". Cindy is a diminutive of the name Lucinda. The name became a popular first name in its own right.

Cissy

Pronunciation: sis-EE

The name Cissy is of Latin and Old Welsh origin. The meaning of Cissy is "blind, sixth". Cissy is a diminutive of the names Cecilia and Cicely.

Claire

Pronunciation: clare

The name Claire is of Latin origin. The meaning of Claire is "bright, famous".

The Norma invaders introduced the name to Britain in the original form of, Clara. The name was revived in the 19th century as the French form of Clare.

Clara
Pronunciation: KLAR-a
Clara is of Latin origin. The meaning of the name Clara is "bright, famous". Clara is a feminine form of the Latin adjective *clarus*. The name has largely been replaced by the names Chiara, Claire and Clare.

Clare
Pronunciation: clare
The name Clare is of Latin origin. The meaning of Clare is "bright, famous". The name was a popular medieval English form of the name Clara.

Clarissa
Pronunciation: kla-RISS-ah
Clarissa is of Latin origin. The meaning of the name Clarissa is "most bright, most famous". Clarissa is a Latinate form of the name Clarice. Samuel Richardson popularised the name in his novel *Clarissa* (1748).

Claudia
Pronunciation: KLAW-dee-ah

The name of Claudia is of Latin origin. The meaning of Claudia is "lame". Claudia is a feminine form derived from the Roman family name Claudius. A biblical name; borne by a Christian woman of Rome greeted by Paul in his second letter to Timothy (2 Timothy 4). The name dates back to the 16th century.

Claudine

Pronunciation: klaw-DEEN

The name Claudine is of French origin. The meaning of Claudine is "lame". Claudine is a French feminine and diminutive form of the name Claude. The name was popular throughout the 20th century.

Cleo

Pronunciation: KLEE-oh

Cleo is of Greek origin. The meaning of the name Cleo is "glory of the father". Cleo is a diminutive of the Greek name Cleopatra. The name became a popular first name in its own right.

Clíodhna

Pronunciation: KOR-ee

The name Clíodhna is of Irish Gaelic origin. The meaning of Clíodhna is unknown. The name is born in

Irish legend, Clíodhna was one of the three beautiful daughters of the poet Libra.

Coco

Pronunciation: KO-ko

Coco is of French origin. The meaning of the name Coco is "people of victory". Coco is a diminutive of Nicolette, and also of names starting with CO-. The name was popularised by the famous fashion designer Gabrielle Coco Chanel (1883-1971).

Cody

Pronunciation: KO-dee

The name Cody is of Irish and Gaelic origin. The meaning of the name Cody is "Helper". Cody is used as both a boy's name, and as a girl's name.

Cole

Pronunciation: kohl

Cole is of Middle English and Old French origin. The meaning of Cole is "charcoal". Originally a surname that was derived from a medieval given name. Cole is used as both a boy's name and as a girl's name.

Colette

Pronunciation: ko-LET

The name Colette is of French and Greek origin. The meaning of Colette is "people of victory". Colette is a diminutive of the name Nicolette. The name is borne by a 15th-century French nun and saint, she was renowned for giving her money to the poor. French writer, Sidonie-Gabrielle Colette (1873-1954) popularised the name.

Colleen
Pronunciation: kah-LEEN
The name Colleen is of Gaelic origin. The meaning of Colleen is "girl, wench". Colleen is an Irish vernacular word, which means girl. The name is also used as a feminine of the masculine name Colin.

Concetta
Pronunciation: CON-cetta
The name Concetta is of Italian and Latin origin. The meaning of Concetta is "conceived, conception". Concetta is an Italian form of a Latin name, *concepta*. The name is a reference to the Immaculate Conception.

Constance
Pronunciation: KAHN-stans

The name Constance is of Latin origin. The meaning of Constance is "constant, steadfast". From the Latin *constantia*, which means 'constancy'. The name was introduced to Britain by the Normans. The name was borne by a virgin saint daughter of Constantine the Great. Diminutive: Connie.

Constantia
Pronunciation: CONST-ant-tia
The name Constantia is of Latin origin. The meaning of Constantia is "constant, steadfast". Constantia is Latin form of Constance. The name was popular with early Christians and also with the Puritans. Diminutive: Connie.

Corey
Pronunciation: KOR-ee

The name Corey is an English surname derived from an Old Norse personal name Kori. Corey is used as both a boy's name, and as a girl's name. The meaning of the name may mean "God, peace".

Corinna, Corinne
Pronunciation: ko-RINN-nah
The name Corinna is of Greek origin. The meaning of Corinna is "maiden". Corinna was an alternative name

for Persephone, and also for a 5th-century poetess. Roman poet Ovid used the name for the woman in his love poetry. The name was later revived in the 16th and 17th centuries.

Cosima

Pronunciation: KOZ-i-ma

The name Cosima is of Greek origin. The meaning of Cosima is "beauty, order". Cosima is a feminine form of Cosmo.

Courtney

Pronunciation: COURT-ney

Courtney is of Old French origin. The meaning of Courtney is "domain of Curtis". The name is both a surname and a place name. Courtney is a Norman baronial name from places in Northern France called Courtenay. Courtney is used as both a boy's name and a girl's name.

Crystal

Pronunciation: KRISS-tal

The name Crystal is of Greek origin. The meaning of Crystal is "ice". Derived from Greek *krustallos*. Crystal is one of the several stone and mineral names that became fashionable in the late 19th century.

D

Dabney

Pronunciation: DAB-nee

The name Dabney is of Old French origin. The meaning of Dabney is "from Aubigny".

Dacey

Pronunciation: DAY-cee

The name Dacey is of Irish and Gaelic origin. The meaning of Dacey is "from the South".

Dacia

Pronunciation: DAY-sha

Dacia is of Latin origin. The meaning of the name Dacia is unknown. Originally a place name, Dacia was a Roman province.

Dada

Pronunciation: DA-da

The name Dada is of Nigerian origin. The meaning of Dada is "curly haired".

Dagmar

Pronunciation: DAG-mar

The name Dagmar is of Old German and Scandinavian origin. The meaning of Dagmar is "glorious, day's glory". Dagmar is a royal name in Denmark.

Dagny

Pronunciation: DAG-ny

The name Dagny is of Old Norse origin. The meaning of Dagny is "new day". The name possibly relates to the Old German name Dagmar.

Dahlia

Pronunciation: DAL-yah

Dahlia is of Swedish and Scandinavian origin. The meaning of the name Dahlia is "Valley".

Daisy

Pronunciation: DAY-zee

The name Daisy is of Old English origin. The meaning of Daisy is "day's eye". The name was first used as a diminutive of the French name, Marguerite. Daisy is reference to the flower of the same name that opens during the day. The name was popular during the 19th century when botanical names became fashionable.

Henry James also popularised the name in his novel *Daisy Miller* (1878).

Damaris

Pronunciation: DAM-a-ris

The name Damaris is of Greek and Latin origin. The meaning of Damaris is "calf, to tame". A biblical name; borne by an Athenian woman who heard Paul speak at Mar's Hill, she was converted by Saint Paul (Acts 17). The name was adopted by the Puritans.

Dana

Pronunciation: DAY-nah

The name Dana is of Old English origin. The meaning of Dana is "from Denmark". Borne in mythology; Dana was the Celtic goddess of fertility. The name is also used a Scandinavian feminine form of Daniel.

Daniella

Pronunciation: dan-YELL-ah

The name Daniella is of Hebrew and French origin. The meaning of Daniella is "God is my Judge". Daniella is a feminine form of the masculine name Daniel. Daniella is the Latinate form. Diminutives: Dan, Dani.

Danielle

Pronunciation: dan-YELL

The name Danielle is of Hebrew and French origin.
The meaning of Danielle is "God is my Judge".
Danielle is a feminine form of the masculine name
Daniel. The name has been used as a first name since
the 20th century. Daniella is the Latinate form.
Diminutives: Dan, Dani.

Daphne

Pronunciation: DAFF-nee

The name Daphne is of Greek origin. The name
Daphne is of Greek origin. The meaning of Daphne is
"laurel tree". Borne in Greek mythology; by the
daughter of the river god Peneus in Thessaly. Daphne
has vowed to die a virgin as she fled Apollo's advances.
The gods felt sorry for Daphne and turned her into a
laurel tree. The name was popular in the 18th and 20th
centuries.

Dara

Pronunciation: DAR-ah

The name Dara is of Hebrew origin. The meaning of
Dara is "charity, nugget of wisdom".

Darcy
Pronunciation: DAR-cee
The name Darcy is of Irish and Gaelic origin. The meaning of Darcy is "dark". An adopted Norman baronial surname (D'Arcy). The name was introduced to Britain during the Norman Conquest. Darcy is used as both a boy's name, and as a girl's name. Darcy is also a Norman place name.

Daria
Pronunciation: DAR-ee-ah
The name Daria is of Greek and Persian origin. The meaning of Daria is "maintains possessions well". Daria is a feminine form of the masculine name Darius.

Darrell
Pronunciation: DA-rr-ELL
The name Darrell is of French and English origin. The meaning of Darrell is unknown. Originally an adopted surname, derived from a French place name, Arielle (French region of Calvados). The name is used as both a girl's name and as a boy's name.

Davina
Pronunciation: dah-VEE-nah

Davina is of Hebrew and Scottish origin. The meaning of the name Davina is "beloved". Davina is a Scottish feminine form of the name David. The name dates back to the 17th century. Diminutives: Vina, Vinia.

Dawn

Pronunciation: dorn

Dawn is of Old English origin. The meaning of the name Dawn is "the first appearance of light". The name is a direct vocabulary adoption. The name dates back to the 20th century.

Deborah

Pronunciation: DEB-er-ah

The name Deborah is of Hebrew origin. The meaning of Deborah is "Bee". A biblical name; borne by two figures in the Old Testament. One is a prophetess and judge who summoned Barak to battle against an invading army (Judges 4), the other is the nurse of Rebekah (Genesis 35). The name was adopted by the Puritans. Diminutives: Deb, Debbie, Debby, Debs.

Dee

Pronunciation: dee

The name Dee is of Welsh origin. The meaning of Dee is "swarthy". Dee is a diminutive of any name beginning with the letter 'D'.

Delia

Pronunciation: DEEL-yah

The name Delia is of Greek origin. The meaning of Delia is "visible, from Delos". The name derives from Delos, which is the smallest of the Greek islands of the Cyclades. Delia is also used as a diminutive of names ending in –delia.

Delilah

Pronunciation: dee-LYE-lah

Delilah is of Hebrew origin. The meaning of the name Delilah is "amorous, seductive". A biblical name; borne in the Old Testament by the mistress of Samson, she famously persuaded Samson into revealing the secret of his superhuman strength. She then betrayed him by cutting off his hair as he slept (Judges 16). The name was adopted by the Puritans.

Della

Pronunciation: DEL-ah

The name Della is of German origin. The meaning of Della is "noble". Della is a diminutive of Adela. The name has been a popular first name since the late 19th century.

Delora

Pronunciation: del-OR-ah

The name Delora is of Latin origin. The meaning of Delora is "from the seashore".

Delphine

Pronunciation: DEL-fee-ne

The name Delphine is of French origin. The meaning of Delphine is "woman of Delphia, dolphin". Derived from the Latin name Delphina. The name is French form of a name which refers to the Greek town of Delphia, home of Apollo's coracle. The Greeks believed that Delphi was the earth's womb.

Denise

Pronunciation: de-NEES

Denise is of French origin. The meaning of the name Denise is "follower of Dionysius". Denise is a French feminine form of the name Denis. The name was first used in Britain in the 12th century.

Dervla

Pronunciation: DER-vlah

The name Dervla is of Irish and Gaelic origin. The meaning of Dervla is "poet's daughter". From the Irish Gaelic name Deirbhile. The name has undergone a revival in Ireland.

Desdemona
Pronunciation: des-de-mona
The name Desdemona is of Greek origin. The meaning of Desdemona "wretchedness". Desdemona is Latinate form of Greek *dysaimon*, which means, 'ill-starred, miserable'. Shakespeare used the name in *Othello* (1604). Desdemona was the beautiful wife of Othello, wrongly accused of adultery which led to her murder.

Devon
Pronunciation: DEV-en
Devon is of English origin. The meaning of the name Devon is uncertain. Devon is originally an adopted surname, English county name, and the name of several towns in America. The name is used as both a boy's name and as a girl's name.

Diana
Pronunciation: dy-ANN-ah
The name Diana is of Latin origin. The meaning of the Diana is "divine". Borne in mythology; Diana was an

ancient Roman goddess of fertility, hunting and the moon. Her name was possibly derived from Latin *divinus*. The name has been used as a first name since the 16th century. The name was made famous by the Princess of Wales, Diana (1961-1997).

Diane

Pronunciation: DIA-ane

The name Diane is of French and Latin origin. The meaning of Diane is "divine". Diane is French form of Diana, the name dates back to the Renaissance.

Dillan

Pronunciation: DILL-an

The name Dillan is of Irish and Gaelic origin. The meaning of Dillan is "like a lion, loyal". The name is a variant of Dillon. Dillan is used as both a boy's name and as a girl's name.

Dinah

Pronunciation: DYE-nah

Dinah is of Hebrew origin. The meaning of the name Dinah is "judgement". A biblical name: borne by the daughter of Jacob and Leah.

Dolores

Pronunciation: dor-LOR-iss

The name Dolores is of Spanish origin. The meaning of Dolores is " Maria of the sorrows". From Spanish, 'Maria de los Dolores', which is a reference to the Virgin Mary. Diminutives: Lola, Lolita.

Dominica, Domenica

Pronunciation: dom-ih-NEEk-ah

The name Dominica is of French and Latin origin. The meaning of Dominica is "Lord". Dominica is a feminine form of the masculine name Dominic.

Dominque

Pronunciation: dom-ih-NEEK

The name Dominque is of is of French and Latin origin. The meaning of Dominque is "Lord". Dominque is French form of the masculine name Dominic.

Donna

Pronunciation: DON-nah

Donna is of Italian origin. The meaning of the name Donna is "woman". The name was American coinage of the 1920's.

Dora

Pronunciation: DOR-ah

The name Dora is of Greek origin. The meaning of Dora is "gift". Dora is a diminutive of the names Pandora, Dorothea, Dorothy and Theodora. The name became a popular first name in its own right.

Dorothea

Pronunciation: DOR-o-thee-ah

The name Dorothea is of Greek origin. The meaning of Dorothea is "gift of God". Saint Dorothea was a virgin martyr, she was killed under Diocletian in c. 300. Diminutives: Dora, Thea.

Dulcie

Pronunciation: DUL-cie

The name Dulcie is of Latin origin. The meaning of Dulcis is "sweet". From Latin *dulcis*. The name was revived in the 19th century.

E

Eartha

Pronunciation: ER-thah

The name Eartha is of Old English origin. The meaning of Eartha is "earth".

From Old English *eorthe*. The name was used by the Puritans in the 17th century.

Edina

Pronunciation: ED-ina

The name Edina is of Old English origin. The meaning of Edina is unknown. The name may possibly be a variation of Edwina, or of Aithne.

Effie

Pronunciation: EFF-ee

Effie is of Greek origin. The meaning of the name Effie is "well spoken". Effie is a diminutive of Euphemia. The name is also used as a nickname for Efrata and Evelyn.

Eileen

Pronunciation: eye-LEEN

The name Eileen is of Irish origin. The meaning of
Eileen is unknown. Eileen is an anglicised form of the
Irish name Eibhlin. Diminutive: Eily.

Eithne

Pronunciation: EE-na

The name Eithne is of Irish and Gaelic origin. The
meaning of Eithne is either, "little fire" or "kernel".
The name is borne by several figures in Irish legend.

Elaine

Pronunciation: ee-LAYNE

The name Elaine is of Greek origin. The meaning of
Elaine is "sun ray". Elaine is a French form of the
name Helen. In Arthurian legend, the name was borne
by a character who fell in love with Lancelot. The name
underwent a popular revival in the late 19th century.

Eleanor

Pronunciation: EL-a-nor

Eleanor is of Old French and Old German origin. The
meaning of the name Eleanor is "sun ray, other".
Eleanor is a French form of the name Helen. The name
was brought to Britain in the 12th century by Henry II

wife, Eleanor of Aquitaine. Diminutives: Ellie, Nell, Nellie, Nelly.

Elena

Pronunciation: eh-LAYN-ah

Elena is of Greek origin. The meaning of the name Elena is "sun ray". Elena is a variation of the name Helen. The name dates back to the 12th century. The name is considered to be an Italian and Spanish form of Helen.

Elise

Pronunciation: el-LEES

Elise is of French and Hebrew origin. The meaning or the name Elise is "God is my oath". Elise is a French diminutive of Elizabeth. The name became popular in its own right, particularly during the 19th century.

Elizabeth

Pronunciation: ee-LIZ-a-beth

The name Elizabeth is of Hebrew origin. The meaning of Elizabeth is "God is my oath". A biblical name; borne in the Old Testament by the wife of Aaron. In the New Testament the Greek form, Elisabeth was borne by the wife of Zacharias, and mother of John the Baptist. The Greek form of Elisabeth was replaced in the 16th century by Elizabeth, probably due to the reign of Queen Elizabeth I of England. Diminutives: Bess, Bessie, Bessy, Beth, Eliza, Libby, Lisbeth, Liz, Liza, Lizbeth, Lizzie, Lizzy, Tetty.

Ella

Pronunciation: EL-ah

The name Ella is of Old German origin. The meaning of Ella is "all". The name is derived from the Old German name Alia. The name was introduced to Britain by the Normans. The name was later revived in the 19th century.

Ellen

Pronunciation: EL-en

The name Ellen is of Greek origin. The meaning of Ellen is "sun ray". Ellen is the most common variant of the name Helen. The name is also used as a diminutive of Eleanor. The name was first used as an independent name in the 16th century. Diminutives: Ellie, Nell, Nellie, Nelly.

Eloise

Pronunciation: el-o-WEE

The name Eloise is of Old German origin. The meaning of Eloise is "famous warrior". Eloise is the French variant of the name Louise.

Elsa

Pronunciation: EL-sah

The name Elsa is of Hebrew origin. The meaning of Elsa is "God is my oath". Elsa is originally a German diminutive of the name Elisabeth. The name became a popular first name in its own right.

Emanuela

Pronunciation: e-man-u-elah

The name Emanuela is of Hebrew origin. The meaning of Emanuela is "God is with us". Emanuela is a feminine form of the masculine name Emanuel.

Emily

Pronunciation: EM-i-lee

Emily is of Latin origin. The meaning of the name Emily is "rival, eager". Emily is a feminine form of the Roman family name Aemilius. Boccaccio, a 14th-century writer popularised the name with the form, Emilia. Chaucer used the name in the form Emelye in *The Knight's Tale*. The name was extremely popular during the 18th 19th and 20th centuries. Diminutives: Millie, Milly.

Emma

Pronunciation: EM-ah

The name Emma is of Old German and Old French origin. The meaning of Emma is "entire, universal". The name was introduced to Britain in the 11th century by Emma of Normandy. The name was a royal name in medieval England. The name was revived in the 18th century, possibly due to Jane Austen's romance novel, *Emma* (1815). Emma has been one of the most favoured names for girls in Britain since the 1970's.

Emmeline

Pronunciation: EM-a-leen

The name Emmeline is of Old French and Old German origin. The meaning of Emmeline is "entire, work". Emmeline is the Old French form of the Old German name Ameline. The name was introduced to Britain by the Normans. The name was made famous by Emmeline Pankhurst, a British political activist and leader of the British suffragette movement. The Suffragette's helped women to win the right to vote.

Erica

Pronunciation: AIR-a-ka

The name Erica is of Old Norse origin. The meaning of Erica is "complete ruler". Erica is a feminine form of the masculine name Eric. Erica is also the name of a species of plants, which includes heather and rhododendrons. The name was revived during the 19th century, when botanical names became fashionable.

Erin

Pronunciation: AIR-en

Erin is of Gaelic and Irish origin. The meaning of the name Erin is "Ireland". Derived from the Irish Gaelic name Éirinn. Erin is an ancient poetic name for Ireland.

Esmè, Esmèe

Pronunciation: EZ-may

The name Esmè is of Old French origin. The meaning of Esmè is "esteemed". From Latin *aestimatus*. The name was introduced to Scotland from France in the 16th century. The name was originally used for both sexes, it is now mainly given to females.

Esmeralda

Pronunciation: ez-mer-AHL-dah

The name Esmeralda is of Spanish origin. The meaning of Esmeralda is "Emerald". Victor Hugo popularised the name with his heroine in the classic, *The Hunchback of Notre Dame* (1831). Esmeralda was a gypsy girl loved by Quasimodo.

Estella, Estelle
Pronunciation: EST-el-lah
The name Estella is of Old French origin. The meaning of Estella is "star". Charles Dickens popularised the name within his epic novel, *Great Expectations* (1861). Estelle is the modern French form.

Esther
Pronunciation: ESS-tar
The name Esther is of Persian origin. The meaning of Esther is "star, myrtle". A biblical name; borne in the Old Testament by a young beautiful Hebrew woman. She became the wife of the Persian king Ahasuerus in the 5th century BC after he had rejected his disobedient wife, Vashti. Her story is told in the Old Testament book and in the Apocrypha's Rest of Esther. The name has traditionally been given to girls born during the period of Purim. The name was popular with the Puritans in the 17th century.

Étain

Pronunciation: E-tain

The name Étain is of Irish Gaelic origin. The meaning of Étain is unknown, it could possibly mean "jealously". Étain is a traditional Irish Gaelic name. Borne in Irish legend by a fairy princess whose wooing by the mortal King Eochaidh, was turned into an opera, *The Immortal Hour* (1914).

Ethelinda

Pronunciation: e-thelin-da

The name Ethelinda is of Old English origin. The meaning of Ethelinda is "noble serpent". The name was revived in the 19th century.

Etta

Pronunciation: ETT-ah

The name Etta is of English origin. The meaning of Etta is "happy".

Eva

Pronunciation: AY-vah

The name Eva is of Hebrew origin. The meaning of Eva "alive". Eva is a Latinate form of the name Harriet Stowe popularised the name with her novel, *Uncle*

Tom's Cabin (1852). Eva (Evangeline) was the name of her heroine. Diminutives: Evie, Evita.

Eve

Pronunciation: eve

Eve is of Latin and Hebrew origin. The meaning of the name Eve is "alive". A biblical name; borne in the Old Testament by the first woman on earth. Eve is described as, 'the mother of all living'. Diminutives; Eveleen, Evie.

Evelyn

Pronunciation: EV-e-lyn

Evelyn is of Norman origin. Anglicised form of the Norman French feminine name Aveline. Evelyn is used as both a boy's name, and as a girl's name. The named was adopted as a boy's name in the 17th century. Originally a surname and used as a given name.

F

Fabia

Pronunciation: fah-BIA

The name Fabia is of Latin origin. The meaning of Fabia is "bean". A Latin feminine form of the Roman family name Fabius.

Fabiana

Pronunciation: fah-BE-ann-ah

The name Fabiana is of Latin origin. The meaning of Fabiana is "bean". A Latin feminine form of the Roman family name Fabius.

Fabiola

Pronunciation: fah-bee-OH-lah

The name Fabiola is of Latin origin. The meaning of Fabiola is "bean". A Latin feminine form of the Roman family name Fabius. Fabiola is a feminine diminutive of the masculine name Fabian. Saint Fabiola was a 4th-century member of the Fabius family, who founded the first hospital for sick and needy pilgrims. Queen Fabiola of Belgium was a Spanish princess.

Fadia

Pronunciation: FAD-ee-a

The name Fadia is of Arabic origin. The meaning of Fadia is "savior". Fadia is a feminine form of Fadi.

Fadila

Pronunciation: FAD-il-ah

The name Fadila is of Arabic origin. The meaning of Fadila is "moral excellence". Fadila is a feminine form of Fadile.

Faida

Pronunciation: FAI-da

The name Faida is of Arabic origin. The meaning of Faida is "plentiful".

Faith

Pronunciation: faith

The name Faith is of Middle English origin. The meaning of Faith is "belief". Faith is one of the three great Christian virtues, with hope and charity. The name is also one of the several abstract nouns denoting admirable personal qualities. The name was used throughout the 16th century and popular among the Puritans.

Fallon

Pronunciation: FAL-en

The name Fallon is of Irish and Gaelic origin. The meaning of Fallon is "superiority, leader". An adopted surname, anglicised from the Irish surname O Fallamhain, meaning 'leader'. Originally an occupational surname for a textile worker. The name was popularised by the American television series *Dynasty*.

Fanny

Pronunciation: FAN-ee

The name Fanny is of Latin origin. The meaning of Fanny is "from France". Fanny is diminutive of Frances. The name was extremely popular in the 18th and 19th centuries.

Farah

Pronunciation: FAH-rah

Farah is of Arabic origin. The meaning of the name Farah is "pleasant, joy".

Farrah

Pronunciation: FAH-rah

The name Farrah is a modern coinage of the Arabic name Farah, which means "pleasant, joy". The name was popularised by American actress Farrah Fawcett.

Fatima
Pronunciation: FAH-tee-mah
The name Fatima is of Arabic origin. The meaning of Fatima is "baby's nurse, abstainer". Borne by the Prophet Muhammad's favourite daughter, wife of Haidar, she was the only daughter to bear children.

Fay
Pronunciation: fay
The name Fay is of uncertain origin. The meaning of Fay is "belief, fairy". The name is possibly a diminutive of Faith.

Faye
Pronunciation: faye
The name Faye is of uncertain origin. The meaning of Faye is "belief, fairy". The name is possibly a diminutive of Faith.

Felicity
Pronunciation: fa-LISS-a-tee

The name Felicity is from Old French and Latin origin. The meaning of Felicity is "good fortune, lucky". The name is derived from Latin *Felicitas*. The name was a virtue name and one of the several abstract nouns denoting admirable personal qualities. The name was first used in the 17th century and was popular with the Puritans.

Fern
Pronunciation: fern
The name Fern is of Old English origin. The meaning of Fern is "fern". From Old English *fearn*, denoting a green shade-loving plant. Fern is also used as a nickname for Fernanda.

Ffion
Pronunciation: FEE-on
The name Ffion is of Welsh origin. The meaning of Ffion is "white, fair". The name is a Welsh form of Fiona.

Fifi
Pronunciation: FEE-fee
The name Fifi is of French origin. The meaning of Fifi is "Jehovah increases". Fifi is French variant of the

name Josephine. The name is also used as diminutive for Fiona.

Fina

Pronunciation: FI-na

The name Fina is of Spanish origin. The meaning of Fina is "Jehovah increases". Borne in the 13th century by a woman of San Gimignano, in Tuscany. Fina was a young girl whose claim to be recognized as a saint lay in the perfect resignation with which she accepted bodily suffering. Fina was not martyred, instead she died of a physical disease. For six years, she lay on a plank in one position, unable to turn or move. Her feast day is 12 March.

Finella

Pronunciation: fin(el)-la

The name Finella is of Gaelic origin. The meaning of Finella is "white, fair". Finella is an Anglicised Scottish form of the Gaelic name Fionnuala.

Finola

Pronunciation:f(i)-no-la

The name Finola is of Gaelic origin. The meaning of Finola is "white, fair". Finola is an Anglicised form of the Gaelic name Fionnuala.

Fiona

Pronunciation: fee-OWN-ah

The name Fiona is of Scottish and Gaelic origin. The meaning of Fiona is "white, fair". Fiona is a Latin form of Gaelic *fionn*. The name was first by James Macpherson (1736-1796) in his Ossianic poems. William Sharp later used the name Fiona Macleod, as a pen-name for his romantic novels.

Fionnuala

Pronunciation: fya-NOO-lah

The name Fionnuala is of Irish Gaelic origin. The meaning of Fionnuala is "white, fair". Borne in Irish legend; Fionnuala was the daughter of King Lir. Who was transformed into a swan and condemned to wander over the lakes and rivers until Christianity came to Ireland.

Flavia

Pronunciation: FLAH-vee-ah

The name Flavia is of Latin origin. The meaning of Flavia is "yellow hair". Flavia is a feminine form of the Roman family name, Flavius. The name was also borne by several early saints.

Fleur

Pronunciation: F-leur

The name Fleur is of Old French origin. The meaning of Fleur is "Flower".

Flick

Pronunciation: F-li-CK

The name Flick is of Latin origin. The meaning of Flick is "lucky". Flick is also a byname from Felicity.

Flo

Pronunciation: flo

The name Flo is of Latin origin. The meaning of Flo is "flowering, in bloom". Flo is a diminutive of the names Flora and Florence.

Flora

Pronunciation: FLO-ra

The name Flora is of Latin origin. The meaning of Flora is "Flower". From the Roman family name Florus, derived from *flos*. Borne by the Roman goddess of spring and flowers. Her festivals, the Floralia were held on the 28th April- 3rd May. Flora is also the name of a ninth-century Spanish martyr saint. Diminutives: Flo, Florrie.

Florence

Pronunciation: FLOR-ens

Then name Florence is of Latin origin. The meaning of Florence is "flowering, in bloom". Florence is a medieval form of the Latin name Florentius. Florence Nightingale (1820-1910) popularised the name during the 19th century. She was named after the Italian city where she born. The name was later revived in the 20th century. Diminutives: Flo, Florrie, Foss, Flossie, Floy.

Florrie

Pronunciation: FLOR-ee

The name Florrie is of Latin origin. The meaning of Florrie is "flowering, in bloom". Florrie is a diminutive of the name Florence.

Floss

Pronunciation: flo-ss

The name Floss is of Latin origin. The meaning of Floss is "flowering, in bloom". Floss is a diminutive of the name Florence

Fortune

Pronunciation: for-TUNE

Fortune is of Latin origin. The meaning of the name Fortune is "good fate". Borne in mythology; Roman goddess of fortune, chance and happiness. The name was adopted in the 17th century by Puritans.

Frances

Pronunciation: FRAN-siss

Frances is of Latin origin. The meaning of the name Frances is "French". Frances is a feminine form of Francis. Diminutives: Fanny, Fran, Francie, Frankie, Frannie.

Francesca

Pronunciation: fran-CHESS-kah

Francesca is of Italian and Latin origin. The meaning of the name Francesca is "French". Francesca is an Italian feminine form of Francisco. Borne in the 13th century by Francesca di Rimini, the daughter of Guido da Polenta, Count of Ravenna. Francesca married Giovanni Malatesta, however she loved his brother Paolo. When Francesca and Paolo were discovered together, they were put to death in c.1289. Her love story has been retold in literature, Dante told the story in his *Inferno v*. Numerous tragic plays have been written on the subject.

Francine

Pronunciation: fran-SEEN

The name Francine is of French and Latin origin. The meaning of Francine is "French". The name is a familiar form of Françoise, which is the French form of Frances.

Francoise
Pronunciation: fran-co-see
The name Francoise is of Spanish and Latin origin. The meaning of Francoise is "French". Francoise is a Spanish form of the name Frances.

Frederica
Pronunciation: fred-er-EE-kah
The name Frederica is of Old German origin. The meaning of Frederica is "peaceful ruler". Frederica is a Latinate feminine form of the name Frederick.

Freya
Pronunciation: FRAY-ah
Freya is of Old Norse origin. The meaning of the name Freya is "lady, mistress". Borne in Scandinavian mythology; Freya is the goddess of love, marriage and the dead. The fifth day of the week, Friday was named after her.

Frieda

Pronunciation: FREE-dah

The name Frieda is of German origin. The meaning of Frieda is "Lady, peace". Frieda is a diminutive of numerous names that derive from the Old German element *frid*.

Fulgencia

Pronunciation: FUL-gen-cia

The name Fulgencia is of Latin origin. The meaning of Fulgencia is "giving off light".

Fulvia

Pronunciation: FUL-via

The name Fulvia is of Latin origin. The meaning of Fulvia is "dusky".

Fruma

Pronunciation: FRU-ma

The name Fruma is of Yiddish origin. The meaning of Fruma is "deeply religious".

G

Gabriela

Pronunciation: GAB-re-el-AH

Gabriela is of Hebrew origin. The meaning of the name Gabriela is "heroine of God". Gabriela is a feminine form of the name Gabriel. Gabriela is the Latinate form. Gabriella is the Italian form. Diminutives: Gaby, Gabby.

Gabrielle

Pronunciation: gab-ree-ELL

The name Gabrielle is of Hebrew origin. The meaning of Gabrielle is "heroine of God". Gabrielle is a feminine form of the name Gabriel. Gabrielle is the French form. Diminutives: Gaby, Gabby.

Gada

Pronunciation: ga-DAH

The name Gada is of Hebrew origin. The meaning of Gada is "fortunate".

Gaea

Pronunciation: GAY-ah

Gaea is of Greek origin. The meaning of the name Gaea is "the earth". Born in mythology; the womanly personification of the earth and mother of the Titans.

Gaetana

Pronunciation: gae-tan-AH

The name Gaetana is of Italian and Latin origin. The meaning of Gaetana is "from Gaeta". Gaeta is a region in southern Italy.

Gaia

Pronunciation: gab-GA-iah

The name Gaia is of Greek origin. The meaning of Gaia is "the earth". Borne in Greek mythology; the goddess of the earth, she gave birth to the sky, mountains and sea.

Gail

Pronunciation: gayl

The name Gail is of Hebrew origin. The meaning of Gail is "father of exaltation". Gail is a diminutive of the name Abigail. The name became a popular first name in its own right. The name came to Britain in the 20th century.

Galina

Pronunciation: ga-LEEN-ah

Galina is of Greek origin. The meaning of the name Galina is "calm". Derived from the Greek name Galen.

Gaynor

Pronunciation: gay-NOR

The name Gaynor is of Welsh origin. The meaning of Gaynor is "white, soft". Gaynor is a medieval English form of the name Guinevere.

Gavrila

Pronunciation: gav-ril-AH

The name Gavrila is of Hebrew origin. The meaning of Gavrila is "heroine of God".

Gemma

Pronunciation: JEM-ah

Gemma is of Latin origin. The meaning of the name Gemma is "jewel, gem". Derived from the Old Italian word for 'jewel'. The name is borne by Saint, Gemma Galgani (1878-1903). She is known as 'The Daughter of Passion'.

Geneva

Pronunciation: JEN-eve-ah

The name Geneva is of Old French origin. The meaning of Geneva is "juniper tree". The name may refer to the Swiss city, or possibly be a variation of the name Jennifer.

Geneviève

Pronunciation: JEN-a-veev

The name Geneviève is of French origin. The meaning of Geneviève is "white wave". Saint Geneviève (c. 422-512) is the patron saint of Paris. She is said to have defended Paris against the depredations of Attila the Hun with prayer. Her feast day is 3rd January.

Georgette

Pronunciation: jorj-ETT

The name Georgette is of French and Italian origin. The meaning of Georgette is "farmer". Georgette is a French feminine form of the masculine name George.

Georgia

Pronunciation: JOR-jah

Georgia is of Greek and Latin origin. The meaning of the name Georgia is "farmer". Georgia is a feminine form of the masculine name George. The name was influenced by the name of the US state, which was named after King George II of England.

Georgina

Pronunciation: jor-JEE-nah

Georgina is of Latin origin. The meaning of the name Georgina is "farmer". Georgina is a feminine form of the name George. The name was popular during the 18th and 19th centuries.

Georgie

Pronunciation: jorj-EE

Georgie is of Greek and Latin origin. The meaning of Georgie is "farmer". Georgie is a diminutive of Georgette, Georgia, Georgiana or Georgina. Georgia is a feminine form of the masculine name George.

Geraldine

Pronunciation: jare-ul-DEEN

The name Geraldine is of Old German and French origin. The meaning of Geraldine is "spear ruler". Geraldine is a feminine form of the name Gerald. The name was coined in the 16th century by Henry Howard, Earl of Surrey. He used the name in his poems to Lady Elizabeth Fitzgerald, 'the Fair Geraldine'. Diminutives: Geri, Gerry.

Geri

Pronunciation: JER-ee

The name Geri is of English origin. The name is a modern variation of the name Gerry. British singer Geri Halliwell popularised the name during the 1990's.

Germaine

Pronunciation: jer-MAYNE

The name Germaine is of Latin and French origin. The meaning of Germaine is "brother, German". Germaine is a feminine form of the French name Germain. Borne by a 16th-century French saint, Germaine Cousin (1579-1601).

Gerry

Pronunciation: JER-ee

The name Jerry is of uncertain origin. The meaning of Gerry is "spear ruler". Gerry is a diminutive of the name Geraldine.

Gigi

Pronunciation: JEE-jee

Gigi is of French origin. The meaning of the name Gigi is "bright promise". Gigi is a diminutive of the name Gilberte. The name was popularised by Colette's novel *Gigi* (1944).

Gilda

Pronunciation: JILL-dah

The name Gilda is of Old English origin. The meaning of Gilda is "golden, gilded". The name was popularised in the 1940's with the Hollywood film, starring Rita Hayworth *Gilda* (1946). The film starred Rita Hayworth

Gill

Pronunciation: GILL

The name Gill is of uncertain origin. The meaning of Gill is "bright promise, youthful". Gill is a diminutive of the masculine name Gilbert. The name was popular during the Middle Ages.

Gillian

Pronunciation: GILL-ee-an

The name Gillian is of Latin origin. The meaning of Gillian is "youthful". Gillian is a feminine form of the name Julian. The name was popular during the Middle Ages. Diminutives: Gill Gillie, Gilly.

Gina

Pronunciation: GEE-nah

The name Gina is of uncertain origin. Gina is diminutive of girls' names that end in –gina, such as

Georgina. The name became a popular first name in its own right.

Ginger

Pronunciation: JIN-jer

The name Ginger is of English origin. The meaning of Ginger is "liveliness, ginger". Ginger is a diminutive if the name Virginia. Ginger is also the name of a pungent root used as a spice. The name was popularised in the 20th century by the Hollywood dancer, Ginger Rogers (1911-1995).

Gisela

Pronunciation: gi-sel-LAH

The name Gisela is of Old German origin. The meaning of Gisela is "pledge, hostage". From Old German, *gisil*.

Gita

Pronunciation: gi-TAH

The name Gita is of Hindi and Sanskrit origin. The meaning of Gita is "song".

Glenn

Pronunciation: gl-ENN

The name Glenn is of Scottish Gaelic origin. The name Glenn is "Glen, valley". Originally an adopted surname. The name is used as both a boy's name and as a girl's name.

Glory

Pronunciation: glo-EE

Glory is of Latin origin. The meaning of the name Glory is "glory". The name is an anglicised form of the Latin name Gloria.

Glyn

Pronunciation: glin

The name Glyn is of Irish and Gaelic origin. The meaning of Glyn is "valley of water". Glyn is a place name. The name is also a variant of Glen. Glyn is used as both a boy's name and as girl's name

Goldie

Pronunciation: GOLD-ee

Goldie is of English origin. Goldie is a modern by name for one who has blonde hair. Hollywood actress Goldie Hawn popularised the name.

Grace

Pronunciation: grayce

Grace is of Latin origin. The meaning of the name Grace is "blessing, heavenly favour". The name is one of the several abstract nouns denoting admirable personal qualities that became popular first names among the Puritans during the 16th century. The name was revived in the 19th century. Diminutives: Gracie.

Gráinne

Pronunciation: gron-YAH

The name Gráinne is of Irish Gaelic origin. The meaning of Gráinne is "love". Borne in Irish legend; Gráinne was the daughter of King Cormac.

Greta

Pronunciation: GREH-tah

The name Greta is of German origin. The meaning of Greta is "pearl". Greta is a German diminutive of the name Margareta. Hollywood actress, Greta Garbo (1905-1992) popularised the name during the 20th century.

Gretchen

Pronunciation: GREH-chen

Gretchen is of German origin. The meaning of the name Gretchen is "pearl". Gretchen is a German diminutive of the name Margaret. The name became a popular first name in its own right.

Guinevere
Pronunciation: GWIN-a-veer
The name Guinevere is of Welsh origin. The meaning of Guinevere is "fair and smooth". Borne in Arthurian legend by Arthur's unfaithful wife, Queen Guinevere.

Gulielma
Pronunciation: guile-l-MAH
The name Gulielma is of Italian and Old German origin. The meaning of Gulielma is "will helmet". Gulielma is a feminine form of Wilhelm.

Gunhilda
Pronunciation: gun-HIL-dah
The name Gunhilda is of Old Norse origin. The meaning of Gunhilda is "Battle maid".

Gustava
Pronunciation: gust-av-AH
The name Gustava is of Swedish origin. The meaning of Gustava is "staff of the gods". Gustava is a feminine form of the name Gustave, a royal name in Sweden.

Gwen

Pronunciation: gwyn

Gwen is of Welsh origin. The meaning of the name Gwen is "fair, holy, white". Gwen was originally a diminutive of the name Gwendolyn. The name became a popular first name in its own right. The name was popular during the 19th and 20th centuries.

Gwenda

Pronunciation: gwyn-DAH

Gwenda is of Welsh origin. The meaning of the name Gwenda is "fair, good".

Gweyneth

Pronunciation: gwyn-ETH

The name Gweyneth is of Welsh origin. The meaning of Gweyneth is "blessed, happy". The name was popular during the 19th and 20th centuries. Diminutive: Gwyn.

Gwyn

Pronunciation: GW-in

The name Gwyn is of Welsh origin. The meaning of Gwyn is "fair, blessed, holy, white". The name is used as both a boy's name, and as a girl's name.

Gypsy

Pronunciation: GYP-see

The name Gypsy is of Old English origin. The meaning of Gypsy is "Gypsy". The tribe of Romany was called 'gypsy', as they were thought to have originated in Egypt.

H

Hannah

Pronunciation: HAN-ah

Hannah is of Hebrew origin. The meaning of the name Hannah is "God has favoured me". A biblical name; borne by the mother of the prophet Samuel (I Samuel 1). Unable to conceive, she asked God to bless her with a child, and her prayer was answered. Therefore the name connotes, 'God has graced me with a son'. The name was adopted by the Puritans in the 17th century. Hannah was a popular girls' name in the 20th century.

Harriet

Pronunciation: HARE-ee-et

The name Harriet is of Old German origin. The meaning of Harriet is "home leader". The name is an anglicised form of Henriette. Harriet is also a feminine form of the masculine name Henry. Diminutives: Hal, Hattie, Hatty, Hettie, Hetty.

Hayley

Pronunciation: HAY-ley

The name Hayley is of Old English origin. The meaning of Hayley is "hay meadow". The name is an adopted surname, originally from a place name. The name became popular in 20th century when Mary Hayley Bell and Sir John Mills named their daughter Hayley Mills in 1946. Hayley Mills went on to become a famous Hollywood actress.

Hazel

Pronunciation: HAY-zel

The name Hazel is of Old English origin. The meaning of Hazel is "the hazel tree". The name was introduced as a first name during the 19th century, when Hazel enjoyed a popular surge as a first name as plant names became fashionable. The name also refers to a specific eye colour.

Heather

Pronunciation: HEH-ther

The name Heather is of Middle English Origin. The meaning of Heather is unknown. From Old English *hadre*, which donates as a species of moorland shrub with purple and white flowers that, thrives on peaty barren lands. Heather is one of the most popular of the flower names that became fashionable during the 19th century.

Hebe
Pronunciation: HE-be
The name Hebe is of Greek origin. The meaning of Hebe is "youthful beauty". Borne in Greek mythology; Hebe was a daughter of Zeus and Hera, she was the goddess of youth and cup-bearer to the gods. The name was adopted in the 19th century for a species of plant that is native to New Zealand.

Heidi
Pronunciation: HYE-dee
Heidi is of Old German origin. The meaning of the name Heidi is "exalted nature". The name is a Swiss diminutive of Adelheid, from the Old German name Adelaide. Johanna Spyri popularised the name with her beloved children's novel, *Heidi* (1881). Heidi was the name given to the orphaned heroine.

Helen
Pronunciation: HEL-en
Helen is of Greek origin. The meaning of the name Helen is "sun ray". The name is an Anglicised form of the Greek name Helene. In classical legend Paris

abducted Zeus's mortal daughter, Helen of Troy, an act that resulted in the Trojan War. Helen was, 'the face that launched a thousand ships'. Diminutives: Ena, Hels, Lena, Nell, Nellie, Nelly.

Helena
Pronunciation: HEL-en-a

Helena is of Latin origin. The meaning of Helena is unknown. The name is a Latinate form of Helen. Saint Helena (c. 248-328) was the mother of Constantine the Great. Her purity allowed her to find the True Cross at Jerusalem. Her feast day is 18th August.

Heloise
Pronunciation: HEL-oh-ees

The name Heloise is of French and Old German origin. The meaning of Heloise is "famous warrior". The name was popularised by the true story of the French philosopher Peter Abelard (1079-1142), and his seventeen year old student and lover, Hèloíse. After Abelard's castration, he entered the monastery of Saint Denis. Hèloíse later became a nun.

Henrietta, Henriette
Pronunciation: HEN-ree-ett

The name Henriette is of Old German origin. The meaning of Henriette is "home leader". Henriette is a feminine form of Henry. Henriette is a French form of Henry that was introduced to Britain in the 17th century, after Charles I married the French Princess Henriette-Marie in 1625. Diminutives: Etta, Ettie, Etty, Hen, Hennie.

Hermione
Pronunciation: her-MY-oh-nee
The name Hermione is of Greek origin. The meaning of Hermione is "daughter of Hermes, messenger". The name is a feminine form Hermes, the Greek messenger of God. Borne in mythology; Hermione was the daughter of Helen and Menelaus. Shakespeare also used the name in *A Winter's Tale* (1611).

Hero
Pronunciation: HE-ro
The name Hero is of Greek origin. The meaning of Hero is unknown. Borne in Greek legend by a priestess of Venus and beloved by Leander. He swam to her nightly across the Hellespont until one night when he accidently drowned. Hero then drowned herself in the same sea as Leander following his death. Shakespeare

also used the name Hero in *Much Ado About Nothing* (1598).

Hilary

Pronunciation: HILL-a-ree

The name Hilary is of Latin origin. The meaning of Hilary is "cheerful". Medieval form of the Latin name Hilarius. Borne by a 4th-century saint and a 5th century pope. The name was given to both girls and boys name, although it is increasingly rare for boys.

Holly

Pronunciation: HAH-lee

Holly is of Old English origin. The meaning of the name Holly is "the holy tree". From Old English *holen*, which denotes a species of evergreen plant with prickly leaves. Holly was one of the numerous flower and plant names that became popular first names during the 19th century. The name is often given to girls who are born at Christmas time. Audrey Hepburn popularised the name when Capote's novel, *Breakfast at Tiffany's* (1958) was turned into a film in 1961. Hepburn played the fascinating heroine, Holy Golightly.

Honor

Pronunciation: AHN-er

The name Honor is of Latin origin. The meaning of Honor is "woman of honor". Honor was one of the several abstract nouns denoting admirable personal qualities that became popular among Puritans in the 16th century. The name was used as both a girl's name and as a boy's name.

Honey

Pronunciation: HUN-ee

Honey is of Old English origin. The meaning of the name Honey is "nectar". The name is often used as a nickname for endearment.

Hope

Pronunciation: HO-pe

Hope is of Old English origin. The meaning of the name Hope is "belief". One of the three great Christian virtues (faith, hope, & charity). The name is one of the several abstract nouns that symbolizes admirable personal qualities. The name was popular among the Puritans in the 16th century.

I

Ianthe

Pronunciation: eye-AH-thee

The name Ianthe is of Greek origin. The meaning of Ianthe is "violet flower". Borne in Ovid's *Metamorphoses*, written in the 1st century, Ianthe was a Cretan girl who married Iphis.

Ida

Pronunciation: EYE-dah

Ida is of Greek and Old German origin. The meaning of the name Ida is "hardworking". From Old German *id*, which means 'work'. The name was introduced to Britain by the Norman's. Borne in Greek mythology; a Greek nymph who cared for the infant Zeus on Mount Ida.

Idris

Pronunciation: E-dris

The name Idris is of Arabic and Welsh origin. The meaning of Idris is "fiery leader, Prophet". Borne in Welsh legend by a giant magician, astronomer and prince whose observatory was on Cader Idris. Described in the Koran, the Arabic name was borne by a man described as 'a true man' and 'a prophet', he was also the founder of the first Shiite dynasty (788-974). The name is used as both a boy's name and as a girl's name.

Ilsa

Pronunciation: I-lsa

Ilsa is of German origin. The meaning of the name Ilsa is "God is my oath". Ilsa is a diminutive of the Hebrew name Elisabeth.

Iman

Pronunciation: ee-MAHN

The name Iman is of Arabic origin. The meaning of Iman is "belief, faith".

Imogen

Pronunciation: I-mo-gen

The name Imogen is of Irish and Gaelic origin. The meaning of Imogen is "maiden". From the Celtic name Innogen. The name was first used by Shakespeare in his play, *Cymbeline* (1609). Imogen was the name of the heroine.

India

Pronunciation: IN-dee-ah

The name India is of English origin. Originally the name of the country. India was first used a name in Margaret Mitchell's epic novel *Gone With The Wind* (1936).

Ingrid

Pronunciation: ING-rid

The name Ingrid is of Old Norse origin. The meaning of Ingrid is "fair". Borne in Norse mythology; Ing was the God of earth's fertility. The name was popularised by the Hollywood actress Ingrid Bergman (1915-1982).

Iola

Pronunciation: eye-OH-lah

The name Iola is of Greek origin. The meaning of Iola is "violet colored dawn".

Iolana

Pronunciation: eye-oh-LAH-nah

Iolana is of Hawaiian origin. The meaning of the name Iolana is "to soar like the hawk".

Iolanthe

Pronunciation: eye-oh-LAHN-thee

The name Iolanthe is of Greek origin. The meaning of Iolanthe is "violet flower".

Ione

Pronunciation: eye-OHN

The name Ione is of Greek origin. The meaning of Ione is "violet". Ione is also a flower name. The name may have become popular as a first name during the 19th century, when botanical names became fashionable.

Irene

Pronunciation: eye-REEN

The name Irene is of Greek origin. The meaning of Irene is "peace". Borne in Greek mythology; Irene was a goddess of peace and wealth. Saint Irene (4th century) was one of the three sisters martyred for their faith in Macedonia.

Iris

Pronunciation: EYE-riss

Iris is of Greek origin. The meaning of the name Iris is "Rainbow". Borne in Greek mythology; Iris was a goddess of the rainbow and messenger of the gods. She rode on rainbows that formed as a bridge, linking heaven and the earth so that she could deliver

messages from Olympus. The name was revived in the 19th century. Iris is also a flower name.
Pronunciation: eye-REEN

Irma

Pronunciation: IR-ma
The name Irma is of Old German origin. The meaning of Irma is "entire, universal".

Isabel

Pronunciation: iz-a-bel
Isabel is of Hebrew origin. The meaning of the name Isabel is "God is my oath". Isabel is a Spanish variant of the name Elizabeth. The name was brought to Britain from the France in the form of Isabella by Edward II (1296-1358) French wife. The name was popular throughout Britain until the end of the 17th century. Diminutives; Bel, Bell, Bella, Belle, Ib, Ibbie, Ibby, Isa, Iz, Izzie, Izzy, Tibby.

Isabella

Pronunciation: IZ-a-bel-LA
Isabella is of Hebrew origin. The meaning of the name Isabella is "God is my oath". Isabella is a Latinate form of Isabelle. The name has been a popular throughout Britain since the 18th century.

Isadora

Pronunciation: IZ-a-DOR-ah

The name Isadora is of Greek and Latin origin. The meaning of Isadora is "gift of Isis". The name is a feminine form of Isidore. Acclaimed American dancer, Isadora Duncan (1887-1927) popularised the name.

Isla

Pronunciation: EYE-la

The name Isla is of uncertain origins. Isla is the name of a Scottish river.

Isra

Pronunciation: eyes-ra

The name Isra is of Arabic origin. The meaning of Isra is "night journey". The name is a reference to Muhammad's journey to Jerusalem, in which he met Moses and Jesus.

Itzel

Pronunciation: it-zel

The name Itzel is of Spanish origin. The meaning of Itzel is "star of the aurora sky". Itzel is also the name of a Mayan princess.

Ivana

Pronunciation: ee-VAH-nah

Ivana is of Hebrew and Slavic origin. The meaning of the name Ivana is "God is gracious". Ivana is a feminine form of the masculine names Ivan and John.

Ivette

Pronunciation: ee-VET

The name Ivette is of French origin. The meaning of Ivette is unknown. The name is a variant of Yvette.

Ivonne

Pronunciation: ee-VON

Ivonne is of French origin. The meaning of the name Ivonne is unknown. Ivonne is variant of the name Yvonne.

Ivory

Pronunciation: EYE-vree

Ivory is of Latin origin. The meaning of the name Ivory is "creamy white colour". Ivory is the name used for the hard tusk on animals, which is also used for carving fine art and jewelry.

Ivy

Pronunciation: EYE-vee

The name Ivy is of Old English origin. Ivy is a name from nature, an evergreen climbing plant which represents fidelity and eternity.

J

Jacinta

Pronunciation: JAC-in-ta

The name Jacinta is of Spanish origin. The meaning of Jacinta is "hyacinth". Jacinta is Spanish for of the Greek name Hyacinth. The name was originally used for both sexes however, today it is mostly used as a girl's name.

Jacqueline, Jacquelyn

Pronunciation: JAK-ah-lin

The name Jacqueline is of French and Hebrew origin. The meaning of Jacqueline is "he who supplants". Jacqueline is a feminine form of Jacques. The name was introduced to Britain in the 13th century. Diminutives: Jackie, Jacky, Jacqui.

Jade

Pronunciation: JAY-de

The name Jade is of English origin. The meaning of Jade is "precious stone". Jade is also a jewel name, of a green stone which was believed to have magical powers of providing protection against disorders of the intestines. The name was derived from archaic Spanish *piedra de ijada*, which means, 'stone of the side'.

Jamie

Pronunciation: JAY-mee

The name Jamie is of Hebrew origin. The meaning of Jamie is "he who supplants". Jamie is a diminutive of the masculine name James. The name became a popular first name in its own right. Jamie is used as both a girl's name and as a boy's name.

Jancis

Pronunciation: JAN-cis

The name Jancis is a modern blend of Jan and Frances. The name was probably first used by Mary Webb in her novel *Precious Bane* (1924).

Jane, Jayne

Pronunciation: jayn

The name Jane is of Hebrew origin. The meaning of Jane is "God is gracious". Jane is a feminine form of the masculine name John, derived from the Old French name Jehane. Henry VIII's (d 1537) third wife, Jane Seymour popularised the name during the 16th century. The name was extremely popular in the 18th and 19th

centuries. Charlotte Brontë contributed to the popularity of the name with her renowned novel, *Jane Eyre* (1847).

Janet

Pronunciation: JAN-et

The name Janet is of Scottish origin. The meaning of Janet is unknown. Janet is a feminine form of the masculine name John, originally a medieval diminutive of Jane. The name was popular throughout Scotland and underwent a revival in the 20th century.

Diminutives: Jan, Jennie, Jenny.

Janice

Pronunciation: JAN-iss

The name Janice is originally a diminutive of the name Jane. The name was influenced by names that end in –ice, such as Candice and Bernice. The name became popular in its own right during the early 20th century.

Jasmine

Pronunciation: JAZ-min

Jasmine if of Old French and Persian origin. The meaning of the name Jasmine is "Jasmine". From Arabic *Jasamine*, donating a species of an ornamental climbing plant, which has delicate yellow and white flowers. Disney popularised the name with the film *Aladdin* (1990). Princess Jasmine was the name of the heroine.

Jean

Pronunciation: jeen

Jean is of Hebrew origin. The meaning of the name Jean is "God is gracious". Jean is a feminine form of the masculine name John. The name was popular throughout Britain during the 20ᵗʰ century.

Diminutives: Jeanie, Jeannette, Jeannie.

Jena

Pronunciation: JEN-ah

Jena is of Arabic and Sanskrit origin. The meaning of Jena is "little bird, endurance".

Jeanette

Pronunciation: je-NET

The name Jeanette is of Hebrew origin. The meaning of Jeanette is "God is gracious". Jeanette is a diminutive of the Hebrew name Jean. The name became a popular first name in its own right.

Jeanne

Pronunciation: je(an)-ne

The name Jeanne is of French and Hebrew origin. The meaning of Jeanne is "God is gracious". Jeanne is a feminine form of the masculine name John.
Diminutives: Jeannette, Jeannine.

Jemima
Pronunciation: je-MYE-mah
Jemima is of Hebrew origin. The meaning of the name Jemima is "dove". A biblical name; borne in the Old Testament by the eldest of Job's daughters. The name was adopted by the Puritans. Beatrix Potter popularised the name with her heroine, Jemima Puddleduck.

Jennifer
Pronunciation: JEN-ee-fer
The name Jennifer is of English origin. The meaning of Jennifer is "fair and smooth". Jennifer is a variant of Guinevere. The name was popular throughout Britain during the 20th century.

Jessica
Pronunciation: JESS-a-kah
The name Jessica is of Hebrew origin. The meaning of Jessica is "He sees". The name may be a Shakespearean

invention for the daughter of Shylock in *The Merchant of Venice* (1596). Diminutives: Jess, Jessie.

Jessie

Pronunciation: JESS-ee

The name Jessie is of Hebrew origin. The meaning of Jessie is "He sees". Jessie is a Scottish diminutive of the name Janet. The name dates back to the 18th century. Jessie is also a diminutive of the name Jessica.

Jillian

Pronunciation: JIL-ee-an

The name Jillian is of unknown origin. Jillian is a modern variation of the name Gillian. Diminutives: Jill, Jilly.

Jinny

Pronunciation: JIN-ee

Jinny is of uncertain origin. The name is a variation of Jenny or a diminutive of the name Virginia.

Joan

Pronunciation: jone

The name Joan is of Hebrew origin. The meaning of Joan is "God is gracious". Joan is a feminine form of the masculine name John. Borne by the only female pope, supposedly of the 13th century. However, her existence is still in dispute. The name was replaced by Jane by the 17th century. Hollywood actress Joan Crawford popularised the name during the 20th century.

Joanna

Pronunciation: joh-AN-ah

Joanna is of Latin origin. The meaning of Joanna is "God is gracious". Joanna is a feminine form of the masculine name John. Derived from the Latin name Johanna. A biblical name; borne by several women who were disciples of Christ. The Puritans adopted the name. The name was later revived in the 18th century. Diminutive: Jo, Joey.

Joanne

Pronunciation: JOH-anne

The name Joanne is of uncertain origin. From the Old French name Johanne, derived from the Latin name Johanna. The name was first used as a first name in French-speaking communities in the US. The name became popular during the 20th century. Diminutives: Jo, Joey.

Jocasta

Pronunciation: JO-cast-ah

The name Jocasta is of Greek origin. The meaning of Jocasta is "shining moon". Borne in Greek mythology; Jocasta was a daughter of Meneceus and Queen consort of Thebes, Greece. She was also the wife of Laius, mother of Oedipus, and both mother and grandmother of Antigone, Eteocles, Polynices and Ismene. She unknowingly became the wife of her own son, when the truth was revealed she hung herself.

Jocelin, Joceline

Pronunciation: JOS-e-lin

The name Jocelin is of Old German origin. The meaning of Jocelin is "one of the Goths". The name was introduced to Britain by the Normans. Jocelin is used as both a boy's name, and as a girl's name. Diminutives: Joss, Jossy.

Jocelyn

Pronunciation: JOS-e-lyn

The name Jocelyn is of Old German origin. The meaning of Jocelyn is "one of the Goths". The name was introduced to Britain by the Normans. Jocelyn is used as both a boy's name, and as a girl's name. Diminutives: Joss, Jossy.

Johanna

Pronunciation: joh-HAHN-ah

Johanna is of Latin and Hebrew origin. The meaning of the name Johanna is "God is gracious". The name is originally a Latinate and feminine form derived from Johannes (John).

Jordan

Pronunciation: JOR-dan

Jordan is of Hebrew origin. The meaning of the name Jordan is "down-flowing". From the name of the river in the Middle East where Christ was baptized by John the Baptist. The name has been used as a first name since the Crusades. The name underwent a popular revival in the 1980's. Jordan is used as both a boy's name, and as a girl's name.

Josephine

Pronunciation: JOH-sa-feen

The name Josephine is of Hebrew origin. The meaning of Josephine is "Jehovah increases". Josephine is a feminine form of the masculine name Joseph.
Napoleon Bonaparte's wife, Empress Josèphine (1763-1814) popularised the name across Europe.
Diminutives: Fifi, Jo, Joey, Josa, Josette, Josie, Josy, Posie, Posy.

Joy

Pronunciation: joy

The name Joy is of Old French origin. The meaning of Joy is "joy". The name is a direct adoption of the English vocabulary. The name was used during the Middle Ages and was popular with the Puritans. The name was later revived in the 19 century.

Judith

Pronunciation: JOO-dith

The name Judith is of Hebrew origin. The meaning of Judith is "Jewess, from Judea". A biblical name; borne in the Old Testament by a wife of Esau. Judith was a central figure in the Apocrypha's Book of Judith. The name popular during the 18th and 20th centuries. Diminutives: Jodi, Jodie, Jody, Jude, Judi, Judy.

Judy

Pronunciation: JOO-dee

The name Judy is of Hebrew origin. The meaning of Judy is "Jewess, from Judea". Judy is a diminutive of the name Judith.

Julia

Pronunciation: joo-lee-AH

The name Julia is of Latin origin. The meaning of Julia is "Jove's child" Julia is a feminine form of the Roman family name Julius. Shakespeare used the name in *The Two Gentlemen of Verona* (1594). The name was extremely popular in Britain during the 18th century. Diminutives: Jules.

Juliana
Pronunciation: joo-lee-AH-NAH
The name Juliana is of Latin origin. The meaning of Juliana is "youthful, Jove's child". Juliana is a feminine form of Julian, the name dates back to the Middle Ages.

Julianne
Pronunciation: joo-lee-AH-ne
The name Julianne is a 20th-century coinage of uncertain origin. Julianne is a combination of the names Anne and Julie.

Julie
Pronunciation: JOO-lee
The name Julie is of French origin. The meaning of Julie is "youthful, Jove's child". Julie is a French form of the Latin name Julia. The name was first used in

Britain in the 20th century. Julie became one of the most popular girl's names during the 1070's.

Julienne

Pronunciation: JOO-lee-ene

The name Julienne is of French origin. The meaning of Julienne is "youthful, Jove's child". Julienne is a French feminine form of the masculine name Julian.

Juliet

Pronunciation: joo-lee-ET

The name Juliet is of Latin origin. The meaning of Juliet is "youthful, Jove's child". Juliet is a diminutive of the name Julia. Shakespeare popularised the name with the infamous love story, Romeo and Juliet (1595).

June

Pronunciation: joon

June is the sixth month of the year. The name was possibly derived from the Latin Iunius. The name is often associated with the Latin name Juno. June is known as the bridal month. June was the most successful of the names that were taken from the months of the year. The name was first adopted as a first name in the early 20th century.

Juno

Pronunciation: joo-NO

The name Juno is of Latin origin. The meaning of Juno is "queen of heaven". Borne in Roman mythology; Juna was a Roman goddess, wife and sister of Jupiter and the queen of heaven. She is identified with the Greek goddess Hera, as patron of women and marriage.

Justine

Pronunciation: juss-Tine

The name Justine is of Latin origin. The meaning of Justine is "fair, upright". Justine is a feminine form of the masculine name Justin. Originally a French from of the Latinate name Justina. Lawrence Durrell popularised the name with his novel, *Justine* (1957).

K

Kacie

Pronunciation: KAY-see

The name Kacie is of American origin. The meaning of Kacie is "alert, vigorous". Kacie is a variant of the name Casey.

Kadenza

Pronunciation: KAD-en-za

The name Kadenza is of Latin origin. The meaning of Kadenza is "with rhythm".

Kady

Pronunciation: KAY-dee

The name Kady is of American origin. The meaning of Kady is unknown. Kady is a variant of the name Katy.

Kai

Pronunciation: kye

Kai is of Hawaiian origin. The meaning of the name Kai is "the sea".

Kaila

Pronunciation: KYE-lah

The name Kaila is of Hebrew and Hawaiian origin. The meaning of Kaila is "the laurel crown".

Kaitlin

Pronunciation: KAYT-len

Kaitlin is of Irish origin. The meaning of the name Kaitlin is "pure". Kaitlin is a phonetic form of the name Caitlin, an Irish form of Catherine.

Kamala

Pronunciation: KAM-al-ah

The name Kamala is of Sanskrit origin. The meaning of Kamala is "pink". Kamala is a feminine form of the masculine name Kamal. In classical Hindu texts, Kamala is a byname of the goddess of Lakshmi. The name is also borne by the wife of Shiva.

Karen

Pronunciation: KARE-en

The name Karen is of Danish origin. The meaning of the name Karen is "pure". Karen is a variation of the name Katherine. Karen became one of the most popular girls' names in Britain during the 1970's.

Kate

Pronunciation: KAY-te

The name Kate is a variation of Katherine. The name has become a popular first name by its own right.

Katherine, Katharine

Pronunciation: KATH-er-rin

Katherine is of Greek origin. The meaning of the name Katherine is "pure". Katherine is a Latin form of Catherine. Kathrine is the English spelling, Katharine is the Scottish spelling. The early Latin forms Katerina and Caterina became Katharine and Catherine.

Kathleen

Pronunciation: kath-LEEN

The name Kathleen is of Irish origin. The meaning of Kathleen is "pure". Kathleen is a variation of Catherine, which was influenced by the Irish Gaelic name Caítlin. The name was first used outside of Ireland in the 19th century.

Kathryn

Pronunciation: KATH-ryn

The name Kathryn is of Greek origin. The meaning of Kathryn is "pure". Kathryn is a variant of the names Catherine and Kathrine.

Katrina

Pronunciation: ka-TREE-nah

Katrina Is of Greek origin. The meaning of the name Katrina is unknown. Katrina is a variation of the names Catriona and Catrina.

Katya

Pronunciation: KAT-ya

Katya is of Greek and Russian origin. The meaning of the name Katya is "pure". Katya is a Russian form of the Greek name Katherine.

Kay, Kaye

Pronunciation: kay

The name Kay is of Greek origin. The meaning of Kay is "pure". Diminutives of Katherine and Kathleen. The name became a popular first name in its own right.

Kayleigh

Pronunciation: kay-LEE

The name Kayleigh is of Irish and Gaelic origin. The meaning of Kayleigh is "slim and fair". Kayleigh is a variant of the names Cayla and Kaylee.

Kellie, Kelly

Pronunciation: KELL-ee

The name Kelly is of Irish and Gaelic origin. The meaning of Kelly is "strife, warlike". Originally an Irish surname. The name is an anglicised form of the ancient Irish Gaelic name Ceallach.

Kendall

Pronunciation: KEN-dal

The name Kendall is of Old English origin. The meaning of the Kendall is "the Kent River valley". An adopted surname, from a Cumbrian place name, Kendal. The name is used as both a boy's name, and as a girl's name. Kendal has been used as a given name since the 19th century.

Kerenza

Pronunciation: KER-en-za

The name Kerenza is of English origin. The meaning of Kerenza is "love, affection". Kerenza is a variant of the Cornish name Kerensa.

Kerry

Pronunciation: KARE-ee

The name Kerry is of Irish and Gaelic origin. The meaning of Kerry is "black". Kerry is also a place name of an Irish county. The name was first used by Irish immigrants to Australia for their sons. Kerry is used as both a girl's name and as a boy's name.

Khadija

Pronunciation: kah-DEE-jah

The name Khadija is of Arabic origin. The meaning of Khadija is "early baby". Khadijah bint-Khuwaylid was the first wife of Prophet Muhammad and mother of all his children. She was named in Koran as one of the four perfect women.

Kiara

Pronunciation: kee-AR-ah

Kiara is of Irish origin. The meaning of the name Kiara is "black". Kiara is a variant of the Irish name Ciara. The name is also a feminine form of Kieran.

Kiera

Pronunciation: kee-RAH

The name Kiera is of Irish origin. The meaning of Kiera is "black, lord". Kiera is a variant of the Irish name Ciara and is a modern feminine form of Ciaran. Kiera is also a variant of the Greet name Kira.

Kim

Pronunciation: KIM

The name Kim is of English origin. The meaning of Kim is "gold". Originally a diminutive of Kimball or Kimberley. The name is used as both a boy's name and as a girl's name.

Kimberley

Pronunciation: KIM-ber-lee

The name Kimberley is of English origin. The meaning of Kimberley is "Cyneburg's field". Kimberley is used as both a girl's name and as a boy's name.

Kira

Pronunciation: KEER-ah

Kira is of Greek origin. The meaning of the name Kira is "Lord". Kira is a variant of the name Kyra.

Kitty

Pronunciation: KIH-tee

The name Kitty is of Greek origin. The meaning of Kitty is "pure". Kitty is a diminutive of the Greek name Katherine. The name has been used a first name since the 15th century. The name was also used as a slang term for a woman of dubious morals during the 17th century.

Kirsten

Pronunciation: KERS-ten

Kirsten is of Latin and Scandinavian origin. The meaning of the name Kirsten is "follower of Christ". Kirsten is a Scandinavian form of the name Christine.

Kirstie, Kirsty

Pronunciation: KERS-tee

The name Kirsty is of Scottish origin. The meaning of Kirsty is "follower of Christ". Scottish diminutives of Christina or Christine.

Kristen

Pronunciation: KRISS-ten

Kristen is of Latin origin. The meaning of the name Kristen is "follower of Christ". Kristen is a variant of Christine.

Kristin

Pronunciation: KRISS-tin

Kristin is of Latin origin. The meaning of the name Kristin is "follower of Christ". Kristin is a variant of Christina and Christine. The name is also a feminine form of Christianus.

Kylie

Pronunciation: KYE-lee

The name Kylie is of Australian origin. The meaning of Kylie is "boomerang". The name was probably coined as a feminine form of the masculine name Kyle. The name was most popular during the 1980's. The name was made famous by Australian actress and singer, Kylie Minogue.

Kynthia

Pronunciation: kyn-THIA

The name Kynthia is of Greek origin. The meaning of Kynthia is "from Mount Kynthos". Kynthia is a variant of the Greek name Cynthia.

Kyoko

Pronunciation: kee-OH-koh

Kyoko is of Japanese origin. The meaning of the name Kyoko is "mirror".

Kyra

Pronunciation: KEER-ah

Kyra is of Greek origin. The meaning of the name Kyra is "Lord". Kyra is a feminine form of the masculine name Kyros.

L

Lacey

Pronunciation: LAY-see

Lacey is of Old French origin. The meaning of the name Lacey is unknown. Originally a nobleman's surname. The name was brought to Britain by the Normans.

Ladonna

Pronunciation: la-DAH-nah

The name Ladonna is of Italian origin. The meaning of Ladonna is "Lady". Ladonna is a modern form of the Italian name Donna.

Laetitia

Pronunciation: le-TISH-ah

The name Laetitia is of Latin origin. The meaning of Laetitia is "joy". Diminutives: Lettie, Letty, Tisha.

Laila

Pronunciation: LAY-lah

The name Laila is of Arabic origin. The meaning of Laila is "night beauty".

Lakeisha

Pronunciation: lah-KEE-shah

Lakeisha is of uncertain origin. The meaning of the name Lakeisha is "cassia tree". Lakeisha is an elaborated form of the name Keisha.

Laine

Pronunciation: layn

The name Laine is of English origin. The meaning of Laine is "path, roadway". Laine is a variant of the surname Lane. The name is also used as a short form of the name Marlaine and Melanie.

Lainey

Pronunciation: layn-EE

The name Lainey is of French origin. The meaning of Lainey is "bright, shining light". Lainey is a diminutive of the Old French name Elaine.

Lakshmi

Pronunciation: la-KSH-mi

The name Lakshmi is of Hindi and Sanskrit origin. The meaning of Lakshmi is "good sign, good omen". Borne by the goddess of beauty, good fortune, and wealth. Lakshmi is the wife of Vishnu and the mother of Kama.

Lana

Pronunciation: LAHN-ah

Lana is of modern coinage. The name is possibly a variant of the Old German name Alana, which means "precious". American actress Lana Turner (1921-1995) popularised the name.

Lara

Pronunciation: LAR-ah

Lara is of Latin origin. The meaning of the name Lara is "protection". Lara is a diminutive of the name Larissa. Lara is also a Spanish surname and a place name. Boris Pasternak popularised the name in his novel, *Dr Zhivago* (1957).

Larissa

Pronunciation: la-RISS-ah

Larissa is of Latin origin. The meaning of the name Larissa is "cheerful". The name was borne by a Greek martyr of the Eastern Church.

Laura

Pronunciation: LAW-rah

The name Laura is of Latin origin. The meaning of Laura is "the bay, the laurel plant". Laura is a feminine form of *laurus*. The love poet Petrarch (1304-1374) addressed his sonnets to a Laura.

Laurel

Pronunciation: LAWR-el

The name Laurel is of Latin origin. The meaning of Laurel is "the bay, the laurel plant". A nature name derived from the name of the tree.

Lauren

Pronunciation: LAWR-en

The name Lauren is of Latin origin. The meaning of Lauren is "the bay, the laurel plant". Lauren is a variant of the name Laura. The name is also a feminine form of the masculine name Lawrence. Hollywood actress Lauren Bacall (1924-2014) popularised the name during the 20th century.

Lavinia

Pronunciation: la-vee-NEE-ah

The name Lavinia is of Latin origin. The meaning of Lavinia is unknown. Borne in mythology by the daughter of Latinus, king of the Latini. Lavinia became the wife of Aeneas and the ancestress of Romulus and Remus. The name was popular during the Renaissance, and later revived in the 18th century.

Layla
Pronunciation: LAY-la
The name Layla is of Arabic origin. The meaning of Layla is "wine". Layla is a variation of the Arabic name Leila.

Leah
Pronunciation: LAY-ah
Leah is of Hebrew origin. The meaning of the name Leah is "delicate, cow". A biblical name; borne by Jacob's first wife and the mother of Jacob's twelve sons (Genesis 29). The name was revived by the Puritans,

Leanne, Leanna
Pronunciation: lee-AN-ah
The name Leanne is of English origin. The meaning of Leanne is unknown. The name is either a combination of the name Lee and Anna or possibly a variation of the name Liane.

Leanora

Pronunciation: LEE-nor-ah

The name Leanora is of Italian origin. The meaning of Leanora is "compassion, light". Leanore is the Italian form the Old German name Eleanor.

Leda

Pronunciation: LEE-dah

The name Leda is of Greek origin. The meaning of Leda is "joy, happiness". Borne in Greek mythology; Leda was the Queen of Sparta and the mother of Helen of Troy and Clytemnestra.

Lee

Pronunciation: LEE

Lee is of Old English origin. The meaning of the name Lee is "wood, meadow, clearing". An adopted surname and place name. Lee was first used as a first name in the 19th century, probably in honour of the Confederate general Robert E. Lee (1807-1870). The name is used as both a boy's name and as a girl's name.

Leila

Pronunciation: LEE-lah

The name Leila is of Arabic origin. The meaning of Leila is "night beauty".

Lena

Pronunciation: LEE-nah

The name Lena is originally a byname from female names ending in –lena, such as Helena. The name became a popular first name in its own right.

Leona

Pronunciation: LEE-oh-nah

Leona is of Latin origin. The meaning of the name Leona is "Lion". Leona is a feminine form of the masculine name Leon.

Leonie

Pronunciation: LEE-oh-nee

Leonie is of Latin origin. The meaning of the name Leonie is "Lion". Leonie is a feminine form of the masculine name Leon. Leonie is the French form.

Leonora

Pronunciation: lee-a-NOR-ah

The name Leonora is of Greek and Italian origin. The meaning of Leonora is "compassion, light". Leonora is the Italian form of the name Eleanor. Beethoven popularised the name is his opera *Fidelio* (1814). Diminutives: Leo, Nora, Norah.

Lesley

Pronunciation: les-LEE

The name Lesley is of Scottish origin. The meaning of Lesley is "Holly garden". Originally a Scottish surname derived from a place called Lesslyn in Aberdeenshire. Lesley is a variant of the name Leslie.

Liesel

Pronunciation: LIE-sel

The name Liesel is German and Hebrew origin. The meaning of Liesel is "God is my oath". Liesel is a German diminutive of the name Elizabeth.

Lili

Pronunciation: LIL-ee

Lili is of German and Hebrew origin. The meaning of the name Lili is "lily, God is my oath". Lili is a German diminutive of the name Elizabeth. The name became a popular first name in its own right.

Lilian

Pronunciation: LIL-e-an

The name Lilian is of Latin origin. The meaning of Lilian is "lily". Lilian is also a variant of the name Lily. Diminutives: Lily.

Lily

Pronunciation: LIL-ee

Lily is of Greek and Latin origin. The meaning of the
name Lily is "lily". From Greek *leirion*, which denotes
a species of slender plants with trumpet shaped
flowers. The lily is a symbol of innocence and purity.
The name became popular during the 19th century,
when botanical names became fashionable.

Lina

Pronunciation: LY-na

The name Lina is of Arabic and Latin origin. The
meaning of Lina is "palm tree". Lina is a diminutive of
names that end with –lina, such as Selina.

Linda

Pronunciation: LIN-dah

The name Linda is of Spanish origin. The meaning of
Linda is "pretty". Linda is also a byname for the names
Belinda and Melinda. Diminutives: Lin, Lindie, Lindy.

Lindsay

Pronunciation: LIN-d-say

Lindsay is of Old English origin. The meaning of the
name Lindsay is "Lincoln's marsh". Sir Walter de
Lindesay brought the name to Scotland from Lindsey,

Lincolnshire. The name is used as both a boy's name and as a girl's name.

Lisa

Pronunciation: LEE-sah

Lisa is of Hebrew origin. The meaning of the name Lisa is "God is my oath". Lisa is a variation of the name Liza. The name was popular throughout the 20th century.

Livia

Pronunciation: LIV-iah

Livia is of Latin origin. The meaning of the name Livia is "olive, tree". Livia is a feminine form of the Roman clan name Livius.

Lois

Pronunciation: LOH-iss

The name Lois is of Greek origin. The meaning of Lois is "superior". A biblical name; borne in the New Testament by the grandmother of Timothy.

Lola

Pronunciation: LOH-lah

The name Lola is of unknown origin. The meaning of Lola is "sorrows". Lola is a Spanish diminutive of the name Dolores.

Lolita

Pronunciation: LOH-e-tah

The name Lolita is of unknown origin. The meaning of Lolita is "sorrows". Lolita is a Spanish diminutive of the name Dolores.

Lorna

Pronunciation: LOR-nah

The name Lorna is of Scottish origin. The meaning of Lorna is unknown. The name was invented by R D Blackmore for his novel *Lorna Doone* (1869). The name was possibly derived from an area of Argyll, Scotland called Lorne.

Lorraine

Pronunciation: lor-AYN

The name Lorraine is of French origin. The meaning of Lorraine is "from Lorraine". Originally an adopted French surname derived from the district of Alsace-Lorraine.

Louisa

Pronunciation: LOH-e-sah

The name Louisa is of Latin origin. The meaning of Louisa is "famous warrior". Louisa is Latinate feminine form of the name Louis. The name was popular during the 17th century. Diminutives: Lou, Louie, Lulu.

Louise

Pronunciation: loo-EEZ

The name Louise is of Old German and French origin. The meaning of Louise is "famous warrior". Louise is a French feminine form of the masculine name Louis. Saint Louise (16th century) was the co-founder of the nursing order Daughter of Charity. The name was adopted in Britain during the 17th century. Diminutives: Lou, Louie, Lulu.

Lucia

Pronunciation: LOU-cee-ah

Lucia is of Italian and Latin origin. The meaning of the name Lucia is "light". Lucia is a feminine form of the Latin name Lucius.

Lucilla

Pronunciation: LOO-sil-lah

The name Lucilla is of Latin origin. The meaning of Lucilla is "light". Lucilla is a Latin byname for Lucia. The name was borne by several saints. The name was popular with the Romans and later revived in the 19th century.

Lucille

Pronunciation: loo-SEEL

Lucille is of French origin. The meaning of Lucille is "light". Lucille is the French form. The name was made popular by American actress Lucille Ball (1911-1989).

Lucinda

Pronunciation: loo-SEEN-dah

The name Lucinda is of Latin origin. The meaning of Lucinda is "light". Lucinda is a variant of the Latin name Lucy.

Lucy

Pronunciation: LOO-see

The name Lucy is of Latin origin. The meaning of Lucy is "light". Lucy is an anglicised form of the Old French name Lucie. The name is borne by a fourth-century saint. Saint Lucy is patroness of sight. Diminutives: Loose, Luce.

Lulu

Pronunciation: LOO-loo

The name Lulu is of Spanish and German origin. The meaning of Lulu is "famous warrior". Lulu is a byname of Luisa, Luise and Louise. The name became a popular first name in its own right.

Lydia

Pronunciation: LED-ee-ah

The name Lydia is of Greek origin. The meaning of Lydia is "woman of Lydia, from Lydia", a town in Asia Minor. A biblical name; borne by a woman who was converted to Christianity by Saint Paul (16:14).

Lyn, Lynn

Pronunciation: lyn

The name Lyn is of uncertain origin. The meaning of Lyn is "pretty". Lyn is a variant of the name Linda.

Lynette

Pronunciation: le-NET

The name Lynette is of Welsh origin. The meaning of Lynette is "idol, nymph". Originally adopted from the medieval French form of Eluned. Lord Tennyson (1859-1885) popularised the modern form of the name in *Idylls of the King.*

Lyra

Pronunciation: LY-rah

The name Lyra is of Greek origin. The meaning of Lyra is "lyre". Lyra is a variant of the Greek name Lyris.

M

Mackenzie

Pronunciation: ma-KEN-zee

The name Mackenzie if of Gaelic and Irish origin. The meaning of Mackenzie is "son of the wise ruler". An adopted Scottish surname, from Gaelic Mac Coinnich. Mackenzie is used as both a boy's name, and as a girl's name.

Madelaine

Pronunciation: MAD-el-aine

The name Madelaine is of French and Hebrew origin. The meaning of Madelaine is "woman from Magdala". Magdala is a village by the Sea of Galilee. Madelaine is a medieval French form of the name Magdalene.

Magdalen, Magdalene

Pronunciation: MAG-da-len

The name Magdalen is of Hebrew origin. The meaning of Magdalen is "woman from Magdala". Magdala is a village by the Sea of Galilee. A biblical name; borne by

Saint Mary Magdalene, a reformed prostitute and follower of Jesus.

Mahalia
Pronunciation: ma-HAL-yah
The name Mahalia is of Hebrew origin. The meaning of Mahalia is "tenderness".

Maia, Maya
Pronunciation: MA-ia
Maia is of Greek origin. The meaning of the name Maia is "great, mother". Maia is a variation of the name Mary. Borne in Greek mythology; Maia was a beautiful nymph and mother of Hermes. In Roman mythology, she is eldest and most beautiful of the Pleiades. The month of May was named in honour of her. In Buddhist philosophy, Maya gave birth to Buddha in the shape of a little white elephant.

Mallory
Pronunciation: MALL-or-ee
The name Mallory is of Old French origin. The meaning of Mallory is "unfortunate". The name is used as both a boy's name and as a girl's name.

Márie

Pronunciation: mar-EE

The name Márie is of Irish Gaelic origin. The meaning of Márie is unknown.

Maisie

Pronunciation: MAY-zee

Maisie if of English origin. The meaning of the name Maisie is "pearl". Maisie is a diminutive of the names Margaret, Marjorie and Mary.

Manon

Pronunciation: MAN-awn

The name Manon is of French origin. The meaning of Man is "star of the sea". Manon is a French diminutive of the name Marie.

Manuela

Pronunciation: mahn-WAY-lah

The name Manuela is of Spanish and Hebrew origin. The meaning of Manuela is "God is with us". Manuela is a feminine form of the name Manuel.

Mara, Marah

Pronunciation: MAHR-ah

The name Mara is of Hebrew origin. The meaning of Mara is "bitter". A biblical name; adopted by Naomi, mother-in-law of Ruth. She claimed the name Mara after the death of her husbands and sons.

Marcella, Marcelle
Pronunciation: mar-SELL-ah
Marcella is of Latin origin. The meaning of the name Marcella is "dedicated to Mars". Marcella is a feminine form of a Roman family name Marcellus. Marcelle is the French form. Saint Marcella from the 4th century was killed during the sack of Rome.

Marcia
Pronunciation: MAR-shah
Marcia is of Latin origin. The meaning of the name Marcia is "dedicated to Mars". Marcia is a feminine form of the Roman family name Marcius. Diminutives: Marcie, Marcy.

Maretta
Pronunciation: mar-ee-et-AH
The name Maretta is is of Scottish origin. The meaning of Maretta is "star of the sea". Maretta is an anglicised form of Mairead and the Scottish Gaelic form of the name Margaret.

Margaret

Pronunciation: MARG-ar-et

The name Margaret is of Greek origin. The meaning of Margaret is "pearl". Derived from the Latin name Margarita, which was derived from Greek *margaron*. Saint Margaret of Antioch was a 3rd-century virgin martyr, is renowned for fighting the devil in the shape of a dragon. Diminutives: Daisy, Madge, Maggie, Marge, Margie, Margy, Marji, Marjie, May, Meg, Meggie, Peg, Peggy.

Margarita

Pronunciation: MARG-ar-ee-TAH

The name Margarita is of Spanish origin. The meaning of Margarita is "pearl". Margarita is a Spanish form of Margaret. The name became a popular first name in its own right.

Margherita

Pronunciation: MARG-er-ee-TAH

The name Margherita is of Italian origin. The meaning of Margherita is "pearl". Margherita is an Italian form of Margaret. The name became a popular first name in its own right.

Marguerite

Pronunciation: mar-gue-rite

The name Marguerite is of French origin. The meaning of Marguerite is "pearl". Marguerite is French variation of the name Margaret. The name was first adopted during the 19th century. Diminutives: Margot.

Maria

Pronunciation: mah-REE-ah

Maria is of Latin origin. The meaning of the name Maria is "star of the sea". Maria is Latinate form of the name Mary. The name was revived during the 20th century, possibly due to the popularity of the American musical, *West Side Story*.

Mariah

Pronunciation: mah-ri-AH

Mariah is of Latin origin. The meaning of the name Mariah is "star of the sea". Mariah is a variant of the name Maria. The name dates back to the 19th century. The name was popularised by American singer Mariah Carey.

Marian

Pronunciation: mar-ee-AHN

The name Marian is of French origin. The meaning of Marian is "star of the sea". Marian is a French diminutive of the name Marie. The name became a popular first name during the Middle Ages. The name was later revived in the 19th century.

Marie

Pronunciation: mah-REE

The name Marie is of French origin. The meaning of Marie is "star of the sea". Marie is a French form of the Latin name Maria. The name became a popular first name in its own right.

Mariella

Pronunciation: mar-EE-el-AH

Mariella is of German origin. The meaning of the name Maiella is "star of the sea". Mariella is originally a German diminutive of the name Mary.

Marietta

Pronunciation: MAR-e-ett-AH

The name Marietta is of Italian origin. The meaning of Marietta is "star of the sea". Marietta is an Italian diminutive of the name Mary. Mariette is the French form.

Marilyn

Pronunciation: MARE-a-lin

Marilyn is of English origin. The meaning of the name Marilyn is "star of the sea". Marilyn is a variation of the name Mary. The name was popularised in the 20th century by Hollywood actress Marilyn Monroe (1926-1962).

Marina

Pronunciation: mah-REE-nag

The name Marina is of Latin origin. The meaning of Marina is "from the sea". Possibly derived from Latin *marinus*, or from a Latin family name that is related to Marius. The name was borne by the 14th-century martyr of the Greek Church. Shakespeare used the name in *Pericles, Prince of Tyre* (1619).

Marissa

Pronunciation: ma-RISS-ah

The name Marissa is of Latin origin. The meaning of Marissa is "of the sea", Marissa is a diminutive of the name Mary.

Marlene

Pronunciation: mar-LEEN

The name Marlene is of German origin. The meaning of Marlene is "star of the sea". The name was introduced to Britain by Lili Marlene. German and Hollywood actress Marlene Dietrich (1901-1992) popularised the name during the 20th century.

Marnie

Pronunciation: marn-EE

Marnie is of Scandinavian origin. The meaning of the name Marnie is "from the sea". Marnie is a variant of the Latin name Marina. The name is also a diminutive of Marna.

Martha

Pronunciation: MAR-tha

Martha is of Aramaic origin. The meaning of the name Martha is "Lady". A biblical name; borne in the New Testament by the sister of Lazarus and Mary of Bethany. She is the patron saint of the helping professions. The name was revived by the Puritans.

Martina, Martine

Pronunciation: mar-TEEN-ah

The name Martina is of Latin origin. The meaning of Martina is "dedicated to Mars". Martina is a feminine form of the masculine name Martin. Martina is the

Latinate form, Martine is the French form. The name was borne by two saints.

Mary

Pronunciation: MARE-ee

The name Mary is of Latin origin. The meaning of Mary is "star of the sea". Mary is a medieval Anglicization of the French name Marie. A biblical name; borne by the virgin mother of Christ, Mary became the object of great worship in the Catholic Church. Mary Magdalene and Mary of Bethany are also mentioned in the Bible. Diminutives: Maidie, Maisie, Mamie, May, Mimi, Minnie, Moll, Molly, Poll, Polly.

Matilda

Pronunciation: mah-TIL-dah

The name Matilda is of Old German origin. The meaning of Matilda is "mighty in battle, strength". From Old German *mahti*. The name was introduced to Britain in the 11th century by Queen Matilda, wife of William the Conqueror. Diminutives: Mattie, Matty, Tilda, Tilly.

May

Pronunciation: may

The name May is of English origin. The meaning of May is "the fifth month". The name is derived from the Latin Maius. May is of the names of months that were adopted as first names in the early 20th century. May is a diminutive of the name Mary.

Maybelle

Pronunciation: MAY-belle

The name Maybelle is of English origin. The meaning of Maybelle is "lovable". Maybelle is a variant of the English name Mabel.

Maxine

Pronunciation: mak-SEEN

The name Maxine if of Latin origin. The meaning of Maxine is "greatest". Maxine if a feminine form of the name Max.

Megan

Pronunciation: MEG-an

Megan is of Welsh origin. The meaning of the Megan is "pearl". Megan is a Welsh diminutive of Meg.

Mehetabel

Pronunciation: meh-et-a-bel

The name Mehetabel is of Hebrew origin. The meaning of Mehetabel is "God makes happy". A biblical name; borne by a figure mentioned in the Old Testament.

Melanie

Pronunciation: MEL-a-nee

The name Melanie is of French and Greek origin. The meaning of Melanie is "black, dark". The name is derived from the French form of the Latin name Melania. The name is borne by two Roman saints. The name was introduced to Britain in the 17th century. Margaret Mitchell popularised the name in her epic novel, *Gone With The Wind* (1936). Melanie Wilkes is wife of Ashely Wilkes and Scarlet O' Hara's best friend.

Melba

Pronunciation: MEL-bah

The name Melba is of Australian origin. The name is derived from the Australian place name Melbourne. The name was possibly created as a surname by diva Nellie Melba (1861-1931).

Melinda

Pronunciation: ma-LIN-dah

The name Melinda is of Latin origin. The meaning of Melinda is "sweet". The name is an 18th-century coinage, a combination of the names Mel and Linda. The name was also influenced by the name Greek name Melissa and is often associated with bees, honey and sweetness.

Melissa

Pronunciation: ma-LISS-ah

Melissa is of Greek origin. The meaning of the name Melissa is "bee, honey". Borne in Greek mythology by a princess of Crete, who introduced mankind to honey. Diminutives: Mel.

Melody

Pronunciation: MEL-a-dee

The name Melody is of Greek origin. The meaning of Melody is "song, music". Melody is a direct adoption from the English vocabulary, which denotes a musical tune. The name was first used in the 13th century.

Mercedes

Pronunciation: mer-SAY-dees

Mercedes is of Spanish origin. The meaning of the name Mercedes is "mercies". Derived from Maria de Las Mercedes, a Spanish title for the Virgin Mary.

Mercedes is also the name of the German luxury car. Diminutives: Mercy, Sadie.

Mercy

Pronunciation: MER-see

Mercy is of English origin. The meaning of the name Mercy is "compassion". The name is a direct adaptation from the English vocabulary. The virtue name was adopted by the Puritans in the 17th century. Mercy is also a diminutive of the name Mercedes.

Merlin

Pronunciation: MER-lin

Merlin is of Welsh origin. The meaning of the name Melvin is "sea fortress". From Latinate form, Merlinus, of the Old Welsh name Myrddin. Borne in Arthurian legend by magician Merlin Ambrosius. The name is used as both a boy's name and as a girl's name.

Mia

Pronunciation: MEE-ah

Mia is of Latin and Scandinavian origin. The meaning of the name Mia is "star of the sea". Mia is a Scandinavian diminutive of the Latin name Maria. The name was popularised in the 20th century by Hollywood actress Mia Farrow.

Michaela

Pronunciation: mih-KAY-lah

The name Michaela is of Hebrew origin. The meaning of Michaela is "who is like God?" Michaela is a feminine form of the masculine name Michael.

Michelle

Pronunciation: mee-SHELL

Michelle is of French and Hebrew origin. The meaning of the name Michelle is "who is like God?" Michelle is a feminine form of the French name Michel. The name was popularised by the Beatles in the 20th century.

Diminutives: Chelle, Mich, Michy, Shell, Shelley, Shelly.

Mignon

Pronunciation: mig-NON

The name Mignon is of French origin. The meaning of Mignon is "cute, dainty".

Millie, Milly

Pronunciation: mill-EE

Millie is of Latin and Old German origin. The meaning of Millie is "rival, bee, honey". Millie is a diminutive of the names Camila, Mildred and Millicent.

Mimi

Pronunciation: MEE-mee

Mimi is of French origin. The meaning of the name Mimi is "star of the sea". Mimi is a diminutive of the name Mary.

Mina

Pronunciation: MEE-nah

The name Mina is of German origin. The meaning of the name Mina is "love". Mina is a diminutive of the names Philomena and Wilhelmina.

Minerva

Pronunciation: mi-NER-vah

The name Minerva is of Latin origin. The meaning of Minerva is "the mind". Borne in mythology; Minerva was the Roman goddess of wisdom, arts, crafts and war. She is equivalent to the Greek goddess Athena.

Minna

Pronunciation: min-NAH

The name Minna is of Old German origin. The meaning of Minna is "determined protector". Minna is a diminutive of the name Wilhelmina.

Minnie

Pronunciation: min-EE

Minnie is of uncertain origin. The meaning of Minnie is "star of the sea, determined protector". Minnie is a diminutive of the names Mary and Wilhelmina. The name became a popular first name in its own right. Walt Disney made popularised the name in the 20th century, by using it for the name of Mickey Mouse's girlfriend.

Mirabella

Pronunciation: mira-bel-LAH

The name Mirabella is of Latin origin. The meaning of Mirabella is "wonderful". The name was popular in medieval Britain.

Miranda

Pronunciation: mer-ANN-dah

The name Miranda is of Latin origin. The meaning of Miranda is "worthy of admiration". The name was used by Shakespeare in *The Tempest* (1612). Miranda was the name of the innocent heroine, raised and educated on an isolated island by her magician father.

Miriam

Pronunciation: MEER-ee-em

The name Miriam is of Hebrew origin. The meaning of Miriam is "star of the sea". Miriam is an old-fashioned form of the name Mary. A biblical name; borne by the sister of Moses and Aaron. The name was adopted by the Puritans. The name was later revived in the 18th century.

Mitzi

Pronunciation: MIT-zee

Mitzi is of German origin. The meaning of the name Mitzi is "star of the sea". Mitzi is originally a German diminutive of the Latin name Maria.

Modesty

Pronunciation: MAH-dess-tee

The name Modesty is of Latin origin. The meaning of Modesty is "modest, without conceit". Modesty is a virtue name.

Mohana

Pronunciation: mo-HAN-ah

The name Mohana is of Sanskrit origin. The meaning of Mohana is "attractive, enchanting".

Moira

Pronunciation: MOY-rah

The name Moira is of English origin. The meaning of Moira is "star of the sea". Moria is the Irish Gaelic form of the name Mary.

Moll

Pronunciation: moll

The name Moll is of Latin origin. The meaning of Moll is "star of the sea". Moll is a diminutive of the names Mary and Molly.

Molly

Pronunciation: moll-EE

The name Molly is of Latin origin. The meaning of Molly is "star of the sea". Molly is a diminutive of the names Mary.

Mona

Pronunciation: MOH-nah

The name Mona is of Irish Gaelic origin. The meaning of Mona is "aristocratic, noble". Mona is an anglicised form of the Irish Gaelic name Muadhnait. Mona is sometimes used as a diminutive of the name Monica. The name is also an Italian short form of Madonna. Leonardo da Vinci popularised the name with his famous painting, *Mona Lisa*.

Monica

Pronunciation: MAH-ni-kah

Monica is of Latin origin. The meaning of the name
Monica is "advisor, alone". Borne by the mother of
Saint Augustine, she prayed for her son and saved him
from self-destruction. American sitcom, Friends
(1994-2004) popularised the name with its character
Monica Geller.

Monique

Pronunciation: mon-EEK

The name Monique is of French and Latin origin. The
meaning of Monique is "advisor". Monique is French
form of the Latin name Monica.

Morwenna

Pronunciation: mor-WEN-ah

The name Morwenna is of Welsh origin. The meaning
of Morwenna is "maiden". The name is borne by a 5th
century Cornish saint.

Myra

Pronunciation: MYE-rah

The name Myra is of Greek origin. The meaning of the
name Myra is "myrrh". The name was a poetic and
literary invention by the English poet Fulke Greville

(1554-1628). The name was popular during the 19th century.

N

Nadia

Pronunciation: NAH-d'-yah

The name Nadia is of Russian origin. The meaning of Nadia is "hope". The name is an Anglicization of Nadya, diminutive of the Russian name Nadezhda. The name is popular in Russia.

Nadine

Pronunciation: nay-DEEN

Nadine is of Russian origin. The meaning of the name Nadine is unknown. The name is a French diminutive of Nadia. The name was first used in the 20th century, when Diaghilev's Ballets Russes was established in Paris.

Naida

Pronunciation: NAY-da

The name Naida is of Greek origin. The meaning of Naida is "water nymph".

Nancy

Pronunciation: NAN-cee

Nancy is of Hebrew origin. The meaning of the name Nancy is "grace". The name is originally a diminutive of the name Constance. However, during the 18th century the name was regarded as a diminutive of Anne. Diminutives: Nan, Nance.

Naomh

Pronunciation: nay-OHM

The name Naomh is of Irish Gaelic origin. The meaning of the Naomh is "holy".

Naomi

Pronunciation: nay-OH-mee

The name Naomi is of Hebrew origin. The meaning of Naomi is "pleasant". A biblical name; borne in the Old Testament an ancestress of Jesus and mother in law to Ruth. The name has long been popular with Jewish families.

Natalia, Natalya

Pronunciation: NAT-al-ee-a

Natalia is of Russian origin. The meaning of the name Natalia is "birthday". Derived from Latin *natale domini*. The name refers to the birthday of Christ.

Saint Natalia was Saint Adrian's wife. Diminutives: Talia, Talya, Tally.

Natalie

Pronunciation: NAT-a-lee

The name Natalie is of Latin origin. The meaning of Natalie is "birthday". The name is a French form of Natalya. The name dates back to the 20th century when Diaghilev's Ballet Russes was first established in Paris.

Natasha

Pronunciation: na-TAH-shah

The name Natasha is of Russian origin. The meaning of Natasha is "birthday". Natasha is a diminutive of the name Natalya. The name became a popular first name in its own right. The name became famous with Leo Tolstoy's epic novel *War and Peace* (1865-9). Natasha was the name of the heroine. Diminutives: Tash, Tasha.

Neila

Pronunciation: NEE-lah

The name Neila is of Hebrew origin. The meaning of Neila is "closing". The name is a feminine form of the masculine name Neil.

Nelinia

Pronunciation: NEL-ee-nee-a

The name Nelinia is of Scottish origin. The meaning of Nelinia is "Champion". Nelinina is a feminine form of the masculine name Neil.

Neima

Pronunciation: NEE-ma

The name Neima is of Hebrew origin. The meaning of Neima is "melody".

Neiva

Pronunciation: NEE-vah

The name Neiva is of Spanish origin. The meaning of Neiva is "snow". Neiva is a feminine variant of the word, nieve.

Neka

Pronunciation: NEE-ka

The name Neka is of Native American Indian origin. The meaning of Neka is "wild goose".

Nelia

Pronunciation: NEE-lee-a

Nelia is of Latin origin. The meaning of the name Nelia is "horn". Nelia is a diminutive of the Latin name Cornelia.

Nell
Pronunciation: N-ell
The name Nell is a diminutive of the Old French & Old German name, Eleanor. The meaning of the name Nell is "horn, sun ray". Nell can also be a variant for the names Helen, Ellen and Nelly. Diminutives: Nellie, Nelly.

Nelly
Pronunciation: NEL-ee
Nelly is of English origin. The meaning of the name Nelly is "sun ray". Nelly is a diminutive of the names Helen and Eleanor.

Nemera
Pronunciation: NEM-er-a
The name Nemera is of Hebrew origin. The meaning of Nemera is "leopard".

Neneca
Pronunciation: NE-ne-KA

The name Neneca is of Spanish origin. The meaning of Neneca is "industrious". Neneca is a variant of the Old German name Amelia.

Neoma
Pronunciation: NE-oo-ma
The name Neoma is of Greek origin. The meaning of Neoma is "new moon".

Nera
Pronunciation: NEE-ra
The name Nera is of Hebrew origin. The meaning of Nera is "candle".

Nereida
Pronunciation: ne-RAY-dah
Nereida is of Greek and Spanish origin. The meaning of the name Nereida is "sea nymph". Borne in Greek mythology; the Nereids were mermaids of the sea.

Nerissa
Pronunciation: NEE-riss-a
The name Nerissa is of Italian origin. The meaning of Nerissa is "black haired".

Nerola

Pronunciation: NE-rol-a

The name Nerola is of Italian origin. The meaning of Nerola is "orange flower".

Nerys

Pronunciation: NER-iss

The name Nerys is of Welsh origin. The meaning of Nerys is "noblewoman".

Nessa

Pronunciation: NESS-a

The name Nessa is of Scottish Gaelic origin. The meaning of Nessa is unknown. Nessa is a diminutive of the Greek name Agnes. The name was borne in Scottish legend by the mother of Conchobhar. Nessa is also used as a variant of the Greek name Vanessa.

Nettie

Pronunciation: NEH-tee

The name Nettie is of English origin. The meaning of Nettie is unknown. Nettie is a diminutive of all girls' names ending –net.

Niamh

Pronunciation: NI-amh

The name Niamh is of Irish Gaelic origin. The meaning of Niamh is "brightness". Borne in Irish mythology by the lover of Oisín was carried off to the land of eternal youth.

Nicola
Pronunciation: NIC-o-la
Nicola is of Greek origin. The meaning of the name Nicola is "people of victory". The name is a Latinate and Italian feminine form of the name Nicholas. Diminutives: Nic, Nik, Nicki, Nicky, Niki,, Nikki, Nico.

Nicole
Pronunciation: ni-KOHL
The name Nicole is of Greek origin. The meaning of Nicole is "people of victory". The name is a French feminine form of the name Nicholas.

Nigella
Pronunciation: NI-gel-la
The name Nigella is of English origin. The meaning of Nigella is "Champion". Nigella is a Latinate feminine form of the name Nigel.

Nikita

Pronunciation: nih-KEE-tah

Nikita is of Greek origin. The meaning of the name Nikita is "unconquered". Nikita is a Russian masculine name, derived from the Greek name Aniketos. The name was borne by an early pope. The name is regarded as a girl's name in the English-speaking world; however it is still in use as a boy's name in Russia.

Nina

Pronunciation: NEE-nah

The name Nina is of Spanish and Hebrew origin. The meaning of Nine is "little girl". The name was originally a diminutive of girls' names that ended with –nina. The name became a popular first name in its own right. Christopher Columbus named one of his three ships Nina. Diminutive: Ninka.

Nisha

Pronunciation: NEE-shah

The name Nisha is of Hindi origin. The meaning of Nisha is "night",

Nissa

Pronunciation: NISS-a

The name Nissa is of Hebrew origin. The meaning of Nissa is "to test".

Nixie

Pronunciation: NIX-ee

The name Nixie is of Old German. The meaning of the name Nixie is "water sprite".

Noelani

Pronunciation: no-ah-LAH-nee

The name Noelani is of Hawaiian origin. The meaning of Noelani is "mist of heaven".

Noelle

Pronunciation: noe-ELL

Noelle is of Old French origin. The meaning of the name Noelle is "Christmas". Noelle is a feminine form of Noel.

Nokomis

Pronunciation: n(o)-KO-mis

The name Nokomis if of Native American Indian origin. The meaning of Nokomis is "daughter of the moon".

Nolan

Pronunciation: NO-lan

The name Nolan is of Irish and Gaelic origin. The meaning of Nolan is "Champion". Nolan is an adopted surname.

Nona

Pronunciation: NOH-nah

The name Nona is of Latin origin. The meaning of Nona is "ninth". The name was originally given to a family's ninth baby.

Nora

Pronunciation: NOR-ah

Nora is of English origin. The meaning of the name Nora is "woman of honor". In Scotland, Nora is used as a feminine form of the name Norman.

Nordica

Pronunciation: NOR-dic-a

The name Nordica is of Latin origin. The meaning of Nordica is "from the North".

Noreen

Pronunciation: nor-EEN

The name Noreen is of Irish origin. The meaning of Noreen is unknown. Noreen is a variant of the name Nora.

Norell

Pronunciation: no-RELL

The name Norell is of Scandinavian origin. The meaning of Norell is "from the North". The name is originally a surname.

Norma

Pronunciation: NOR-mah

Norma is of Latin origin. The meaning of the name Norma is "the standard, norm". The name was possibly invented by Felice Romani. The name became popular in the 19th century, after Vincenzo Bellini's 1832 tragic opera, *Norma*. The name was popularised by Hollywood actress Norma Jeane Mortenson, also known as Marilyn Monroe (1926-1962).

Nova

Pronunciation: NOH-vah

The name Nova is of Latin origin. The meaning of Nova is "new". In astronomy, a nova is a star that releases bursts of energy.

Nuala

Pronunciation: NOO-la

The name Nuala is of Irish origin. The meaning of Nuala is unknown. The name was originally a diminutive of Fionnuala. The name is now widely used as a first name in its own its own right.

Nura

Pronunciation: NOOR-ah

The name Nura is of Arabic and Aramaic origin. The meaning of Nura is "light".

Nydia

Pronunciation: NIH-dee-ah

The name Nydia is of Latin origin. The meaning of Nydia is "nest". Taken from the word *nidus*. The name was popularised by Edward Bulwer-Lytton's epic novel, *The Last Days of Pompeii* (1834). Nydia was the name of a blind woman who died whilst saving her beloved one.

Nina

Pronunciation: NEE-nah

The name Nina is of English origin. The meaning of Nine is unknown. Nine is a feminine form of Nyles.

Nyree

Pronunciation: ny-REE

The name Nyree is of Maori origin. The meaning of the Nyree is unknown. The name dates back to before Christ.

Nysa

Pronunciation: NY-sa

The name Nysa is of Greek origin. The meaning of Nysa is "ambition".

O

Oceana

Pronunciation: oh-see-AH-nah

The name Oceana is of Greek origin. The meaning of Oceana is "ocean". The name is a feminine form of *Oceanus.*

Octavia

Pronunciation: ock-TAHV-yah

The name Octavia is of Latin origin. The meaning of Octavia is "eighth". The name is a feminine form of Octavius, from Latin *octavus.* Octavia was sometimes given to the eighth or child or daughter.

Odele

Pronunciation: OH-del

The name Odele is of Greek origin. The meaning of Odele is "song". The name is also possibly a variant of Adele.

Odelia

Pronunciation: oh-DEEL-yah

The name Odelia is of Hebrew origin. The meaning of Odelia is "praise God". Borne by an 8th-century French saint.

Odessa

Pronunciation: oh-DESS-ah

The Odessa is of Greek origin. The meaning of Odessa is "long journey". The name is a variant of Odysseus.

Odila

Pronunciation: oh-DIL-a

The name Odila is of Old German origin. The meaning of Odila is "fortunate in battle".

Ofra

Pronunciation: OF-ra

The name Ofra is of Hebrew origin. The meaning of Ofra is "fawn". The name is variant of Ophrah.

Oksana

Pronunciation: OK-sana

The name Oksana is of Hebrew and Russian origin. The meaning of Oksana is "praise God".

Ola

Pronunciation: Oh-lah

The name Ola is of Old Norse origin. The meaning of Ola is "ancestor's relic". Ola is a variant of the Greek name Olesia.

Oleisa

Pronunciation: oh-LEE-sa

Oleisa is of French origin. The meaning of the name Oleisa is "God is my oath". Oleisa is a variant of the Hebrew name Elizabeth.

Olena

Pronunciation: oh-LEE-na

The name Olena is of Greek and Russian origin. The meaning of the name Olena is "sun ray". The name is a variant of Helen.

Olesia

Pronunciation: OL-ee-SEE-a

Olesia is of Greek origin. The meaning of the name Olesia is "man's defender".

Olethea

Pronunciation: oh-lee-THEE-ah

The name Olethea is of Greek origin. The meaning of Olethea is "truth". Olethea is a variant of the Greek name Alethea.

Olga

Pronunciation: OL-gah

The name Olga is of Old Norse and Scandinavian origin. The meaning of Olga is "blessed, holy". The name is a Russian form of Helga. Saint Olga was a 10th century Christian and Princess from Kiev.

Olina

Pronunciation: oh-LEE-nah

The name Olina is of Hawaiian origin. The meaning of Olina is "joyous".

Olinda

Pronunciation: oh-LIN-dah

The name Olinda is of Greek origin. The meaning of Olinda is "wild fig".

Olivia

Pronunciation: oh-LIV-ee-ah

The name Olivia is of Latin origin. The meaning of Olivia is "olive tree". The name is possibly a Latinate feminine form of Oliver. The name was used by Shakespeare in his play *Twelfth Night* (1602). Saint Olivia was venerated in Italy as patron the saint of olive trees.

Olwen

Pronunciation: OL-wen

The name Olwen is of Welsh origin. The meaning of
Olwen is "white footprint". Borne in the medieval
story of *Culhwch and Owen*, Olwen was so beautiful
that wherever she stepped four white flowers would
suddenly appear.

Olympia

Pronunciation: oh-LIM-pee-ah

Olympia is of Greek origin. The meaning of the name
Olympia is "from Mount Olympus". The name is a
modern adaptation of the ancient name, Peloponnesus,
which was the site of the early Olympic games.

Ondine

Pronunciation: ON-dine

The name Ondine is of Latin origin. The meaning of
Ondine is "little wave".

Ondrea

Pronunciation: ON-dree-ah

The name Ondrea is of Czechoslovakian origin. The
meaning of Ondrea is unknown. Ondrea is a variant of
the name Andrea.

Oneida

Pronunciation: ON-ee-da

The name Oneida is of Native American Indian origin. The meaning of Oneida is "long awaited".

Onella

Pronunciation: ON-el-la

The name Onella is of Greek origin. The meaning of Onella is "light".

Oona

Pronunciation: OO-nah

The name Oona is of Irish and Scottish origin. The meaning of Oona is "one". The name is an anglicised form of the Irish Gaelic name Úna.

Opal

Pronunciation: OH-pel

The name Opal is of Hindi and Sanskrit origin. The meaning of Opal is "gem". Opal is a type of semi-precious stone. The gemstone is suitable for an a baby born in October. Opals have been associated with bad luck for centuries.

Ophelia

Pronunciation: oh-FEEL-yah

The name Ophelia is of Greek origin. The meaning of Ophelia is "help". Ophelia is a feminine form of Greek *ophelos*. Shakespeare used the name is his play, *Hamlet* (1601). Ophelia was the ill-fated lover of Hamlet. The name was popular during the 19th century.

Ophrah
Pronunciation: OHF-rah
Ophrah is of Hebrew origin. The meaning of the name Ophrah is "young deer, gazelle". A biblical name; borne by several male figures. The name is now used as both a boy's name and as a girl's name.

Oracia
Pronunciation: OR-a-cee-a
Oracia is of Spanish origin. The meaning of the name Oracia is unknown. The name is a feminine form of the Latin clan name, Horace.

Oralee
Pronunciation: OR-a-lee
The name Oralee is of Hebrew origin. The meaning of Oralee is "my light". Oralee is a variant of the English name Auralee.

Oriana

Pronunciation: or-ee-AHN-ah

The name Oriana is of Latin origin. The meaning of Oriana is "Sunrise". From Latin *oriri*. The name first appeared in the 14th-century romance, *Amadis de Gaul*.

Orla

Pronunciation: OR-lah

The name Orla is of Irish, Gaelic and Celtic origin. The meaning of Orla is "Princess".

P

Paloma

Pronunciation: pa-LOH-mah

Paloma is of Latin origin. The meaning of the name Paloma is "dove". Paloma is a Spanish name.

Pamela

Pronunciation: PAM-eh-lah

The name Pamela was invented by the poet Sir Philip Sidney (1554-86). He used the name for his heroine in his book, Arcadia (1590). Samuel Richardson popularised the name with his novel, *Pamela* (1740).

Pandora

Pronunciation: pan-DOE-ah

Pandora is of Greek origin. The meaning of the name Pandora is "all gifts". Borne in Greek mythology; Pandora was the beautiful, but foolish first mortal, created by the Greek god of fire to avenge the theft of fire by Prometheus. Pandora was given charge of a mysterious box and told never to open it up. However Pandora could not resist opening the box, and in doing so she released all of humankind's ills into the world, followed by one counterpart, Hope.

Paris

Pronunciation: PARE-iss

The name Paris is of Greek origin. In Greek mythology, Paris was the name of the young prince of Troy, whose love affair with Helen caused the Trojan war. Paris is used as both a boy's name and as a girl's name. The name was also an English given surname for immigrants from the capital of France.

Pascale

Pronunciation: PAS-cale

The name Pascale is of French and Hebrew origin. The meaning of Pascale is "pertaining to Easter". Pascale is the feminine form of the French name Pascal. Early Christians often gave the name to children born at Passover.

Patience

Pronunciation: PAY-shuns

The name Patience is of English origin. The meaning of the name Patience is "enduring, forbearing". Patience is one of the several abstract nouns denoting admirable qualities. The name was popular among Puritans in the 16th century.

Patricia

Pronunciation: pa-TRISH-ah

The name Patricia is of Latin origin. The meaning of Patricia is "noble". Patricia is a feminine form derived from *patricius*, which means 'nobleman'. The name is also a feminine form of Patrick. Diminutives: Pat, Patsy, Pattie, Patty, Tricia, Trish.

Patsy

Pronunciation: PAT-see

The name Patsy is of Latin origin. The meaning of Patsy is "noble, patrician". Patsy is a diminutive of the name Patricia.

Paula

Pronunciation: PAW-lah

The name Paula is of Latin origin. The meaning of Paula is "small". Paula is a feminine form of the masculine name Paul. A 4th-century Saint Paula founded a number of convents in and around Bethlehem.

Paulette

Pronunciation: PAWL-ette

The name Paulette is of Latin origin. The meaning of Paulette is "small". Paulette is a French diminutive form of the Latin name Paula.

Paulina

Pronunciation: pawl-EEN-ah

The name Pauline is of Latin origin. The meaning of Paulina is "small". Paulina is Latinate diminutive form of the name Paula.

Pauline

Pronunciation: pawl-EEN

The name Pauline is of Latin origin. The meaning of Pauline is "small". The name is a French form of Paulina.

Penelope

Pronunciation: pen-NELL-a-pee

Penelope is of Greek origin. The meaning of the name Penelope is "weaver". Borne in Greek mythology; Penelope was the wife of Odysseus. She passed his ten-year absence in spinning, loyally fending off all suitors. She was the model of domestic virtues. The name has

come to signify a loyal, and intelligent woman.
Diminutives: Pen, Penny.

Pepita

Pronunciation: p(e)-pi-ta
The name Pepita is of Spanish origin. The meaning of
Pepita is "Jehovah increases". Pepita is a feminine
form of Joseph.

Peta

Pronunciation: PET-ah
The name Peta is of Spanish and Greek origin. The
meaning of Peta is "rock". Peta is a variant of the
Spanish name Papita. The name is also a variant of the
Greek name Petra. Peta is a modern feminine form of
the masculine name Peter.

Petra

Pronunciation: PEH-trah
The name Petra is of Greek origin. The meaning of
Petra is "rock". Petra is a feminine form of the
masculine name Peter, derived from Greek *petra*.

Petrova

Pronunciation: PET-rova

The name Petrova is Greek and Russian origin. The meaning Petrova is "rock". Petrova is a Russian feminine form of the name Peter.

Petula

Pronunciation: pe-tu-LAH

Petula is of Latin origin. The meaning of the name Petula is "to ask, to seek". Possibly derived from the Latin *petulare.*

Philippa

Pronunciation: FIL-lip-ah

The name Philippa is of Greek origin. The meaning of Philippa is "horse lover". Philippa is a feminine form of the masculine name Philip. Diminutives: Phil, Phillie, Philly, Pip, Pippa, Pippi, Pippy.

Philomena

Pronunciation: pa-LOH-mah

Philomena is of Greek origin. The meaning of Philomena is "beloved". The name was borne by two early Roman saints. Diminutives: Mena, Mina, Phil, Phillie, Philly.

Phoebe

Pronunciation: FEE-bee

Phoebe is of Greek origin. The meaning of the name Phoebe is "bright, radiant". Borne in Greek mythology; it was the title given to the Greek goddess of the moon, Artemis. The name became popular in the 18th century.

Pia
Pronunciation: PEE-ah

The name Pia is of Latin origin. The meaning of Pia is "pious". The name is a feminine form of the Latin adjective *pius*.

Pilar
Pronunciation: pee-LAR

The name Pilar is of Spanish origin. The meaning of Pilar is "pillar". From Nuestra Señora del Pilar, which means, 'Our Lady of the Pillar'? In the Catholic tradition, it is a reference to a legendary appearance of the Virgin Mary standing on a pillar at Saragossa.

Pippa
Pronunciation: PIPP-a

Pippa is of Greek origin. The meaning of the name Pipa is "lover of horses". Pippa is a diminutive of the Greek name Phillipa.

Polly

Pronunciation: PAH-lee

The name Polly is of English and Irish origin. The meaning of Polly is "star of the sea". Polly is a variant of the name Molly, which is a nickname for Mary.

Pollyanna

Pronunciation: POLL-ee-ann-a

The name Pollyanna was invented by Eleanor Porter for the heroine in her children's book, *Pollyanna* (1913).

Poppy

Pronunciation: POP-ee

The name Poppy is of Latin origin. The meaning of Poppy is unknown. From Latin *papaver*, donating a species of flower that has papery leaves.

Posy

Pronunciation: POH-see

The name Posy is of English origin. The meaning of Posy is "a bunch of flowers". Posy is also used a nickname for Josephine.

Primrose

Pronunciation: PRIM-rose

The name Primrose is of Latin origin. The meaning of Primrose is "first rose". From Latin *prima rosa*. Primrose is also a botanical name of a 19th-century yellow flower which blooms early in spring, particularly on banks and in woodlands.

Princess
Pronunciation: PRIN-sess
The name Princess if of English origin. Princess is a title name used by Royalty.

Priscilla
Pronunciation: pris-SILL-ah
Priscilla is of Latin origin. The meaning of the name Priscilla is "ancient". Priscilla is a feminine diminutive of the Roman family name Priscus. A biblical name: Priscilla was a first-century Christian missionary. The name was adopted by the Puritans. Diminutives: Cilla, Pris.

Prudence
Pronunciation: PROO-dens
The name Prudence is of Latin origin. The meaning of Prudence is "caution, discretion". The name was popular during the 16th, 17th and 19th centuries.

Prunella

Pronunciation: PRU-nell-a

The name Prunella is of Latin origin. The meaning of Prunella is "small plum".

Psyche

Pronunciation: p-sy-che

The name Psyche is of Greek origin. The meaning of Psyche is "breath, of the soul". Borne in mythology; Psyche was a mortal girl who fell in love with Cupid.

Purity

Pronunciation: PUR-it-ee

The name Purity if of Middle English origin. Purity is a virtue name.

Q

Qiturah

Pronunciation: KWIT-ur-ah

The name Qiturah is of Arabic origin. The meaning of Qiturah is "incense, scent".

Queenie

Pronunciation: KWE-nee

The name Queenie is of English origin. The meaning of Queenie is "Queen". From Old *cwen*, which means 'woman'. Queenie was a name used to by contemporaries to refer to Queen Victoria. The name was popular during the 20th century.

Quenby

Pronunciation: KWIN-bee

The name Quenby is of Old English origin. The meaning of Quenby is "Queen's settlement". Quenby is also a place name.

Querida

Pronunciation: kare-EE-sah

The name Querida is of Spanish origin. The meaning of Querida is "beloved".

Questa

Pronunciation: KWES-ta

The name Questa is of French origin. The meaning of Questa is "one who seeks".

Quiana

Pronunciation: kee-AHN-ah

The name Quiana is of American origin. The meaning of Quiana is "silky". The name is also possibly a variant of the name Hannah or Ayana.

Queta

Pronunciation: KAY-tah

The name Queta is of Spanish origin. The meaning of Queta is unknown.

Quilla

Pronunciation: KWIL-la

The name Quilla is of Middle English origin. The meaning of Quilla is "feather".

Quincey

Pronunciation: KWIN-cey

Quincey is of Old French origin. The meaning of the name Quincey is "estate of the fifth son". Adopted surname, originally a baronial name from Cuinchy in northern France. Quincey can be used as a both a girl's name, and as a boy's name.

Quinn

Pronunciation: KWIN

The name Quinn is of Irish and Gaelic origin. The meaning of Quinn is "counsel". An adopted Irish surname, from the Gaelic name O Cuinn, meaning 'decedent of Conn'. Quinn has been used a given name from very ancient times. Quinn is used as both a girl's name and as a boy's name.

Quintina

Pronunciation: KWIN-te-na

Quintina is of Latin origin. The meaning of the name Quintina is "fifth".

Quirina

Pronunciation: KW-ree-na

The name Quirina is of Latin origin. The meaning of Quirina is "Warrior".

R

Rachana

Pronunciation: ra-SHA-nah

Rachana is of Hindi origin. The meaning of the name Rachana is "creation".

Rachel

Pronunciation: RAY-cehl

The name Rachel is of Hebrew origin. The meaning of Rachel is "ewe, female sheep". A biblical name; borne in the Old Testament by the wife of Jacob, and mother of Benjamin and Joseph. She was described as being 'beautiful in form and countenance'. She died whilst giving birth to Benjamin. The name was popularised in hit TV series, *Friends* (1994-2004). Diminutives: Rach, Rae.

Radha

Pronunciation: RAD-ha

The name Radha is of Hindi and Sanskrit origin. The meaning of Radha is "success". In Hindu religion,

Radha was the name of a cowherd who became the favourite consort of Krishna.

Rae

Pronunciation: ray

The name Rae is of Hebrew origin. The meaning of Rae is "ewe, female sheep". Rae is a diminutive of the name Rachel.

Rafaela

Pronunciation: rah-fah-AY-lah

The name Rafaela is of Spanish origin. The meaning of Rafaela is "God has healed". Rafaela is a feminine form of the masculine name Raphael.

Raphaela

Pronunciation: rah-fah-AY-lah

The name Raphaela is of Spanish origin. The meaning of Raphael is "God has healed". Raphael is a feminine form of the masculine name Rephael.

Ramona

Pronunciation: ra-MOH-nah

The name Ramona is of Spanish and Old German origin. The meaning of Ramona is "protecting hands".

Ramona is a feminine form of the masculine name Roman, the Spanish form of Raymond.

Raquel

Pronunciation: rah-KELL

Raquel is of Spanish and Portuguese origin. The meaning of the name Raquel is "ewe, female sheep". Raquel is a Spanish form the name Rachel.

Rebecca

Pronunciation: ree-BEK-ah

The name Rebecca is of Hebrew origin. The meaning of Rebecca is "to bind". Rebecca is a Latin form of the Hebrew name Rebekah. The name was popularised in the 20th century, possibly due to Daphne du Maurier's novel *Rebecca* (1938). The novel was later made into a film by Alfred Hitchcock in 1940. Diminutives: Becca, Becky.

Regan

Pronunciation: REE-gan

Regan is of Gaelic origin. The meaning of the name Regan is unknown. Shakespeare used the name for one of the king's three daughters in *King Lear* (1606).

Renata

Pronunciation: REN-at-ah

The name Renata is of Latin origin. The meaning of Renata is "Reborn". Renata is a Latinate form of the name Renèe. The name was adopted by the Puritans.

Rene, Renie

Pronunciation: REN-ee

The name Rene is of Greek origin. The meaning of Rene is "peace". Rene is a diminutive of the Greek name Irene.

Rhiannon

Pronunciation: ree-ANN-on

The name Rhiannon is of Welsh origin. The meaning of Rhiannon is "goddess, great queen". Borne in mythology; by a figure in the *Mabinogian*, the collection of Welsh legends.

Rhoda

Pronunciation: ROH-da

The name Rhoda is of Greek and Latin origin. The meaning of Rhoda is "rose". From Greek *rhodon*. A biblical name; borne by a servant girl who was one of the early Christian disciples. The name was popular during the 18th and 19th centuries.

Rhona

Pronunciation: ROH-nah

Rhona is of uncertain origin. Rhona is a feminine form of the masculine name Ronald.

Rica

Pronunciation: REE-kah

The name Rica is of Old Norse origin. The meaning of Rica is "complete ruler". Rica is a diminutive of any girl's name ending –rica, such as Erica or Frederica.

Rika

Pronunciation: re-KAH

The name Rika is of Old Norse origin. The meaning of Rika is "complete ruler". Rika is a diminutive of any girl's name ending –rica, such as Erica or Frederica.

Rita

Pronunciation: REE-tah

The name Rita is of Spanish origin. The name is originally a diminutive of Margarita, the Spanish form of Margaret. The Italian Saint Rita is regarded as the patron saint of unhappy marriages and desperate cases.

Roberta

Pronunciation: roh-BER-tah

The name Roberta is of Old English and Old German origin. The meaning of Roberta is "bright fame". Roberta is a feminine form of the masculine name Robert. Diminutives: Bobbie, Bobby.

Robin

Pronunciation: RAH-bin

Robin is of English origin. The meaning of the name Robin is unknown. The name is a 20th-century adoption of a well establish boy's name for girls. Robyn is also used a nickname for males named Robert. Robyn is also the name of a red-breasted songbird.

Róisín

Pronunciation: ROE-sheen

The name Róisín is of Irish Gaelic origin. The meaning of Róisín is "little rose".

Romaine

Pronunciation: ROE-may-ne

The name Romaine is of French origin. The meaning of Romaine is "woman of Rome".

Ros

Pronunciation: ros

The name Ros is of Old German origin. The meaning of Ros is "gentle horse, horse protector". Ros is a diminutive of Rosalind, Rosamund or any name beginning with Ros-.

Rosa

Pronunciation: ROH-za

Rosa is of Latin origin. The meaning of the name Rosa is "rose". Rosa is a Latinate form of Rose.

Rosalie

Pronunciation: ROH-za-lee

The name Rosalie is of French origin. The meaning of Rosalie is "rose garden". Rosalie is a French name derived from the Latin name Rosa. Saint Rosalie was a 12th-century virgin martyr of Palermo, Sicily.

Rosalind

Pronunciation: RAH-za-lind

The name Rosalind is of Old German origin. The meaning of Rosaline is "gentle horse". Shakespeare popularised the name in *As You Like It* (1603). Rosalind was the name of the heroine. Diminutives: Ros, Roz.

Rosaline

Pronunciation: ROZ-a-lin

The name Rosaline is of French origin. The meaning of Rosaline is "gentle horse". Rosaline is a variation of the name Rosalind.

Rosamond

Pronunciation: ROH-za-mond

The name Rosamond is of Old German origin. The meaning of Rosamond is "horse protector". The name dates back to the Middle Ages.

Rosamund

Pronunciation: ROH-za-mund

The name Rosamund is of French origin. The meaning of Rosamund is "horse protector". The name was associated with the Latin *rosa mundi*, which means, 'rose of the world'. An epithet that was given to the Virgin Mary. Diminutives: Ros, Rosa, Roz.

Rosanna

Pronunciation: ROSE-an-ah

The name Rosanna is an 18th-century coinage combining the names Rose and Anna together.

Rosanne

Pronunciation: ROSE-anne

The name Rosanne is a 19th-century coinage combining the names Rose and Anne together.

Rose

Pronunciation: rohz

The name Rose is of Latin origin. The meaning of Rose is "rose". Rose is derived from Latin, *rosa*. The name denotes a shrub of the genus rosa, fragrant flowers with thorny stems. The name was introduced to Britain by the Normans in the 11th century. Diminutives: Rosie.

Rosemary

Pronunciation: ROHZ-mare-ee

The name Rosemary is of Latin origin. The meaning of Rosemary is "dew of the sea". Rosemary is also the name of a fragrant herb. Diminutives: Romey, Romy.

Rosetta

Pronunciation: ROE-set-ah

Rosetta is of Latin origin. The meaning of the name Rosetta is "rose". Rosetta is a variation of the name Rose. Originally an Italian diminutive, that dates back to the 19th century.

Rosheen

Pronunciation: ROE-she-n

The name Rosheen is of Irish Gaelic origin. The meaning of Rosheen is "little rose". Rosheen is an Anglicization of the Irish Gaelic name Roísín.

Rosie

Pronunciation: ROSE-ee

The name Rose is of Latin origin. The meaning of Rosie is "rose". Rosie is a diminutive of all names that contain the element, 'Rose'.

Rosina

Pronunciation: ROS-in-ah

The name Rosina is of Latin origin. The meaning of Rosina is "rose". Originally a Spanish diminutive, Rosina is a variation of the name Rose.

Rowan

Pronunciation: ROH-an

The name Rowan is of Gaelic origin. The meaning of Rowan is "red berry tree". Rowan is used as both a girl's name and as a boy's name.

Rowena

Pronunciation: roh-EEN-ah

The name Rowena is of Old German origin. The meaning of Rowena is "fame and happiness". Rowena is also possibly a variation of the Welsh name Rhonwen.

Roxanne
Pronunciation: roks-ANN
Roxanne is of Persian origin. The meaning of the name Roxanne is "Dawn". The name is borne by a Persian wife of Alexander the Great. Diminutive: Roxy.

Ruby
Pronunciation: ROO-bee
The name Ruby is of English origin. The meaning of Ruby is "the red gemstone". From Latin *rubus*. Ruby is the name of a precious red stone, considered by the Ancients to be an antidote to poison and a protection from the plague. Some people consider Rubies to be bad luck. Rubies are the birthstone of July.

Ruth
Pronunciation: rooth
The name Ruth is of Hebrew origin. The meaning of Ruth is "friend". A biblical name; borne in the Old Testament by the loyal wife of Boaz. Ruth was the young Moabite widow and daughter-in-law of Naomi.

The name was popular during the 17th century.
Diminutives: Ruthi, Ruthie.

S

Sabrina

Pronunciation: sa-BREE-nah

Sabrina is of Celtic origin. The meaning of Sabrina is unknown. Sabrina is a Roman name for the River Severn. Borne in mythology; the name of the illegitimate daughter of King Locrine of Wales. She was drowned in the river Severn by her father's ex-wife, Gwendolen. The Old Man of the Sea took pity on her and turned her into a river goddess.

Sadie

Pronunciation: SAY-dee

The name Sadie is of Hebrew origin. The meaning of Sadie is "Princess". Sadie is a diminutive for Sarah and Mercedes. The name was first used as a first name at the beginning of the 20th century.

Saffron

Pronunciation: SAFF-ron

Saffron is of Arabic origin. Derived from Arabic
zafaran. Saffron is the most expensive of all spices.
Saffron is also a bright orange/yellow colour dye.

Sally

Pronunciation: SAL-ee

The name Sally is of Hebrew origin. The meaning of
Sally is "Princess". Sally is a diminutive of Sarah, often
used in its own right. The name was popular in the 18th
and 20th centuries. Diminutives: Sal.

Samantha

Pronunciation: sa-MAN-thah

The name Samantha is of English origin. The meaning
of Samantha is "listen, God heard". American Actress
Samantha Eggar popularised the name during the
1960's with the hit TV show, *Bewitched*.

Sanchia

Pronunciation: san-CHIA

The name Sanchia is of Spanish origin. The meaning of
Sanchia is "holy, sacred". Sanchia is a variant of the
Latin name Sancia. The name was introduced into
Britain during the 13th century.

Sandie, Sandy

Pronunciation: SAN-dee

Sandy is of uncertain origin. The meaning of the name Sandy is "man's defender". Diminutives of Alexandra, Cassandra and Sandra.

Sandra

Pronunciation: SAN-drah

The name Sandra is of English origin. The meaning of Sandra is "man's defender". Sandra is a variation of the Alexandra, via the Italian form, Alessandra.

Saorise

Pronunciation: seer-sha

The name Saorise is of Irish Gaelic origin. The meaning of Saorise is "freedom".

Sapphire

Pronunciation: SAFF-ire

The name Sapphire is of English origin. From Old French *safir*, derived from Greek *sappheiros*. Sapphire is a jewel name and the birthstone for September. A Sapphire is a transparent blue precious stone.

Sara, Sarah

Pronunciation: SARE-ah

The name Sarah is of Hebrew origin. The meaning of Sarah is "Princess". A biblical name; borne by the wife of Abraham and mother of Isaac, whom she conceived when she was 90 years old. Originally called Sarai, she was given the name Sarah at God's command. Sarah lived an adventurous and nomadic life. She was described as being exceptionally beautiful. The name became popular in the 16th century.

Sarina

Pronunciation: sa-REE-nah

The name Sarina is of Latin origin. The meaning of Sarina is "Princess". Sarina is a variant of the Hebrew name Sarah.

Sarita

Pronunciation: sa-RE-ta

The name Sarita is of Hebrew origin. The meaning of Sarita is "Princess". Sarita is a variant of the Hebrew name Sarah.

Sasha

Pronunciation: SAH-shah

Sasha is of Greek and Russian origin. The meaning of the name Sasha is "man's defender". Sasha is a Russian diminutive of the name Alexandra. Sasha is used as both a girl's name and as a boy's name.

Saskia

Pronunciation: SAS-kee-a

Saskia is of Danish and Old German origin. The meaning of the name Saskia is "the Saxon people". Saskia was the name of the wife of the Dutch painter, Rembrandt (17th century).

Scarlett

Pronunciation: SCAR-let

The name Scarlett is of Old French origin. The meaning of Scarlett is "red". An adopted surname derived originally from Old French *escarlate*, which means 'scarlet cloth'. Margaret Mitchell popularised the name in her epic novel, *Gone With The Wind* (1936). Scarlett O' Hara was the name of the heroine.

Selena, Selina

Pronunciation: sa-LEEN-ah

The name Selina is of uncertain origin. The meaning of Selina is "the moon". The name was first used in Britain during the Middles Ages.

Selma

Pronunciation: SEL-mah

The name Selma is of Old German and Arabic origin. The meaning of Selma is "safe, peace".

Serena

Pronunciation: ser-REE-nah

Serena is of Latin origin. The meaning of the name Serena is "calm, serene". From Latin *serenus,* meaning 'calm'. Borne by a Christian saint.

Shannon

Pronunciation: SHAN-en

Shannon is of Gaelic origin. The meaning of the name Shannon is "old". Originally an adopted surname, derived from Ireland's principal river.

Sharon

Pronunciation: SHARE-en

The name Sharon is of Hebrew origin. The meaning of Sharon is "a fertile plain". A biblical place name, from the plain of Sharon in the Holy Land. The name was adopted by the Puritans.

Sheba

Pronunciation: SHEE-bah

The name Sheba is of Hebrew origin. The meaning of Sheba is "promise". Sheba is a diminutive of Bathsheba, which is associated with the Queen of Sheba. She visited Solomon in search of information about his God. Balkis, Queen of Sheba, also appears in the Koran. Sheba is the name of a kingdom in southern Arabia noted for its great wealth.

Sheila
Pronunciation: SHEE-lah
The name Sheila is of Irish and Gaelic origin. The meaning of Sheila is "blind". Sheila is an anglicised form of the Irish Gaelic name, Síle.

Shelley
Pronunciation: SHEL-ee
The name Shelley is of Old English origin. The meaning of Shelley is "sloped meadow". An adopted surname and place name from Old English, meaning 'wood on a slope'. Shelley is also used a nickname for Michelle, Rochelle and Shirley. Shelley is used as both a girl's name and as a boy's name.

Sheridan
Pronunciation: SHARE-a-den

The name Sheridan is of Irish and Gaelic origin. The meaning of Sheridan is "seeker". An adopted Irish surname, from O Sirideain. The name was popularised by Irish playwright Richard Brinsley Sheridan (1751-1861). The name is used as both a boy's name and as a girl's name.

Sherry
Pronunciation: SHARE-ee
The name Sherry is of English origin. The meaning of Sherry is "darling, dear". From French chèrie. The name is also a short form of the Hebrew name Sharon.

Shona
Pronunciation: SH-o-na
The name Shona is of Gaelic and Hebrew origin. The meaning of Shona is "God is gracious". Shona is a Gaelic feminine form of the name John.

Sian
Pronunciation: shaahn
The name Sian is of Welsh origin. The meaning of Sian is "God's grace". Sian is a Welsh variant of the name Jane.

Siena

Pronunciation: see-EN-ah

Siena is of Latin origin. The meaning of the name Siena is "from Siena". Originally a place name of the city, Siena in Italy. Siena is also the name of reddish shade of brown.

Sidney, Sydney

Pronunciation: SID-nee

Sidney is of Old English origin. The meaning of the name Sidney is "wide meadow". Sidney is an adopted surname and place name. The name has been used as a first name since the 17th century. Charles Dickens boosted the popularity of the name when he used it for his hero in *A Tale Of Two Cities* (1859). Australian city of Sydney was named in honour of Thomas Townshend. The name is used as both a boy's name and as a girl's name.

Silvia

Pronunciation: SIL-vee-ah

The name Silvia is of Latin origin. The meaning of Silvia is "wood, forest". From the Latin name Silvius. Shakespeare used the name in *The Two Gentlemen of Verona* (1594).

Simone

Pronunciation: sih-MOHN

The name Simone is of Hebrew origin. The meaning of Simone is "hear, listen". Simone is a feminine form of the masculine name Simon. Simone is used as both a girl's name and as a boy's name.

Sinèad

Pronunciation: sha-NADE

The name Sinèad is of Irish Gaelic origin. The meaning of Sinèad is "God is gracious". Sinèad is an Irish Gaelic form of the name Janet.

Siobhan

Pronunciation: sha-VAHN

The name Siobhan is of Irish Gaelic and Hebrew origin. The meaning of Siobhan is "God is gracious". Siobhan is an Irish Gaelic form of the name Joan.

Sky, Skye

Pronunciation: sky

The name Sky is of English origin. Sky is one of several nature names that became popular when nature names were made fashionable during 1960's. Skye is associated to the Isle of Skye in Scotland. Sky is used as both a girl's name and as a boy's name.

Skyler

Pronunciation: SKY-ler

Skyler is of Dutch origin. The meaning of the name Skyler is "fugitive".

Sonia

Pronunciation: SOHN-yah

The name Sonia is of Greek origin. The meaning of Sonia is "wisdom". Sonia is a Russian variation of the name Sophia. Stephen McKenna popularised the name with his novel, *Sonia* (1917).

Sonja

Pronunciation: SON-ja

The name Sonja is of Greek origin. The meaning of Sonja is "wisdom". Sonja is a Russian variation of the name Sophia.

Sophia

Pronunciation: so-FEE-ah

Sophia is of Greek origin. The meaning of the name Sophia is "wisdom". The name was introduced to Britain in the 17th century by the granddaughter of James I.

Sorcha

Pronunciation: SAW-kha

The name Sorcha is of Irish and Gaelic origin. The meaning of Sorcha is "bright".

Sorrel

Pronunciation: s(or)-rell

The name Sorrel is of Old French and Old German origin. The meaning of Sorrel is "sour". From the Old French plant name, *surele*, derived from *sur*, which means 'sour'. This refers to the acid taste of its leaves.

Stacey, Stacie, Stacy

Pronunciation: ST-aa-cee

The name Stacey is of Greek origin. The meaning of Stacey is "Resurrection". Stacey is a diminutive of the Greek name Anastasia, and of the name Eustacia.

Stella

Pronunciation: STELL-ah

The name Stella is of Latin origin. The meaning of Stella is "star".

Stephanie

Pronunciation: STEFF-a-nee

The name Stephanie is of Greek origin. The meaning of Stephanie is "garland, crown". Stephanie is a feminine form of the masculine name Stephan. Diminutives: Steff, Steffi, Steffie, Steph, Stephie.

Stevie
Pronunciation: STE-vie
The name Stevie is of Greek origin. The meaning of Stevie is "garland, crown". The name is originally a diminutive of Stephen. The name is used as both a girl's and as a boy's name.

Summer
Pronunciation: SUH-mer
The name Summer is of Old English origin. Summer is one of several names derived from nature. The name was popularised during the 1960's when nature names became fashionable.

Susanna, Susannah, Suzanna
Pronunciation: SU-zan-ah
The name Suzanna is of Hebrew origin. The meaning of Suzanna is "lily". From the Hebrew name Shushannah.

T

Tabitha

Pronunciation: TAB-i-thah

The name Tabitha is of Aramaic origin. The meaning of Tabitha is "gazelle". A biblical name; borne by a New Testament figure, the Aramaic name of Dorcas. She was a kind woman noted for her good work, who was resurrected by St Peter.

Tacy

Pronunciation: TAY-cee

The name Tacy is of Latin origin. The meaning of Tacy is "silence". The name may possibly a short form of Anastasia.

Taffy

Pronunciation: TAFF-ee

The name Taffy is of Welsh origin. The meaning of Taffy is "loved one".

Tahira

Pronunciation: TA-hi-ra

Tahira is of Arabic origin. The meaning of the name Tahira is "virginal, pure".

Taima

Pronunciation: ta(i)-MAH

The name Taima is of Native American Indian origin. The meaning of Taima is "pearl of thunder".

Talia

Pronunciation: TAL-yah

The name Talia is of Hebrew and Aramaic origin. The meaning of Talia is "heaven's dew". The name is a variant of Taliah. Talia is also a short form of the name Natalia.

Tallulah

Pronunciation: TAL-oo-lah

The name Tallulah is of Native American Indian origin. The meaning of Tallulah is "running water, leaping water". The Choctaws lived near the Tallulah waterfall.

Tamara

Pronunciation: TAM-a-rah

Tamara is of Hebrew origin. The meaning of the name Tamara is "date palm". The name is a Russian variant of Tamar, borne by a 12th-century Queen of Georgia. Diminutives: Tammie, Tammy.

Tamsin

Pronunciation: TAM-sin

The name Tamsin is of English origin. The meaning of Tamsin is unknown. Tamsin is a short form of the Aramaic name Thomsaina, the feminine form of Thomas. The name dates back to the Middle Ages.

Tania, Tanya

Pronunciation: THAN-ya

The name Tania is of Russian origin. The meaning of Tania is unknown. Tania is a Russian diminutive of Tatiana.

Tansy

Pronunciation: TAN-see

The name Tansy is of Greek origin. The meaning of Tansy is "eternal life". From old French *tanesie*, derived from Greek *anthanasi*, which means 'immortal'. Tansy is also the name of a bitter tasting, aromatic herb. The name was adopted as a first name in the 1960's.

Tara

Pronunciation: TAH-rah

Tara is of Gaelic and Sanskrit origin. The meaning of the name Tara is "hill, star". Ancient Tara is the name of a place in County Meath, 'stone of destiny' where Irish kings resided. The name was popularised by the Hollywood film, *Gone with the Wind* (1939). Tara is the name of Scarlett O'Hara's family estate. Borne in Hindu mythology; Tara is one of the names of the wife of Shiva. In Mahayana Buddhism, Tara is the name of the wife of Buddha.

Tatiana

Pronunciation: tat-YAH-nah

Tatiana is of Latin and Russian origin. The meaning of the name Tatiana is "of the family of Tatius". From the feminine for of the Latin name Tatianus. Tatiana is also the name of a 3rd-century saint.

Tegan

Pronunciation: TEA-gan

The name Tegan is of Welsh origin. The meaning of Tegan is "beautiful".

Teresa

Pronunciation: ter-REE-sah

The name Teresa is of Greek origin. The meaning of Teresa is "late summer". The first bearers of the name might possibly have been from the Greek island of Therasia. The name is popular among Roman Catholic saints. Saint Thèrese of Lisieux (1873-97) was a young Carmelite nun who wrote her autobiography whilst she lay dying of tuberculosis. Mother Teresa founded an order of nuns, the Missionaries of Charity, whose sisters help people in need around the world. Mother Teresa's hard work earned her the title, 'the saint of the gutters'.

Theresa

Pronunciation: ter-REE-sah

The name Theresa is of Greek origin. The meaning of Theresa is "late summer". The first bearers of the name might possibly have been from the Greek island of Therasia. The name is popular among Roman Catholic saints.

Tess

Pronunciation: TESS

The name Tess is of Greek origin. The meaning of Tess is "late summer". Tess is diminutive of Teresa and Theresa, the name became popular in its own right.

Tomas Hardy popularised the name with his famous novel, *Tess of the d'Ubervilles* (1891).

Tessa
Pronunciation: TESS-ah
Tessa is of English origin. The meaning of the name Tessa is "fourth child".
Tessa is diminutive of Teresa and Theresa, the name became popular in its own right.

Thea
Pronunciation: THEE-ah
Thea is of Greek origin. The meaning of the name Thea is "goddess". Thea is a short form of Althea, Mathea and Dorothea.

Theodora
Pronunciation: thee-a-DOR-ah
The name Theodora is of Greek origin. The meaning of Theodora is "God's gift". Theodora is a feminine form of the masculine name Theodore.

Tiana
Pronunciation: tee-AHN-ah

Tiana is of Latin and Russian origin. The meaning of the name Tiana is 'of the family of Tatius'. Tiana is a diminutive of Tatiana.

Tiffany

Pronunciation: TIF-a-nee

The name Tiffany is of Greek origin. The meaning of Tiffany is "revelation of God.". Tiffany is variant of the Greek name Theophania. The name refers to manifestations of God, particularly Epiphany. In many Christian countries, females who are born on 6th January (the Feast of Epiphany) are given some form of this name. The name was made popular by the New York jeweler, Tiffany & Co.

Tilda

Pronunciation: TIL-da

The name Tilda is German origin. The meaning of Tilda is "mighty in battle". Tidla is a diminutive of the Old German name Matilda.

Tilly

Pronunciation: TILL-ee

The name Tilly is German origin. The meaning of Tilly is "mighty in battle". Tilly is a diminutive of the Old

German name Matilda. Tilda is also a variant of the name Tilda.

Tina
Pronunciation: TEE-nah
The name Tina is of Latin origin. The meaning of Tina is "follower of Christ". Originally a diminutive for Christiana, the name is now used in its own right.

Toni
Pronunciation: TOH-nee
The name Toni is of English origin. The meaning of Toni is unknown. Toni is a diminutive of Antonia, Antonina and Antoinette.

Tonia, Tonya
Pronunciation: TOHN-yah
The name Tonia is of French origin. The meaning of Tonia is unknown. Tonia is French feminine diminutive of the name Antoine.

Tracie, Tracy, Tracey
Pronunciation: T-race-ee
The name Tracie is of Greek origin. The meaning of Tracie is "late summer". Variations of Teresa. The

name was popularised by the character of Tracey Lord in the film *The Philadelphia Story* (1940).

Trina

Pronunciation: TREEN-nah

Trina is of Scandinavian origin. The meaning of the name Trina is "pure". Trina is diminutive for the Greek name Katrina.

Trinity

Pronunciation: TRIN-ee-tee

The name Trinity is of Latin origin. The meaning of Trinity is "triad". The name refers to the Holy Trinity in Christian faith.

Trista

Pronunciation: TRISS-tah

Trista is of English origin. The meaning of the name Trista is "tryst". Trista is a feminine form of the masculine name Tristan.

Tristana

Pronunciation: TRIST-an-ah

The name Tristana is of Welsh origin. The meaning of Tristana is "tryst". Tristana is a feminine form of the masculine name Tristan.

Trixie

Pronunciation: TRIKS-ee

The name Trixie is of English origin. The meaning of Trixie is "blessed, voyager". Trixie is a diminutive of Beatrix.

Troy

Pronunciation: TR-oy

The name Troy is of Irish and Gaelic origin. The meaning of Troy is "descendant of the footsoldier". An adopted surname that was given to those who migrated to England from Troyes in France, after the Norman conquest of 1066. Troy is also associated with the ancient city In Asia Minor where the Trojan wars were fought. The name is used as both a boy's name and as a girl's name.

Trudi, Trudie, Trudy

Pronunciation: TROO-dee

The name Trudi of Old German origin. The meaning of the name Trudi is "strength, strong spear". The name is frequently used as a nickname for people called Gertrude, Hiltrud and Ermintrude.

Tryphena

Pronunciation: T-ryphe-na

The name Tryphena is of Greek origin. The meaning of Tryphena is "delicacy". A biblical name; Tryphena appears in one of Paul's epistles to the Romans.

Tuesday
Pronunciation: TUES-day
The name Tuesday is of Old English origin. Tuesday is a day of the week. The name was popularised by the hit TV series and Hollywood film *The Addams Family*. Tuesday Addams was the daughter of Mortica and Gomez Addams.

Tulia
Pronunciation: TU-lee-a
Tulia is of Spanish and Latin origin. The meaning of the name Tulia is unknown. Derived from an ancient Roman family name, *Tullius*.

Tyler
Pronunciation: TYE-ler
The name Tyler is of English origin. The meaning of Tyler is "a worker in roof tiles". Originally an occupational name. Tyler is used as both a girl's name and as a boy's name.

Tyra

Pronunciation: TEER-ah

The name Tyra is of Old English origin. The meaning of Tyra is "Thor's battle". The name was made famous by supermodel Tyra Banks.

U

Uberta

Pronunciation: OO-ber-TA

The name Uberta is of Italian origin. The meaning of Uberta is "shining intellect". Uberta is variant of the Old German name Huberta.

Udele

Pronunciation: OO-del-e

The name Udele is of Old English origin. The meaning of Udele is "wealthy".

Ula

Pronunciation: oo-LA

Ula is of Celtic and Hawaiian origin. The meaning of the name Ula is "gem of the sea, wealthy".

Ulani

Pronunciation: uwl-an-EE

The name Ulani is of Hawaiian origin. The meaning of Ulani is "cheerful".

Ulima

Pronunciation: uwl-li-MA

The name Ulima is of Arabic origin. The meaning of Ulima is "wise".

Ulla

Pronunciation: uwl-LA

The name Ulla is of Old Norse origin. The meaning of Ulla is "will, determination".

Ulrica

Pronunciation: uwl-REE-kah

The name Ulrica is of Old German origin. The meaning of Ulrica is "power of the wolf". The name is a feminine form of Ulric.

Ultima

Pronunciation: uwl-ti-MA

The name Ultima is of Latin origin. The meaning of Ultima is "farthest point".

Ulva

Pronunciation: uwl-VA

The name Ulva is of Old German origin. The meaning of Ulva is "Wolf".

Ulyssa

Pronunciation: yoo-LISS-ah

The name Ulyssa is of Latin origin. The meaning of Ulyssa is unknown. The name is a feminine form of the masculine name Ulysses.

Uma

Pronunciation: OO-mah

The name Uma is of Hindi and Sanskrit origin. The meaning of Uma is "flax, turmeric". Borne by the goddess what mediates between Brahma and the other gods. Uma is also a byname for the Indian goddess Sakti, wife of Shiva. The Hebrew meaning of the name Uma is "nation".

Una

Pronunciation: OO-nah

Una is of Latin origin. The meaning of Una is "one". Anglicised form of the Irish Gaelic name, Ūna. The name was borne in Irish legend by the mother of Conn Cètchathach.

Udine

Pronunciation: un-DEE-ne

The name Udine if of Latin origin. The meaning of Udine is "little wave". Borne in mythology, Udine is the name of the spirit of the waters.

Unique
Pronunciation: yoo-NEEK
Unique is of Latin origin. The meaning of the name Unique is "only on".

Unity
Pronunciation: yoo-ni-TEE
The name Unity is of Middle English origin. The meaning of Unity is "oneness". The name was used by the Puritans.

Urania
Pronunciation: yoo-ran-IA
The name Urania is of Greek origin. The meaning of Urania is "heavenly". Borne in Greek mythology; Urania was the eldest of Zeus' and Mnemosyne's nine daughters. Zeus and Mnemosyne slept together for nine consecutive nights and birthed nine Muses, Urania was one of them. Urania was in charge of astronomy, she is often associated with universal love and the Holy Spirit. Urania inherited Zeus' majesty

and power, and the beauty and grace of her
Mnemosyne.

Urbana

Pronunciation: ur-BAN-a

The name Urbana is of Latin origin. The meaning of
Urbana is "of the city". The name is a feminine form of
Urban.

Uriela

Pronunciation: YOO-rie-la

The name Uriela is of Hebrew origin. The meaning of
Uriela is "God's light".

Urit

Pronunciation: YOO-rit

The name Urit is of Hebrew origin. The meaning of
Urit is "brightness".

Ursula

Pronunciation: UR-soo-lah

The name Ursula is of Latin and Scandinavian origin.
The meaning of Ursula is "little bear". Several legends
claim that Saint Ursula was a 4th-century British
princess who went on pilgrimage to Rome with her
maiden companions, they were all massacred by the

Huns at Cologne. Disney made the name famous in their film, *The Little Mermaid (1989)*. Ursula is the name of the evil octopus.

Usha

Pronunciation: oo-shah

The name Usha is of Hindi and Sanskrit origin. The meaning of Usha is "Dawn". Borne in mythology, Usha was the daughter of heaven and the sister of night.

V

Val

Pronunciation: VAL

The name Val is a diminutive of Valda, Valentina, Valerie, or Valma.

Valda

Pronunciation: VAL-da

The name Valda is of Old German origin. The meaning of Valda is "renowned ruler". Valda is a feminine form of the name Waldemar.

Valen

Pronunciation: VA-len

Valen is a variant of the Latin name Valentine. The meaning of the name is "strong", "healthy". Valen is used as a both a boy's name and a girl's name.

Valencia

Pronunciation: vah-LEN-cee-ah

The name Valencia is of Latin origin. The meaning of Valencia is "strong". The name is a feminine form of Valentinus.

Valentina

Pronunciation: val-en-TEE-nah

The name Valentina is of Latin origin. The meaning of Valentina is "strong". The name is a feminine form of Valentine.

Valeria

Pronunciation: val-ER-e-a

Valeria is of Latin origin. The meaning of the name Valeria is "to be healthy". Valeria is a variant of the Latin name Valerie.

Valerie

Pronunciation: VAL-er-ee

The name Valerie is of Latin origin. The meaning of Valerie is "strong, healthy". The name is a French form of the Latin name Valeria. Valerie is a feminine form of Valerius, a Roman family clan name. The name was borne by a 3rd-century saint.

Valeska

Pronunciation: VAL-esk-a

The name Valeska is of Slavic origin. The meaning of Valeska is "splendid leader". The name is a feminine form of Vladislav.

Valkyrie

Pronunciation: VALK-y-ree

The name Valkyrie is of Scandinavian origin. The meaning of Valkyrie is unknown. Borne in mythology; Valkyrie was an attendant of Odin.

Valley

Pronunciation: VAL-ee

The name Valley is of a diminutive of Valerie. Valley is also a geography name, for a low spot in a landscape.

Vallombrosa

Pronunciation: VALL-om-bros-a

The name Vallombrosa is of Italian origin. The meaning of Vallombrosa is "shady valley". Vallombrosa is also a place name of a forest resort near Florence, Italy.

Valonia

Pronunciation: VAL-o-ne-a

The name Valonia is of Latin origin. The meaning of Valonia is "shallow valley". Valonia is also a place name.

Valora

Pronunciation: VAL-o-ra

The name Valora is of Latin origin. The meaning of Valora is "brave, courageous".

Vanda

Pronunciation: VAN-da

Vanda is of Italian and Czechoslovakian origin. The meaning of the name Vanda is "the tribe of vandals". The name became popular in the 20th century.

Vanessa

Pronunciation: va-NESS-ah

The name Vanessa is of Greek origin. The meaning of Vanessa is "Butterfly". The name was invented by the author Jonathan Swift (1667-1745) for his friend Esther Vanhomrigh for *Gulliver's Travels*. He combined the first syllable of her Dutch surname name with Essa.

Vania

Pronunciation: VAHN-yah

Vania is of Latin origin. The meaning of the name Vania is "brings good news". The name is a variant of Ivana.

Vanita

Pronunciation: va-NEE-tah

The name Vanita is of Hindi origin. The meaning of Vanita is "woman".

Vanity

Pronunciation: VAN-ih-tee

The name Vanity is of French origin. The meaning of Vanity is "inflated in pride".

Vanna

Pronunciation: VAN-ah

The name Vanna is of Cambodian origin. The meaning of Vanna is "golden". Vanna is the feminine form of the name John.

Vanora

Pronunciation: VAHN-or-a

The name Vanora is of Old Welsh origin. The meaning of Vanora is "white wave".

Varda

Pronunciation: VAR-da

The name Varda is of Hebrew origin. The meaning of
Varda is "rose".

Vashti

Pronunciation: VA-sh-tee

The name Vashti is of Persian origin. The meaning of
Vashti is "beautiful". A biblical name; Vashti was the
wife of King Ahasuerus of Persia. The king replaced his
wife with Esther after she refused to display her beauty
before his guests.

Vasilia

Pronunciation: VAS-il-a

The name Vasilia is of unknown origin. The meaning
of Vasilia is "royal, kingly". Vasilia is a feminine form
of the Greek name Basil.

Veda

Pronunciation: VEE-da

Veda is of Sanskrit origin. The meaning of the name
Veda is "knowledge". The Vedas are the four sacred
books of the Hindus.

Vedette

Pronunciation: VEE-dett

The name Vedette is of Italian origin. The meaning of Vedette is "sentry".

Vega

Pronunciation: VEE-ga

The name Vega is of Arabic origin. The meaning of Vega is "falling venture". Vega is also the name of the brightest star in the group of stars named, Lyra.

Velika

Pronunciation: VEL-ee-ka

The name Velika is of Slavic origin. The meaning of Velika is "great".

Velma

Pronunciation: VEL-ma

Velma is of English origin. The meaning of the name Velma is "determined protector". Velma is possibly a variant of the name Selma.

Velvet

Pronunciation: VEL-vet

The name Velvet is of English origin. The meaning of Velvet is unknown. Velvet is also the name of a soft fabric, which is associated with luxury.

Venerada
Pronunciation: VEN-er-ada
The name Venerada is of Spanish origin. The meaning of Venerada is "venerated".

Venetia
Pronunciation: ve-NEE-shah
The name Venetia is of Latin origin. The meaning of Venetia is "city of canals". From the Latin name for the city of Venice in Northern Italy. Venetia is also associated with the Roman goddess of love and fertility, Venus.

Venus
Pronunciation: VEE-nus
The name Venus is of Latin origin. The meaning of Venus is "love, fertility". Borne in Roman mythology; Venus is the Roman goddess of love and fertility.

Vera
Pronunciation: VEER-ah

Vera is of Russian and Slavic origin. The meaning of the name Vera is "faith". The name is often used as a nickname for Veronica and Guinevere.

Verbena

Pronunciation: VERB-en-a

The name Verbena is of Latin origin. The meaning of Verbena is "holy plants". The name was originally used to refer to the olive and myrtle plants, which had spiritual significance to the Romans.

Verena

Pronunciation: VER-ee-na

Verena is of Latin origin. The meaning of the name Verena is "true".

Verity

Pronunciation: VARE-i-tee

The name Verity is of Latin origin. The meaning of Verity is "truth". From the Latin word *veritas*. The name was adopted by the Puritans.

Verona

Pronunciation: VER-o-na

The name Verona is a short form of Veronica. The origin of the name is disputed. Verona is also the name of a northern Italian city.

Veronica
Pronunciation: ver-RON-ni-kah
Veronica is of Latin origin. The meaning of the name Veronica is "true image". From Latin *vera icon*. Saint Veronica was an Italian mystic. According to legend, St Veronica wiped the face of Jesus on his way to the cross. A 'true image' of Christ's face was left on the cloth. The name is a Latin form of the Greek name Berenice. The name was first used in Britain in the 17th century, the name was popular with Catholic families. Diminutives: Ronnie, Vero.

Veronique
Pronunciation: VER-on-i-k
The name Veronique is of French origin. The meaning of Veronique is "victory bringer". The name is a French form of Veronica.

Victoria
Pronunciation: vit-TOR-ee-ah
Victoria is of Latin origin. The meaning of the name Victoria is "victory". Victoria is a feminine form of

Latin *victorius*. Borne in mythology; Victoria was a goddess who smiled on the people of ancient Rome for centuries. The name was adopted by early Christians. The name has been associated with Royalty after Queen Victoria (1819-1901) was given the name by her German mother. Diminutives: Vic, Vicki, Vickie, Vicky, Vikki, Vita, Tori, Toria, Tory.

Viola

Pronunciation: VI-o-la

The name Viola is of Latin origin. The meaning of Viola is "violet". Viola is a variant of the Latin name Violet. The name was used by Shakespeare in *Twelfth Night* (1602).

Violet

Pronunciation: VYE-a-let

The name Violet is of Latin origin. The meaning of Violet is "purple". From Latin *viola*. Violet is the name of a low growing plant with purple or white flowers. The name became popular in the 19th century when flower names became fashionable.

Violetta

Pronunciation: VYE-el-et-a

The name Violetta is a variant of the Latin name
Violet. The meaning of Violetta is "purple".

Vivian
Pronunciation: VIV-ian
The name Vivian is of Latin origin. Old French form of
the Latin name Vivianus, from *vivus* which means
"alive", "lively". The meaning of the name Vivian is
"full of life" Vivian is used as both a boy's name and as
a girl's name.

Vivien
Pronunciation: VIV-e-en
Vivien is of Latin origin. The meaning of the name
Vivien is "alive, lively". From the Roman family name
Vivianus. Borne in Arthurian legend; Vivien was the
Lady of the Lake and the mistress of Merlin. She stole
Lancelot when he was a child and raised him herself.

W

Wallis

Pronunciation: WAL-is

The name Wallis if of Old English origin. The meaning of Wallis is "from Wales". Wallis is a variant of the name Wallace. The Duchess of Windsor, Wallis Simpson popularised the name.

Wanda

Pronunciation: WAHN-dah

The name Wanda is of Slavic origin. The meaning of Wanda is "the tribe of the Vandals". An ancient Slavonic tribe named *The Vandals,* were well known for their destructive behavior, which led to the modern term 'vandalism'. The name Wanda was popularised in Ouida's novel, *Wanda* (1883).

Wanetta

Pronunciation: WAN-ett-a

The name Wanetta is of Old English origin. The meaning of Wanetta is "pale-skinned".

Warda

Pronunciation: WAR-da

The name Warda is of Old German origin. The meaning of Warda is "Guardian".

Wava

Pronunciation: WAY-vah

The name Wava is of Slavic origin. The meaning of Wava is "stranger". Wave is a Russian form of the name Barbara.

Waverly

Pronunciation: WAY-ver-lee

The name Waverly is of Old English origin. The meaning of Waverly is "meadow of quivering aspens". Waverly is also a place name.

Wendell

Pronunciation: WEN-dell

The name Wendell is of Old German origin. The meaning of Wendell is "wanderer".

Wendy

Pronunciation: WEN-dee

Wendy is of English origin. The meaning of the name Wendy is "friend". The name was created by J M

Barrie for the heroine of *Peter Pan* (1904). Wendy was a nickname which was given to him by a friend's daughter.

Weslee
Pronunciation: WEZ-lee
The name Weslee is of Old English origin. The meaning of Weslee is "western meadow". Weslee is a feminine form of the name Wesley.

Whitley
Pronunciation: WHIT-lee
The name Whitley is of Old English origin. The meaning of Whitley is "white meadow". Whitley is also a place name.

Whitney
Pronunciation: WHIT-nee
Whitney is of Old English origin. The meaning of the name Whitney is "white island". Whitney is also a place name. Originally used as a boy's name, Whitney became a popular first name for females in the early 1980's.

Wilda
Pronunciation: WIL-da

The name Wilda is of Old English and Old German origin. The meaning of Wilda is "untamed".

Wilhelmina
Pronunciation: WIL-ah-men-ah
The name Wilhelmina is of Old German origin. The Meaning of Wilhelmina is "determined protector".

Willa
Pronunciation: WIL-ah
The name Willa is of Old German origin. The meaning of Willa is "determined protector". Willa is a feminine form of the name William.

Willow
Pronunciation: WIL-oh
The name Willow is of English origin. The meaning of Willow is "grace". Willow is the name of a species of tree, known for its grace.

Wilma
Pronunciation: WIL-ma
The name Wilma is of Old German origin. The meaning of Wilma is "determined protector". Wilma is a short form of the name Wilhelmina. The name became famous with Hanna-Barbera's cartoon serious,

The Flintstones. Wilma Flintstone was a Stone Age housewife.

Wilona

Pronunciation: WIL-oo-na

The name Wilona is of Old English origin. The meaning of Wilona is "longed for".

Winifred

Pronunciation: WIN-a-fred

The name Winifred is of Old English and Welsh origin. The meaning of Winifred is "blessed, peace". Borne by a martyred Welsh Princess, Winifred was traditionally known as the patron saint of virgins.

Winona

Pronunciation: wyw-NOH-nah

The name Winona is of Native American Indian origin. The meaning of Winona is "eldest daughter". From Sioux Indian. The name was made famous by Hollywood actress Winona Ryder.

Winsome

Pronunciation: WIN-sum

The name Winsome is of Old English origin. The meaning Winsome is "agreeable".

Winter

Pronunciation: WIN-ter

The name Winter is of Old English origin. The meaning of Winter is unknown. Winter is also the name of one of the four seasons, Spring, Summer, Autumn, Winter.

Wren

Pronunciation: WREN

The name Wren is of Old English origin. The meaning of Wren is unknown. Wren is also the name of a small brown songbird.

Wyanet

Pronunciation: WHY-an-et

The name Wyanet is of Native American Indian origin. The meaning of Wyanet is "beautiful".

Wyetta

Pronunciation: WHY-ett-a

The name Wyetta is of Old English origin. The meaning of Wyetta is "war strength". Wyetta is a feminine form of the Old English name Wyatt.

Wynne

Pronunciation: WYN-ee

The name Wynne comes from the Welsh word, *gwen*, which means "fair, holy, blessed, white". The meaning of the name Wynne is "friend". Wynne is also a variant of the name Wynn. Wynne is used as both a girl's name and as a boy's name.

Wyome
Pronunciation: WY-o-me
The name Wyome is of Native American Indian origin. The meaning of Wyome is "wide plain".

X

Xanthe

Pronunciation: ZAN-thah

The name Xanthe is of Greek origin. The meaning of Xanthe is "yellow, blonde". From Greek *xanthos.*

Xaviera

Pronunciation: zay-vee-HER-ah

The name Xaviera is of Arabic and Basque origin. The meaning of Xaviera is "bright, splendid". The name is a feminine form of the masculine name, Xavier.

Xeni

Pronunciation: SHEH-nee

The name Xeni is of Guatemalan origin. The meaning of Xeni is "protector of plants". Derived from the name Xeniflóres.

Xenia

Pronunciation: ZAYN-yah

The name Xenia is of Greek origin. The meaning of Xenia is "hospitable".

Xylia

Pronunciation: ZYE-lee-ah

The name Xylia is of Greek origin. The meaning of Xylia is "woodland".

Y

Yaffa
Pronunciation: YA-ffa
The name Yaffa is of Hebrew origin. The meaning of Yaffa is "lovely".

Yakira
Pronunciation: ya-KEE-ra
The name Yakira is of Hebrew origin. The meaning of Yakira is "precious".

Yalena
Pronunciation: yal-EE-na
The name Yalena is of Greek and Russian origin. The meaning of Yalena is "sun ray". Yalena is a variant of the name Helen.

Yaminah
Pronunciation: yah-mi-NAH
The name Yaminah is of Arabic origin. The meaning of Yaminah is "suitable".

Yannick

Pronunciation: YANN-ick

Yannick if of French and Hebrew origin. The meaning of the name Yannick is "God is gracious". The name is used as both a boy's name and as a girl's name. Yannick is variant of the name John.

Yara

Pronunciation: YAH-rah

The name Yara is of Brazilian and Arabic origin. The meaning of Yara is "small butterfly".

Yarina

Pronunciation: ya-RI-na

The name Yarina is of Russian origin. The meaning of Yarina is "peace". Yarina is a variant of the Greek name Irene.

Yarmila

Pronunciation: yar-MIL-LA

The name Yarmila is of Slavic origin. The meaning of Yarmila is "trader".

Yasmin, Yasmine

Pronunciation: yahz-MEEN

The name Yasmin is of Arabic and Persian origin. The meaning of Yasmin is "jasmine flower". The name is a variation of Jasmine.

Yesenia
Pronunciation: yeh-SEE-nee-ah
Yesenia is of Spanish origin. The meaning of Yesenia is unknown. Yesenia is variant of Llesenia.

Ynez
Pronunciation: ee-NEZ
The name Ynez is of French and Spanish origin. The meaning of Ynez is "chaste". Ynez is a variant of the Greek name Agnes.

Yoana
Pronunciation: yo-ANA
The name Yoana is of Hebrew origin. The meaning of Yoana is "God is gracious". The name is a variant of Joanna and a feminine form of the masculine name John.

Yoko
Pronunciation: YO-ko
The name Yoko is of Japanese origin. The meaning of Yoko is "good, positive".

Yolanda

Pronunciation: yoh-LAHN-dah

Yolanda is of Greek and Spanish origin. The meaning of the name Yolanda is "violet flower".

Yolande

Pronunciation: yoh-LAHN-dee

The name Yolande is of Latin origin. The meaning of Yolande is "violet flower". A variation of the French name Iolanthe derived from the Italian name Violanta.

Yonina

Pronunciation: yo-ni-NA

The name Yonina is of Hebrew origin. The meaning of Yonina is "dove".

Yosepha

Pronunciation: yo-se-pha

The name Yosepha is of Hebrew origin. The meaning of Yosepha is "Jehovah increases". The name is a Feminine form of the name Joseph.

Yseult

Pronunciation: yse-(u)-lt

The name Yseult is of French origin. The meaning of Yseult is "fair lady". The name is also a variant of the name Isolde.

Yudit
Pronunciation: YU-dit
The name Yudit is of Hebrew origin. The meaning of Yudit is "praise".

Yuliya
Pronunciation: yu-li-ya
The name Yuliya is of Russian origin. The meaning of Yuliya is "youthful". The name is a variant of Julia.

Yumiko
Pronunciation: yoo-mee-koh
Yumiko is of Japanese origin. The meaning of the name Yumiko is "arrow child".

Yuriko
Pronunciation: yoo-ree-koh
The name Yuriko is of Japanese origin. The meaning of Yuriko is "lily child".

Yvette
Pronunciation: ee-VET

The name Yvette is of French origin. The meaning of Yvette is "yew". The name is a feminine form of the French name Yves.

Yvonne

Pronunciation: ee-VAHN

The name Yvonne is of French and Old German origin. The meaning of Yvonne is "yew". A feminine form of the French name Yves.

Z

Zahavah

Pronunciation: ZA-hav-AH

The name Zahavah is of Hebrew origin. The meaning of Zahavah is "gilded".

Zaida

Pronunciation: ZAY-dah

The name Zaida is of Arabic origin. The meaning of Zaida is "prosperous".

Zaina

Pronunciation: ZAY-nah

Zaina is of Greek origin. The meaning of the name Zaina is "beauty". Zaina is a variant of the name Xenia.

Zalika

Pronunciation: za-LEE-kah

The name Zalika is of Swahili origin. The meaning of Zalika is "well born".

Zandra

Pronunciation: ZAHN-dra

The name Zandra is of Spanish origin. The meaning of Zandra is "man's defender". Zandra is a diminutive of the Greek name Alexandra.

Zaneta

Pronunciation: zah-NEE-tah

The name Zaneta is of Spanish origin. The meaning of Zaneta is unknown. Borne by a saint.

Zara

Pronunciation: ZR-ah

The name Zara is of Arabic origin. The meaning of Zara is "radiance". The name is possibly taken from the Hebrew meaning, 'bright as the dawn'. Zara is a diminutive of the name Sarah.

Zarina

Pronunciation: za-REEN-ah

Zarina is of Persian origin. The meaning of the name Zarina is "golden".

Zea

Pronunciation: ZEE-a

The name Zea is of Latin origin. The meaning of Zea is "grain".

Zarya

Pronunciation: ZAR-ya

The name Zarya is of Slavic origin. The meaning of Zarya is "protector of warriors". Borne in mythology, Zarya is a water priestess and protector of the warriors.

Zefira

Pronunciation: ZE-fir-a

The name Zefira is of Hebrew origin. The meaning of Zefira is "morning".

Zelda

Pronunciation: ZEH-dah

Zelda is of Old German origin. The meaning of the name Zelda is "dark battle". Originally used as a nickname of the Old German name, Griselda.

Zelenia

Pronunciation: ZEL-een-ia

The name Zelenia is of Greek origin. The meaning of Zelenia is "the moon". Zelenia is a variant of the Greek name Selena.

Zena

Pronunciation: ZEE-na

The name Zena is of Greek origin. The meaning of Zena is "guest, stranger". The name is a variant of Xenia.

Zelma

Pronunciation: ZEL-mah

The name Zelma is of Old German origin. The meaning of Zelma is "helmet of God". Zelma is a variant of the name Selma.

Zenobia

Pronunciation: ze-NOH-bee-ah

Zenobia is of Greek origin. The meaning of the name Zenobia is "life of Zeus". Borne by a 3rd-century queen of Palmyra in the Arabian desert. The name was revived in the 19th century.

Zetta

Pronunciation: ZEE-ta

The name Zetta is of Hebrew origin. The meaning of Zetta is "olive".

Zoe

Pronunciation: ZOH ee

Zoe is of Greek origin. The meaning of the name Zoe is "life". Originally a Greek Jewish translation of the Hebrew name Eve, meaning 'life'. The name was borne by a 3rd-century Roman martyr. The name was adopted in Britain in the 19th century, the name has been in regular since.

Zola

Pronunciation: ZO-la

The name Zola is of Italian origin. The meaning of Zola is "lump of earth". The name is possibly a variation of the Greek name Zoe. Zola was adopted as a first name in the late 20th century.

Zora

Pronunciation: ZOR-ah

The name Zora is of Slavic origin. The meaning of Zora is "dawn". Variation: Zorah.

BIBLOGRAPHY

Cresswell, Julia
Bloomsbury Dictionary of First Names
Bloomsbury, London, 1992

Cross. F. L and Livingstone E A, ed
Oxford Dictionary of the Christian Church
Oxford University Press, 1997

Drunkling, Leslie
First names first
J M Dent & Sons Ltd, London 1977

Fergusson, Rosalind
Choose Your Baby's name
Penguin, London 1987

Hall, James
Dictionary of Subjects and Symbols in Art
John Murrary, 1992

Hanks, Patrick and Falvia Hodges
A Concise Dictionary of First Names
Oxford University Press, Oxford, 1997

Holy Bible
Cambridge University Press

Macleod, Iseabail and Terry Freedman
The Wordsworth Dictionary of First Names
Wordsworth Editions Limited, London, 1995

Pickering, David
The Penguin Dictionary of First Names
Penguin, 2004

Room, Adrian
Brewer's Names
Cassell, London, 1992

Stafford, Diane
The Big Book of 60, 000 Baby Names
Sourcebooks, Inc, 2006

Strong, James
Strong's Concordance of the Bible
Thomas Nelson 1980

Withycombe, E G
Oxford Dictionary of English Christian Names
Oxford University Press, Oxford 1977

Printed in Great Britain
by Amazon.co.uk, Ltd.,
Marston Gate.